Revised and Enlarged

Pacific Square-Riggers

Henry B. Hyde

MEDIUM CLIPPER

☐ By the 1860's shipbuilders along the New England Coast realized the ever-pressing need for building vessels to capture the booming California grain trade to the East Coast and European ports. Soon to evolve was the medium clipper, a magnificent type of wooden vessel. They were well-built with full bottom for cargo-carrying capacity, and sturdy to fight the gales off Cape Horn.

These were known as "Down Easters" as they were built in the down east parts of Maine, New Hampshire, Massachusetts and Connecticut.

The Seamen's Bank

PACIFIC
SQUARE-RIGGERS

Revised and enlarged

Pictorial History of the
Great Windships of Yesteryear

by JIM GIBBS

Frontispiece photo, left.
One of the last of the square-riggers to fly the American flag was the graceful **TUSITALA** seen scudding along off Cape Flattery in 1926. A multiple rounder of the Horn and crosser of the equator, the green members of her crew were always in for the usual ceremony when they crossed the line for the first time.

> "Shave him and bash him,
> Duck him and splash him,
> Torture and smash him
> And don't let him go."

The orders were carried out with "brutal" precision. *Photo by Walter P. Miller.*

Schiffer Publishing Ltd

West Chester, Pennsylvania 19380

Ship **FALLS OF CLYDE** sail plan.

Dedication

In remembrance of the late Dr. John Lyman and Captain
P.A. McDonald whose research was most valuable in the
writing of this book.

Front cover:
Sailing into the nuclear age, the vintage iron-hulled bark **STAR
OF INDIA,** built in 1863, is maintained as an historic attraction at
San Diego.

Revised and enlarged
Copyright © 1987 by Jim Gibbs.
Library of Congress Catalog Number: 87-61703.

Printed in the United States of America.
ISBN: 0-88740-106-6
Published by Schiffer Publishing Ltd.
1469 Morstein Road, West Chester, Pennsylvania 19380

This book may be purchased from the publisher.
Please include $2.00 postage.
Try your bookstore first.

To the men who
know the wheel's
kick and the wind's
song, this book is
dedicated.

"If you would keep alive afloat, you must know what you're about; Unless a man is worthy, the sea will surely find him out." Hans Henrik Anderson, seaman at the wheel of the **FALLS OF CLYDE**. *Aderman collection, courtesy San Francisco Maritime Museum.*

Introduction

"A lost era; the traditional way of seafaring; gone forever."

Each year for nearly 65 years—from Gold Rush times until the era of the Panama Canal—a great fleet of sailing ships beat their way around Cape Horn to San Francisco and the Pacific Northwest.

This fleet gradually changed its initial character from the clipper ship type (lean ocean greyhound sailers that sacrificed cargo space for speed) to more capacious "downeasters," so named from a New England colloquialism for the State of Maine. The clipper ships had been built at New York or Boston to reach San Francisco during the 1850s, when the city was young and isolated. Gold rush merchants, awaiting cargoes, were willing to pay extra for speed. By the '60s and '70s these earnings were a thing of the past, and the clippers gave way to downeasters—of which Bath and Thomaston, Maine were two "main" areas of construction. Built firm and stout, these fine wooden ships had a remarkable carrying capacity for their size and at times showed the sailing qualities of their forebears. With about half the crew and twice the payload, such ships put New England on the map and made California a close neighbor by creditable passages around "Ol Cape Stiff."

Contemporary with the New England ships, contesting with them in epic grain races around the Horn, and gradually outnumbering them in San Francisco Bay, on the Columbia River, on Puget Sound, and in British Columbia ports, came iron, and finally steel sailing ships. Built for the most part in the British Isles, many had black hulls with painted mock gunports (a holdover from the days of the pirates to scare them into thinking such merchantment were armed), entered the Golden Gate in the '70s, '80s and '90s to load San Joaquin Valley wheat for Northern Europe. They crowded the wharves and anchorages and made San Francisco into one of the three great sailing ship ports in the world. No fewer than 559 sailing vessels assembled at San Francisco to load a single season's grain harvest in the year 1881, perhaps the all-time record year. Numerous others came to Pacific Northwest ports.

The revised *Pacific Square-riggers* is a sequel to *Windjammers of the Pacific Rim.* Where the first effort concerned, for the main part, those windships of 100 tons and over, built on the West Coast for Pacific Ocean service, this book deals with the square-riggers built elsewhere but which became a representative part of Pacific commerce, basing their operations at West Coast ports. This gallant fleet of sailing vessels represented the majority of the finest and largest sailing vessels ever built. Among them were the California-bound clipper ships, the whalers, the downeasters from New England, the big British, German and French iron and steel vessels, the giant square-riggers commandeered in World War I, and a sprinkling of miscellaneous smaller sailing vessels.

For the most part, however, this book deals with those sailing vessels that eventually came under ownership of West Coast shipping companies, and especially those ships owned on this coast from 1900 until the end of the sailing ship era.

As steamers and motorships began to take their toll on the windship, many of the last of these great winged beauties found their way to the Pacific for less competitive trades. Ports from California to British Columbia became repositories for the old square-riggers. When there was no place for them to sail, they were cut down to barges and many of these aging ships lasted well into the twentieth century.

British bark **HIGHMOOR**, canvas partially furled, off Astoria, Oregon July 6, 1889. It was an era when windships were as common to the Columbia River as powered vessels are in our day. Photo, courtesy Columbia River Maritime Museum.

Among this great fleet were the statuesque grain ships, that for many years, carried the trade from the West Coast to the United Kingdom and Europe; the square-rigged lumber droughers that lifted their cargoes at Washington, Oregon and B. C. lumber ports for the far corners of the world; the coal packers and the grubby uninsured breed that took any kind of cargo that was offered, asking only a breeze to fill their oft-patched canvas.

Space would never permit full, or deserving coverage of such a vast subject, and preciously little has been written concerning those lusty old days of sail. If this effort can do just a little to fill in the great void in our Pacific maritime history then it will have accomplished its purpose. In a nuclear-space age, amid our pleasant surroundings, it is hard for one to imagine the rugged life of the underpaid, underfed, seafarers of old. Among them were both the scum of the earth and the bravest of men—men of every nation and color rubbing elbows in their raw surroundings. Courageous, trusted skippers or fierce masters who loved nothing better than to rule their little floating worlds with an iron fist, once out of sight of land.

Few voyages were ever completed without a bloody fracas among crewmen, illness in the fo'c'sle, hostility between officers and seamen. The captain's word was law and woe to him that challenged that authority. The code of the sea was binding.

It took a peculiar kind of man to furl canvas in a 60-knot gale, out on a yardarm 150 feet above the sea—one hand for the ship, and one hand for himself, with only a wildly swaying foot rope between him and eternity. Freezing weather, bleeding hands and lack of sleep or food were no excuse for not performing well. Woe to the man who shirked his duties.

Nautical scene at the bustling milltown of Port Blakely on Bainbridge Island in Puget Sound back in the days of yore. In the foreground is the sidewheel paddle steam tug **FAVORITE** tied up at the dock. In the background are three square-riggers awaiting cargo. In the center is the foreign flag ship **ASTER.**

Contents

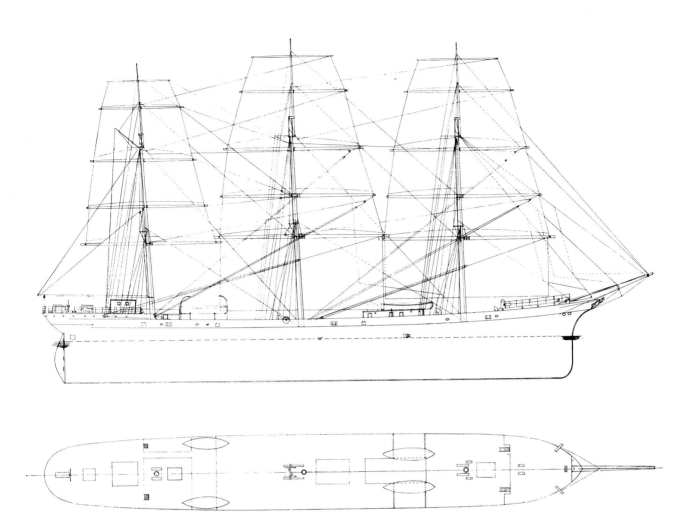

RECHRISTENED BALCULTHA JULY 20, 1955

STAR OF ALASKA

Traced From An Original Rigging Plan By Captain
C A Halvorsen 1909   F W Snow August 1964

MIDSHIP SECTION

Sail plan, deck plan and spar plan for the ship **STAR OF ALASKA** of the Alaska Packers fleet. One of the few surviving commercial square-riggers, she has been restored under her original name **BALCLUTHA,** a museum vessel at San Francisco under the auspices of the San Francisco Maritime Museum, via the direction of Karl Kortum.

Masefield once wrote these words: "As once, long since, when all the docks were filled, With the beauty man has ceased to build." This nostalgic scene was taken on the San Francisco waterfront way back when, showing a British full-rigged ship, left, and an American downeaster, plus two scow schooners which carried cargo around the bay. *Courtesy San Francisco Maritime Museum.*

PREPARED BY WILLIAM FOSTER WILMURT, A.I.A.

Courtesy Maritime Museum Association of San Diego

BARK STAR of INDIA

LAUNCHED as *EUTERPE* on NOVEMBER 14, 1863 at RAMSEY, ISLE of MAN

MARITIME MUSEUM
EMBARCEDERO, SAN DIEGO, CALIFORNIA

THE OLDEST MERCHANTMAN AFLOAT

Length (on Waterline)	205'-0"	Mainmast - Deck to Truck	124'-8"	Tonnage	1197 $^{01}/_{100}$
Beam	35'-0"	Main Yard	72'-0"	Loaded Draft	22'-0"
Depth of Hold	23'-6"	Jibboom	55'-0"	Light Draft	14'-6"

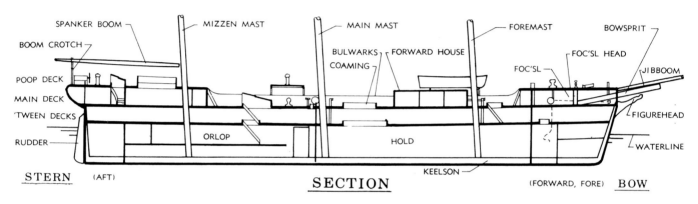

STERN   (AFT)   SECTION   (FORWARD, FORE)   BOW

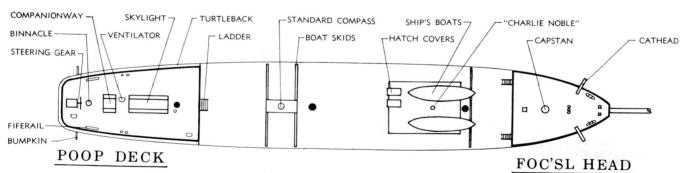

POOP DECK   FOC'SL HEAD

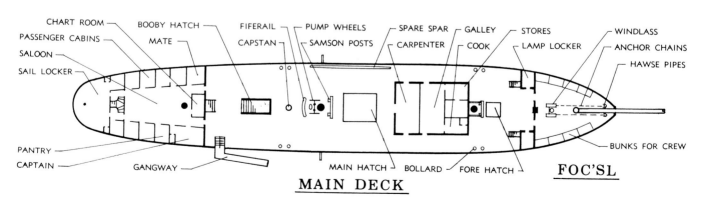

MAIN DECK   FOC'SL

Chapter One

Sail Comes to the Pacific

"He that will learn to pray, let him go to sea."

Who were the first men that went down to the sea in ships? What were the thoughts that raced through their minds as they faced the alluring, compelling, charming, cruel, devastating, heartless, stretches of water—their frail craft open to blessing and destruction in quick succession. Imagine the thrill of the first salt who hoisted a sail to gather in the precious breeze, only to learn that the oar and paddle were not the only means of motivation.

Nor is it hard to imagine the heathen giving homage to false gods, nor the God-fearing practising their faith to protect them on arduous voyages to lonely places. Fear was often present and the weird phenomenon of weather at sea often drove them to their knees to ask deliverance.

The Psalmist understood the suffering of men when they "go down to the sea in ships to do business in great waters . . . they cry Jehovah in their trouble and he bringeth them out of their distreses . . . and bringeth them into their desired heaven."

Paul knew the power of God's delivery in the very jaws of death but he alone stood tall as his vessel was jostled about and eventually wrecked trying to escape the storm.

Despite shipwreck, privation and loneliness, men of the sea drove ever onward, Roman ships going as far as England in the early centuries. And the Polynesians in their frail outriggers conquered many of the islands of the Pacific in ancient times—but records of their conquest of the southern seas are non-existent except for an occasional stone carving or ritual. Man undoubtedly traveled by water soon after he beheld the vast stretches of liquid ocean. His efforts were limited by the sight of land for the areas that shut out all landmarks were greatly feared, and even in Columbus' time men thought the world was square and if he sailed his craft far enough he would drop off into endless space.

Phoenicians, Greeks, Egyptians and Romans took to the sea as a thoroughfare, just because it was there. Iliad and Odyssey tell of ships and sea folk, and their entire world was the Mediterranean. The Vikings in their amazing craft broke away from the Scandinavian shores with assurity, crossing oceans to lands never before seen by white man.

It has been said that the most religious people of the ancient world were sailors, not because they were morally better than landsmen, but because of the fear of the awesome power they felt when facing the rigors of the sea. Their helplessness caused them to fear non-existent gods, for even in Paul's time the crew of his vessel were believers almost to the man in heathen gods, but Paul who had the everlasting faith of the new found Christian predominated.

False security in false gods led sailors of old into twisted superstitions and fears, many of which have flourished down to modern times.

Man's confidence in using the wind for motive power, by comparison to other modes of transportation, increased slowly and it wasn't really until the 14th century that man stepped out to experiment with large, more complex sailing vessels with a variety of sails and more sophisticated rigging.

Before the call of the West was loud and clear, the United States looked for the most part to New England for merchant sailing ships. Timber, crafts-manship, and zeal there abounded, a perfect combination for the curtain raiser on one of the outstanding chapters in American history. The great clipper ships, whalers and the downeasters were fashioned there. Speed and skill were built into them and afforded the incentive for the ruling of the seas by young America. Prior to that era, England had it pretty much its own way. It too, built fine clippers and in the decades to follow progressed further in the building of the best steel and iron square-riggers the world has ever known. Not only were they easy to handle but were commodious and seaworthy. Most traded regularly with the West Coast ports and scores came out west to homeport. Other foreign nations, mostly in Europe, followed in

John Bull's footsteps and also built formidable merchant ships to keep pace with the times.

Along the rugged coast of New England in the early years of America, gaunt-faced men hewed down tall trees and brought them to the nearby shore and laid them in neat rows near little sawmills. These mills abutted the crude log ways where they fashioned mighty ships from fresh hewn pine with oak ribs. The smell of the fresh wood and pine tar delighted the nostrils. The only sounds were the ring of a spike maul and the chipping adz. No blueprints existed, only cunning, learned by experience handed down from father to son.

The labor would go on day after day, fair weather and foul. Long hours ensued, the goal to see their creation launched, outfitted and delivered to roam the seven seas.

When the vessel finally neared completion with the last oakum stuffed in her seams, the tempo of conversation rose—there was mirth and activity around the little yard as the ship was about to take to the brine. The spike mauls and adzes at last were quiet for a day. The skids were cleared and expressions tense. Free of her blocks, the vessel's bow would tremble and then there was the squeal and groan of timbers as she slid stern first into the stream. The vessel would hit the water with a great splash and when it was certain she was afloat, a mighty cheer would ascend. The cradle was empty and on the morrow a new keel would be laid and the entire process repeated. A gentleman's handshake was all that was needed to bind a new contract.

Of such were the scenes in the early American shipyards where were fashioned the windships of yesteryear.

From a meager beginning, the East Coast yards grew with the nation and when eventually the clipper ships were fashioned, the eyes of the world were focussed on America which produced the finest and fastest ships afloat. That era ran from 1850 to 1870, about the time the West Coast was just coming into its own. The nation began building many ships of its own and acquiring whatever it could get its hands on elsewhere to bolster the booming economy. It was the San Francisco gold rush of 1849 that sent droves of ships of every kind and description to the West Coast.

The speed realized by American clipper ships astounded the world. One of the early clipper ships, the *Stag Hound,* slid down the ways at an

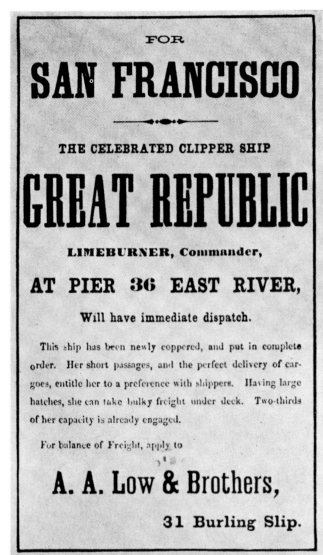

FOR

SAN FRANCISCO

THE CELEBRATED CLIPPER SHIP

GREAT REPUBLIC

LIMEBURNER, Commander,

AT PIER 36 EAST RIVER,

Will have immediate dispatch.

This ship has been newly coppered, and put in complete order. Her short passages, and the perfect delivery of cargoes, entitle her to a preference with shippers. Having large hatches, she can take bulky freight under deck. Two-thirds of her capacity is already engaged.

For balance of Freight, apply to

A. A. Low & Brothers,

31 Burling Slip.

Courtesy of the State Street Trust Company

SAILING CARD FOR THE *GREAT REPUBLIC* 1854

"Immediate dispatch" means she would sail whenever she was fully loaded. Later competition tightened departure dates.

East Boston yard in 1850, a pioneer in size and speed. Following her came the *Flying Cloud,* a miracle of beauty, all copper-sheathed and with slightly raking masts. Perhaps her design and grace were never fully surpassed. Nothing was spared to make her the finest. This latter ship devised and built by Donald McKay was the fastest windship on long passages that ever carried the Stars and Stripes. On her maiden voyage she logged 374 miles for a days run, a good 50 miles more than the average days run for a freighter of the World War II era. These clipper ships of old, turned out by McKay and a host of other famous New England builders, such as Edward and Henry Briggs, Sam Hall and Robert E. Jackson, set numerous records. The *Red Jacket* once ran for six straight days in the Atlantic at 14.7 knots average. The *Lightning* logged 15.5 knots for 3,722 miles and the *James Baines* on an Australian voyage once logged 21 knots for an entire hour. They ranged to Europe, the Orient and to San Francisco in increasing numbers. Every ship, large or small, scheduling a departure for the Golden Gate during the gold rush days was packed to the gunwhales with passengers and cargo.

The competition was something fierce. Big wages were made on the outcome of races and skippers were task masters, demanding and getting everything out of their crews. Though the food on the American ships was considered superior to that on the limejuicers, the work at times was intolerable, the men spending much of their time aloft, night and day, fair or foul weather. Canvas was piled on like dirty laundry. In a gale, the skippers utilized every hunk of canvas they could unfurl to take full advantage of the breeze.

Captain Samuel Samuels once remarked after a near record run in his clipper *Dreadnaught*: "She was on the rim of a cyclone most of the time." No wonder his command got the name of "Wild Boat of the Atlantic."

The notorious Captain Waterman of the clipper *Sea Witch* gained an evil reputation for allegedly having more than once shot a man off the yards for handling sail too slowly. The sheets and halyards attached to the most important sails were often made of chain so sails would not fly loose at night out of the skipper's sight.

As has already been told, seamen were often bullied by the officers, and frightened or slow to learn crewmen were punished in cruel ways.

Hauled out for scraping and painting, the bark **DIAMOND HEAD** around the turn of the century. She was built of iron in England in 1866.

The four-mast steel bark **GIFFORD** is seen here stranded on September 25, 1903, in Mussel Bay, San Francisco. She became a total loss. Cause: thick weather and neglect of the lead. She was inbound to San Francisco from Newcastle with a cargo of coal. The **GIFFORD** was once owned by Briggs, Harvie and Co., of Glasgow and later by Weir & Co. She was built in 1892 by Scott & Co. and was of 2,245 tons. *Photo courtesy San Francisco Maritime Museum.*

No matter how cruel, however, the master's word was law, and nothing short of proven murder would find him guilty once port was reached.

Life for the crew of the clipper ships from the financial side was even more discouraging than the hard work. Wages for the man before the mast was $8 a month — two dollars less than what sailors of New York were paid when they struck unsuccessfully in 1803. As the sailing vessels grew larger, from the 750 ton medium clipper type to the biggest of the clippers, the *Great Republic* of 4,500 tons, more hands were required to work the ship than ever before. When the bedraggled seamen made port they blew their earnings in a single night at

American ship **MAJESTIC,** 1,170 tons, hove down in San Francisco in 1886. Launched at Portland, Maine, in 1866, this handsome vessel was owned by Thayer & Lincoln, Boston, and 12 years later came to the Pacific Coast under ownership of Seattle Coal & Transportation Co. In 1884 she was acquired by A. P. Lorentzen and two years later at the very end of the year she rescued the only three survivors of the ship **HARVEY MILLS** which foundered off Cape Flattery, laden with Seattle coal for San Francisco. The gaunt survivors after days on floating wreckage were nearly dead. Some twenty men of the Mills were drowned. Ironically the Majestic, fully laden with Seattle coal for San Francisco went missing with all hands in December 1892. *Oliver Collection, Bancroft Library, University of California.*

the local pubs, or were drugged and rolled. Many woke up the next day finding themselves in the dank fo'c'sle of another sailing vessel outbound on a long voyage—shanghaied.

The rough and tumble men before the mast were often drunks, misfits and trouble-makers but the hard totalitarian ways of the master and officers quickly whipped them into line. Many kept coming back after each voyage— they knowing no other way of life. Experienced hands were sometimes hard to come by and the green hands were abused, often without letup, working almost constantly around the clock with little time for rest.

After getting seasoned to the life, some of the men often expressed a liking for the windships. Fights and mutiny among seamen were not uncommon and it was the code of the sea never to report one of their number to the officers no matter how severe the offense. These "packet rats" seemed to glory in their ill-treatment and their ability to take punishment. Often referred to as the scum of the earth, they sang their chanties and cursed incessantly. They were a breed all of their own.

The early days on the waterfronts of the Pacific Coast left many black smears on American shipping. Shanghaiing was as common as any household word, and a man's future on the street after dark in places like San Francisco and Port Townsend wasn't worth a plug nickel. Chances are he would end up slugged, beaten up, mugged, drugged or injured on the sodden deck of an outgoing windship bound for a distant port. The word shanghai originated on the West Coast, chiefly at San Francisco where men were provided by crimps to run across the Pacific to Shanghai, China although men were shanghaied in ships bound for any port.

It goes without saying, that it became a big business, a vicious vocation which ran rampant, well out of the clutches of the law. Briberies, reprisals, threats, murders kept the righteous in line. The centers of the evil system were the sailors' boarding houses located in sailor town and operated by those having connections with corrupt city officials to whom protection money was paid. The crimp, in turn, hired runners to whom a stipend was paid for delivery of men at the establishments. The runners also had a close working arrangement with the boatmen who with their dorries and oversized skiffs, frequented the barnacle-infested forest of wooden piling that held the sagging structures up along the waterfront. They cruised this dark world of smelly water like escapists in the underground sewers of Paris. They knew every trap door and shady entrance which alluded what primitive form of law then existed. Sometimes the boatmen freelanced and worked on their own, often robbing and then murdering those traveling between ships and shore. Part of their equipment included knives, revolvers, knuckle dusters, liquor liberally dosed with aphrodisiacs, vials of liquid soap and pornography.

Sometimes masters and officers of vessels were threatened with murder as armies of armed runners swarmed aboard ships as they came to anchor in the bay. Masquerading as the friends of the sailors, they uncorked bottles, spread lewd photos about and dumped liquid soap into the galley food for the last meal before coming ashore. By the time they got finished with the fo'c'sle gang, the victims were higher than a kite and putty in the hands of the runners. Sometimes within hours of arrival in the bay, the deceived sailors were off to sea again on another vessel bound for parts unknown.

Those who got as far as shore fared little better. They usually headed straight for the saloons and illicit houses where the crimps extended their hands while their tainted minds worked out the most convenient way to sell the souls of these unfortunates.

Old Jack didn't have a chance. In the eerie din of the saloons, a sailor who eluded a few of the easier tricks was often flanked by a couple of burly crimps, who with a little muscle could knock the seaman out and hustle him off, virtually undetected.

If belligerent, the bartender's billy club usually put him out of his misery. If he was able to survive a shot of laudanum in his whiskey his blurred eyes made it an unfair fight as he resisted superior forces.

With no representation, no legal rights, the man before the mast was kicked freely about and his complaints always fell on deaf ears. The only protection he had was to travel in a group and to be constantly wary of every stranger. The sailor was grossly underpaid, while the crimps and runners sometimes pocketed more money in a night than a sailor could

make in a decade. Thousands of dollars passed hands on San Francisco's hellish waterfront every night. Some said it was the biggest business in the whole of California during times of crew shortages. All money of the waterfront was blood red, and crime flourished in its most evil forms, the crimps and runners working in close association with prostitutes and bar maids.

Up on Puget Sound, where once flourished Port Townsend's barbary coast, the remnants of some of the old buildings still stand where sailors were shanghaied in droves. At Vancouver, B.C. in olden times, a son sold his father to a short-handed ship, whose master willingly paid blood money. In another case, a clergyman who had never been aboard a ship, was slugged on the street and promptly dumped aboard a departing ship.

Liquor flowed like water and the Babylon of the new world flourished. The righteous believed the constant setbacks of San Francisco—its endless fires, recessions, strife, riots and earthquakes—were acts of God to slow the devil's pace—a modern Sodom or Gomorrah.

The Christian Advocate in early day San Francisco read:

"By actual count, the whole number of places where liquor is sold in this city is said to be 537. . . . Some of these places appear genteel, others are dance houses and such like where Chinese, Mexican, Chilean and other foreign women are assembled."

Columbia River Ho!

Even as San Francisco suffered its growing pains in nautical history, pioneers were eyeing the prospects of the Willamette and Columbia Rivers for the site of a great future seaport where tall ships would come to load full cargoes for the far portals of the world.

Sailing Directions for the West Coast of North America, a nautical guide published in 1853, said of the Columbia River: "Although it possesses at all times a good depth of water, yet it is difficult and dangerous to enter, so much that it can be said to possess but few advantages as a port."

But man accepted the challenge and after decades of toil, sweat, money and tears conquered the river and opened it up as a major area of ship traffic.

Traditionally the port of Portland has been America's chief Pacific Northwest grain port.

A fascinating stern view of the English bark **INVERCLYDE** of Aberdeen, Scotland, photographed by Capt. G. E. Plummer in 1914 off the Strait of Juan de Fuca. Plummer, who became president of the Puget Sound Tug Boat Co., took many famous sailing ship photos off Cape Flattery in his years.

In the days of sail it was a common sight to see the docks along the Willamette lined with tall square-riggers ready to take wheat to the United Kingdom and other far flung sectors of the world.

Trees lined the waterfront along the Willamette River in 1842, and there was but a single trapper's cabin on the site where the Rose City is now located. What few people there were in the area were centered about the Hudson's Bay Company post at Fort Vancouver, a few miles away on the Columbia River, or at fledgling Oregon City near the falls of the Willamette.

Reaching back into the fading chapters of history we find that Captain John Couch on his initial voyage to the Pacific Northwest sailed the brig *Maryland* of Newburyport, Mass.

into the Willamette and up to the small settlement at the falls, in as neat a bit of navigation as one could ask (no engines, no tugs, no assistance except the wind to fill the sails). Couch was forced to drift downstream to a safer haven and there near Ross Island, in the present harbor limits of Portland he dropped the hooks. Here he declared would be an ideal location for a village, and his words of wisdom were to come true.

Three years later this locale attracted the attention of Asa L. Lovejoy and William Overton, who, in 1843 took a claim of 640 acres. Francis W. Pettygrove purchased Overton's share in 1844 and built a log cabin store at the foot of S.W. Washington Street. The partners laid out a town sixteen blocks along the Willa-

Being sucked into the sands of the North Beach Peninsula, Washington, north of the Oysterville beach approach is the French ship **ALICE** wrecked January 15, 1909, laden with a cargo of cement.

mette's west bank bounded on the north side by Washington Street and on the south by Jefferson, extending two blocks up from the river. So the history books tell, neither man could agree on a name for the settlement; Lovejoy favored Boston, Pettygrove, Portland. The former wanted to honor his native Massachusetts town and the latter the big city in his home state of Maine. What to do? Flip a coin—a mere penny at that, and from that flip emerged the name Portland, much to Pettygrove's satisfaction.

Believing his predictions, Captain Couch returned to Oregon in 1844 and took an adjoining claim to the north and four years later established roots there and became a prominent part of the growing west.

From the beginning, Portland was destined to become associated with the maritime industry. In fact even as early as 1841, Swan Island saw the birth of shipbuilding when a group of farmers, under the guidance of Joseph Gale, built a schooner—a small schooner to be sure, but one that was destined to make Oregon history. They appropriately named her the *Star of Oregon,* and shortly after her completion manned and sailed her to San Francisco where as planned they struck up a deal to trade their

Ready to have the torch touched to her aging hull—the former semi-clipper ship **GLORY OF THE SEAS,** the last product of the famous shipbuilder Donald McKay, rests on the beach at Endolyne, south of Seattle, May 13, 1923. She was built at East Boston in 1869, and served under Pacific Coast shipowners from 1906, ending her days as a cold storage ship.

Carried ashore and wrecked at the mouth of the Quinault River, Washington, in December, 1901—
French bark **ERNEST REYER.** All hands were saved but the vessel became a total loss, victim of one
of the worst gales of that decade. *Courtesy Harold Huycke.*

creation for cattle to replenish their stock in the Tualatin Valley. The boom days of the San Francisco goldrush were yet a few years off, but they had little trouble trading their schooner, as lumber to build new ships was a none too plentiful item in early San Francisco.

The prelude to the day of the great windjammer on the Portland waterfront might be traced back to 1846 when John Waymire built the first wharf and a warehouse to go with it at the foot of Washington Street. This marked the beginning of Portland as a deepwater port. But the tall sailing ships were still a long way off. Trading on the Willamette and Columbia was mostly by sail-rigged scows or the Hudson's Bay batteaux. The farm produce was brought to the docks down the old Canyon Road—just a plank roadway supported by logs.

The town began to take on a little lustre in 1850 when the Pacific Mail steamer *Carolina* crossed the Columbia bar and came to Portland from San Francisco with mail, passengers and cargo. It was the biggest event in the early history of the place and every man, woman and child turned out to greet the vessel. They celebrated again the same year when the Astoria-built pint-sized steamer *Columbia* came breezing into Portland and then on to Oregon City. The crowds went wild with excitement and set off fireworks at both ports inasmuch as the arrival had been timed in conjunction with the 4th of July. The trip took 18 hours and the capacity crowd had paid $25 a head for the joy of traveling on the little sidewheeler, despite the fact they had to afford their own blankets and food. The cargo was carried for $25 per ton.

It was the late 19th century and the area had yet to attain a population of 1,000; yet Portland was the largest city north of San Francisco. Henry Corbet and William Ladd established mercantile businesses. They depended on sailing ships such as the bark *Toulon*, skippered by Captain Nathaniel Crosby or Captain Avery Sylvester's brig *Palos* or numerous other less frequent trading ships to handle the trade.

It now became obvious that Portland was the natural meeting place of river steamers and deepwater sailing vessels. The steamers brought farm produce, lumber and other commodities from sections of the upper Columbia and Willamette rivers to Portland's warehouses. Sometimes a little gold-find up river brought encouragement to the town. Tall ships began to arrive with general cargo and supplies so urgently needed by the pioneers. The waterfront gradually became crowded with stately sailing craft and ocean steamers.

Time marched on and progress with it. Through the 1890's and early 1900's, the famous "wheat fleet" of full-rigged ships, and barks from all over the world, annually converged on Portland to take on grain from the vast hinterland. New piers and facilities were hidden behind a vast forest of masts. Not only were the docks occupied with men, ships and cargo but many vessels lay at anchor in the river awaiting their turn. Portland earned the reputation of the bread-basket of the world. Wheat vied with lumber as the big exports at Portland. The lofty windships, mostly of foreign-flag, hauled these transocean cargoes while West Coast-built windjammers, mostly schooners and steam schooners, handled the demands coastwise, to the Pacific Islands and sometimes to the Antipodes.

The sailing ship was the dominant factor in trade till the World War I era. Among them were the handsome steel and iron ships flying the British flag, with a mixture of French, German, Norwegian and other nations represented. And it was to these great winged ships which carried the golden grain from western farms that Portland owed the spreading of its fame as a world seaport.

Back in 1849, all transportation along the West Coast had to be by water; there was no other means. San Francisco had just come into its own with the cry of gold. The permanent white population of the yet-to-be states of Washington and Oregon, then known as Oregon Territory, was virtually nil except for a few pioneers that had ventured into cut the tall timber.

Some little river settlements had started up along the Columbia River, Astoria probably being the oldest and most prominent. If a man wanted to get from San Francisco to the Columbia River he had to go by ship unless he wanted to break trail through impenetrable underbrush, virgin forests, or high mountains.

And so it was with Isaac A. Flint, a Northwest pioneer and minister. He was born in Chenango County, New York in 1816 and had traveled periodically through the years across the United States by land finally arriving in California prior to the goldrush. He made one trip north to Puget Sound in 1847 and while off the Northwest coast was once rescued from the breakers by friendly Indians. His adventures were legion. He returned to San Francisco and after an unsuccessful attempt at finding gold, sought passage to the Columbia River. What we are concerned with here is the journal he left behind telling of that epic voyage from the Golden Gate to the Columbia River aboard the East Coast-built 190 ton bark *Keoka* owned by C. C. White of San Francisco. The account was released a few years back and edited for the Oregon Historical Quarterly by Ted Van Arsdol. Flint died in the Yakima area on March 28, 1892 (an active Christian minister), and his journal was passed on to his grandson, G. Monroe Flint of Chehalis. It is one of the most vivid existing accounts of the hardship suffered by passengers taking passage on sailing ships in those green years of inferior accommodations, no safety regulations, inadequate aids to navigation, and sometimes none too knowledgeable skippers. Excerpts from that account appear here:

HARBOR OF SAN FRANCISCO
November 27, 1849

On board Bark *Keoka* . . . getting ready for sea. Passengers have been coming aboard all day. All the berths in the cabin are taken. Now I will study the character of some of them. Here are some Frenchmen, one of them has a very sour countenance, more gloomy than any storm I wish to meet on the way to the Columbia. I'll notice that young man with the small narrow forehead, keen black eyes and slightly Roman nose.

There is one man who has fallen under the suspicion of dishonesty. His countenance is rather fallen. The conversation is on potatoes. The weather is cloudy. Wind No. W., expect to sail on Thursday.

28th—Ship receiving ballast and water. Wind high this morning. Some harbor sick passengers. Cleared up this evening. Conversation in the cabin neither moral, mental or religious. A feeling of uneasiness in the passengers on account of delay in sailing. 2 o'clock PM got under way with a light breeze, at sundown 10 miles off shore. Five sail in sight.

Sat. Dec. 1st—Land in sight this morning wind ahead, one sail a Bark in sight to the south standing in. The passengers amuse themselves by catching birds which follow the ship and bite a hook. 3 p.m.—Wind rising with signs of a storm. I am seasick today. The crew con-

sists of a Capt., 1st & 2nd mates, steward, cook and seamen. Passengers in cabin 23, Deck 25, housed forward 2 women and 3 children.

Dec. 2nd—A furious N. Wester all day. Spray flying all over us. Some are playing cards, many are sick. No religion on this ship. The most of the passengers are from the state of Missouri. The Capt. is a green 'un.

Dec. 10th—Monday, up to this time a rough sea and abundance of discomfort, made but little headway, Wind North. We are running N.E. We may see the Columbia in 10 days. No prospect sooner.

Sun. 23rd Dec.—Still at sea. Since the 10th there has been a constant succession of furious gales and contrary winds. We have been once nearly in the mouth of the Columbia and with deep regret again stood out to sea. We are enveloped in a thick fog, provisions are scarce and water scarcer still. Three or four are sick. Wind ahead. No hope of getting in without better wind. The vessel rolls so I can scarcely write. The first mate is some of a gentleman and navigator. He is very sick. The Capt. has missed his longitude 60 miles.

Thurs. 28th—We are about 12 miles to the west by north of the cape which has been the scene of much disappointment to us. The sea is very calm scarcely a puff of wind. We have just buried a man (Riley Miller, age 23) in the sea. Three are sick on board. Water nearly gone. A solemn gloom rests on the countenance of nearly all on board. Some appear to care for nothing. 3 miles astern is a brig with all sail set and nearing us very slowly. Ten miles on our windward quarter is another sail, so we have company. I think the old adage (misery loves company) is true. We cannot stand it much longer without distress. Our rations are one spoonful of wormy mouldy beans once in 24 hours.

Mon. 31st—Still at sea. Cape 25 miles on our windward bow. It is under circumstances the most discouraging under which I ever was placed that I write these lines. I have to help the Capt. get the time and reckoning. We are on our last legs. Two or three days of provisions and water. Water is worth more than all gold. We are in great distress. Wind is against us and without a change of wind we must all perish. The passengers are getting peevish. If I ever get in shore I shall long remember this morning when I received my glass of water for a day's allowance. If not, starvation and thirst

After the storm—the ragged remains of the once proud French ship **ALICE** on the North Beach Peninsula. Note man on the yardarm, another high on the foremast and another wading out to survey the dismal sight. *Prentiss photo*

Inbound to Portland for a cargo of grain, the British ship **GLENELG** approaches the Columbia River in days of yore.

Tues. Jan 1, 1850. This morning our anxious eyes are strained to discover the long wished for land, yonder it is. The bald peaks of Saddle Mountain loom up in the mist and fog. The sun is showing its pale, cold sickly face to tell us we have passed another night of horrid gloom and darkness. We took a sea over the starboard side last night which went through the galley carrying the cook's coppers down to the lee scuppers. The old negro cook half drunk pitched down the main hatch head foremost.

At about 10 o'clock P.M. ran over a large fir tree which nearly carried away our rudder. Our larboard rigging is very slack. The Bark looks as if she had been neglected a year. The sailors hands are very sore from the cold. Our fire wood was all gone long ago. One of the passengers whipped the captain last night and they intend to make him run the vessel on the beach tomorrow morning at high tide or throw him overboard. He came to me and said you are the only friend I have on board you have stuck by me to the last, what shall I do? I advised him to run into the little bay south of the Cape Lookout and try to land the passengers there, to which he agreed and I went below to pacify the passengers and crew telling them they would be guilty of mutiny.

Wed. Jan. 2, 1850—We are 10 miles to windward of Cape Lookout. We are willing to land at any place. The jolly boat and canoe have started for shore they are out of sight. One o'clock P.M.—The jolly has come back. The two passengers have reached the land in the canoe 20 miles south of the Columbia. We envy them their good fortune. They have plenty of the greatest beverage this world can offer (good water).

4 P.M.—We have launched the long boat and are off for the shore. The passengers are half crazy every one telling what and how to do. The boat leaks faster than a man can throw it out with a bucket so we must hoist her aboard and caulk her. Got her up and stopped the leaks. I caulked her myself. Dark heavy squalls are coming. Nothing to eat and nothing to cook it with.

Mid-night — got a sea over the starboard quarter nearly carrying away the man at the wheel, staving in the companion door and washing me out of my berth. I feel like a drowned rat and no chance to dry.

Thurs. 3rd—Wind still against us. We hope to reach the shore today. The wind has lulled

will soon put an end to life. Bread is forgotten: in the absence of water. It is impossible for pen or pencil to convey an adequate idea of our feelings at this time.

Every flaw of wind is watched with intense anxiety some 10 or 12 times we have been steering toward the cape with a prospect of getting in and have been as often baffled. God in mercy regard our almost hopeless condition.

and we are standing in under all sail. At 3 o'clock P.M. came to anchor 4 miles off the shore. Preparations are making to try it again in the long boat.

At length we shove off. We intend to affect a landing at the mouth of the Neocoxa if possible. The men at the oars are practicing steady strokes well knowing that the utmost steadiness and skill will be requisite in a few minutes—A mountain sea is running and along the whole line of breakers from south to north not a single opening presents itself—We might as well jump the falls of the Niagara as to cross the outside breakers 30 ft. high and a whole generation of Genesee's and Niagara's would sound like gentle murmurs compared to its thunder. We can count nine successive lines of breakers between us and the beach. Our boat rudder is unshipped.

One rowlock is gone and with heavy hearts and with parched throats we return to the ship.

Fri. 4th—Cape in sight this morning (to windward as usual). But what is that small white speck on our weather bow. A small fore-and-aft schooner. Up goes our colors union down. We are in distress and this is our signal. A spark of hope is kindling in our bosom. The schooner sees us and answered by sending her flag up to her peak and is bearing down upon us in gallant style. Two hours more and she will be along side. Here she is. We hope she can supply us with water. But no. Eighty gallons is all she can give and that is nailed up by common consent and kept for a time of

greater need. We will make a distilling tomorrow to make fresh water if we have no better prospect of getting in the Columbia River.

But she is a pilot boat. Our hopes now are that she will take us off. The Pilot Capt. Cornelius White (of the pilot schooner *Mary Taylor*) is aboard of us, animating the passengers and crew by his presence. He is crowding on the canvas with a vengeance.

Sat. 5th—The pilot boat is out of sight this morning. We are 25 miles off the Cape (Disappointment). 10 o'clock. Sail & Where away. 10 miles on our weather bow. Here she comes and plays around us like a pilot fish about a crippled shark.

If our bark cannot get in the river she (pilot boat) will take us off before we starve to death. Wind is rising. Now for the bar. *Keoka* do your best. 3 o'clock P.M.—the pilot Capt. White is walking the quarter deck with the air of one master of his business.

We are within one mile of the bar. Bout ship away we go all braced up sharp. Knocked off as usual. Ready about says the pilot. Another trial for the channel. Tack ship away we go again. We try it once more. The wind hauls one point in our favor. There is a slight change of wind but it is precious to us. Now she blows. We almost fly.

Hurrah, we are over the dreaded bar at last. Square the yards. Down goes the anchor in Baker's Bay. The pump is put in the cask and all are allowed to drink of the only remaining small cask of water that was received from

French bounty earner **COL. DE VILLEBOIS MAREUIL** crosses the Columbia River bar under tow.

the pilot boat. We have sailed by the log 2,000 miles. There comes a whale boat with provisions and water. (The two members of the ship's company who were landed in the canoe near Cape Lookout came with the whale boat to bring us water and would have crossed the bar that night if we had not got in the river.) A most timely relief. I am devouring a pound or two of raw pork. I can't wait for it to be cooked.

Another night of horrid tempest closes upon us but we are safe at anchor under the lea of Cape Disappointment. Four men from the Brig *Forrest* were lost yesterday on the beach and three from another vessel.

Sun. 6th—Ship at anchor. At 2 o'clock P.M. I left the decks of the *Keoka,* determined never to set foot on them again and in a whale boat with six other men, set sail for Clatsop. The weather was heavy, the bay very rough and in 10 minutes was struck by a squall which nearly capsized us. We run before it some three miles and finally affected a landing on the north shore.

Mon. 7th—At daybreak made choice of crossing the bay rough or smooth rather than lay here and starve. It is not more than 8 miles in a straight line but the way we must go it is 18 or twenty miles, so no time to lose. All aboard and off we go—sunrise—a heavy fog on the bar. We can't see a boat's length ahead and we have no compass so we must go by guess.

The open ocean on our right with breakers, on our starboard bow and a sand bar and breakers on our lee. All at once the fog is blown off and we have a full view Scylla—and Charybdis—sort-of-a-place. The only chance is to keep up to Chinook point: so we pull for it relieving each other every ten minutes or so. 12 P.M. We are abreast of the point. The tide is running out, with a current of eight miles per hour. A furious storm of hail and rain is coming down the river. We can't land, we can't anchor. We are obliged to make the south shore or perish. The men took the oars and I being the weakest took the helm. The wind blew so that we could not carry a rag of sail. We could afford to be blown four miles out of our course and still make land. Every man knew that his life depended upon his effort. Not a word was spoken.

Baker's Bay was as rough as wind could make water. We headed almost straight to the wind and in spite of the utmost exertions it

soon became apparent that we should be swept out the south channel into the breakers. Still we stood on our course in hopes the wind would lull. But on the contrary it seemed to increase. Still we had two chances left. One was to get under the lea of Sandy (Sand) Island and in case we should miss that to anchor just inside the breakers.

The Island seemed to be running up stream with the speed of two race horses, we had but a few rods left, about a dozen rods to the breakers between us and a watery grave. The anchor was dropped and though of only 25 lb. weight, it held on. Who can picture our condition, thoroughly denched with rain and spray, completely exhausted in strength, a gale that no craft could make headway against for a moment, blowing steadily out, large trees floating by us so near that we could touch them with an oar, and if one of those trees had parted our cable nothing could save us and darkness shutting in.

The parting of that little rope will sound our death knell. We knew we could not hold out till morning. The tide would turn in about an hour and be in our favor. The wind begins to lull and then come in puffs. It hauls round a little; we up anchor and set the mainsail. The boat leaps from one sea to another like a frightened horse, one man wants to jump overboard with fear. We put on the main jib which makes it easier to steer. I never saw such rough water. We have gained half a mile when snap goes our sprit; and we are glad of it: for it would have run us under bow foremost. I locked my feet in the baggage to keep from being washed off the stern sheets. I was almost blinded by the water that flew in my face and in sheets over the boat. Four miles up the bay lay a ship at anchor, and we must reach her. The men urged me to keep the boat more off the wind as we took such hard slaps at every plunge. It blows like a hurricane.

Our starboard stays parts; the mast breaks at the thwart; and mainsail and jib goes by the board. But we are within 100 yards of the ship *(Eliza)* and under her lea. I left the helm (the handle being unscrewed from the rudder) to take care of itself, and double banked an oar, and in 15 minutes raised eleven blisters on my hands. We got under her stern: they threw us a line and helped us aboard. She was dragging her anchor and surging heavily.

Capt. Nighton ordered supper for us, dry clothes and dry berths. We ate, drank, we slept till sunrise on Tuesday the 8th day of January.

German bark **ALSTERNIXE,** was one of the few ships to ever escape the awful clutches of dreaded Peacock Spit at the entrance to the Columbia River. She went ashore February 9, 1903. It was touch-and-go but she came off some time later, little damaged. *Photo supplied by Charles Fitzpatrick*

Big barkentine **COLLAROY** hard aground near the entrance to Humboldt Bay, California in June 1889. *Carl Christensen collection.*

On a Sunday, during salvage operations aboard the ill-fated ship **JOHN ROSENFELD** in 1886.

On departing Nanaimo B.C. with a cargo of coal the American ship **JOHN ROSENFELD** grounded on East Point, Saturna Island, February 19, 1886, in tow of the tug **TACOMA.** She went on the reef at high tide with 3,906 tons of coal. Twenty days of court hearing and 2,200 pages of testimony later, a libel suit against the tug owners brought $12,500, plus $2,500 damages to the owners of the Rosenfeld. Further testimony said the ship's master James G. Baker abandoned the wreck recklessly and commenced removing fittings before it was pronounced a total loss. The vessel later slipped off the reef and sank bequeathing her name to the British Columbia outcropping.

The Yankee clipper ship **NIGHTINGALE** was so skillfully constructed that she was exhibited at the World's Fair in London in 1851. In her logbook was recorded a swift run from Melbourne, Australia to New York in 75 days.

Launched in 1851, the clipper ship **FLYING CLOUD** was claimed as the largest merchant ship under the Stars and Stripes. She established half a dozen of the world's unequalled sailing records and reaped huge profits for her owners, making as much as $200,000 on a single voyage. On her maiden run she breezed around the Horn from the East Coast to the Golden Gate in a record smashing 89 days.

Those rip-roaring years in the wake of the California goldrush sent swift clipper ships like the **ADELAIDE** around the Horn under hard-driving masters of sail. The Adelaide was built by A. C. Bell in 1854 at New York.

The clipper ship **SOVEREIGN OF THE SEAS,** launched in 1852, influenced the design of all future clippers. She was built with an almost flat-bottomed hull to allow for greater cargo carrying capacity while still maintaining speed. On her maiden run to San Francisco, with a mainmast that reached over 200 feet into the sky, and able to carry more than 12,000 square feet of canvas, she made San Francisco in 103 days. She once ran from New York to Liverpool in a record 13 days, 13½ hours, and is said to have also attained a record speed for a sailing vessel of 22 knots.

The clipper ship **CONTEST** which was built to satisfy the rush for gold in California, broke many speed records fighting her way around the Horn to San Francisco and from there to the Orient.

One of the last of the typical Yankee clippers was the **SWEEPSTAKES.** She carried two acres of canvas. Launched in 1858, she was not only well known in California but perhaps moreso in old Australia when a goldrush broke out there yielding $80 million in a single year. *Currier & Ives drawings*

Ship **BALCLUTHA** riding out a severe gale in Bristol Channel (England) in the winter of 1894. Note men aloft furling sail. Reproduced from the famous painting by Oswald Brett, *courtesy Don Maskell & Co.*

England's most famous clipper ship, **CUTTY SARK,** built at Dumbarton in 1869 for John Willis of London. Reproduced from a painting by J. Spurling. *Courtesy Don Maskell & Co.*

Over the stern loading at the old Port Blakely mill docks on Bainbridge Island around the turn of the century. From left, American schooner **BLAKELY,** German bark **THALASSA** and Downeaster **BENJ. F. PACKARD.** *Webster & Stevens photo.*

Tall square-riggers at anchor on Chuckanut Bay on Puget Sound awaiting cargoes of coal in 1890.

Wreck of the British bark **PETER IREDALE** on Clatsop Beach, south of the Columbia River bar. She was wrecked October 25, 1906, and her remains are still visible at this writing, opposite old Fort Stevens, long an Oregon tourist attraction. Inbound for the Columbia River to load at Portland, the vessel was in ballast coming from Salina Cruz, Mexico.

The Downeasters

Though the grain trade from Pacific Northwest ports grew in considerable importance in the latter day of the commercial sailing vessel, the so named earlier Downeaster was spawned in New England for the challenge of carrying California grain to world ports. These rugged vessels which took over from the swift clipper ships, were designed to carry a good payload, sacrificing only a modicum of speed. They were known in every port from Calcutta and Cape Town to Hong Kong and Honolulu, and the chronicles of such ships created a colorful era, carving a niche for three decades.

The American flag on the high seas might have been a scarce item had it not been for the California grain trade. Many of the American clipper ships fell pray to the Confederate raiders in the Civil War and others were sold to foreign countries, many carrying with them brilliant records from the California gold rush trade. Their numbers were few with the rise of trade between California and the European market.

Thus came the birth of the Downeaster, a vessel that did not demand a large crew, an economical craft with medium clipper qualities and constructed only a little less rugged than a first-rate fighting vessel of the period. Skilled artisans at such New England ports as Bath, Thomaston, East Boston, Newburyport, Portsmouth and Mystic made their respective yards household words turning out a splendid wooden-hulled vessel with fine lines, smart in appearance and commanding dedicated shipmasters who demanded the utmost from their crews, standing rigging in tiptop shape at all times, and decks holystoned so clean one could scarce find a speck of dust.

The growth in the San Francisco grain trade was quite remarkable and from the late 1860's till the turn of the century the trade flourished with American flag vessels claiming a large share of the business.

According to the *Maritime History of Massachusetts*, the initial consignment of grain from San Francisco was carried by the clipper bark *Greenfield* in 1855. In her wake was the Boston clipper *Charmer*, destined for New York with a full cargo of wheat at $28 a ton. In 1860, San Francisco longshoremen loaded 58,926 barrels of flour and 1,088 tons of wheat on sailing vessels, but within ten years sailing vessels passing out through the Golden Gate carried no less than 243,000 tons of grain and 353,000 barrels of flour. The record was set in 1882, when a bumper crop demanded the services of 559 ships carrying 1,128,031 tons of wheat and barley and 919,898 barrels of flour.

Some splendid passages were made by the grain carriers but ironically in the San Francisco to Europe route one of the best records was set by an American bark built on Puget Sound by skilled builders that had migrated from New England. She was the 1,127 ton *Cassandra Adams,* built at Seabeck, Washington Territory in 1876. She made the passage in 105 days.

The Cape Horn route made heavy demands on the square-riggers in both directions and canvas, rope, masts and spars had to be of the best available material to withstand the gaff. Mostly native woods were utilized in the construction of the Downeasters. Stem, stern-post and other principal segments were created of white oak while the outside planking and interior lining were of pitch-pine which was also used for deck beams. Keel and keelsons were of pitch pine and knees were generally cut from Maine hackmatack fastened with locust treenails. Many of the vessels had brass or copper bolts throughout while others utilized iron bolts. Bottom planking was felted and coppered and deckhouses were of oak planked with white pine. Interior cabins, were tastefully done in bird's eye maple or choice mahogany accompanied by an oyster shell colored paint over pitch pine panelling, but with none of the gingerbread work generally found on the speedy American clipper ships.

Rigging-wise, three skysails were frequently displayed but few Downeasters crossed double top-gallant yards. Nevertheless the three upper yards squared and equally spaced gave them a handsome appearance. Masts were frequently three pitch pine logs bolted together, rounded off, varnished and banded by six inch iron hoops.

Stunsails virtually disappeared with the clipper ship and only three of the standard Downeasters carried them—the *Jabez Howes, Indiana* and *Paul Revere.*

Downeasters were easily recognized from a distance by their large wheelhouses and monkey-poops, caravel built boats, long boats on the skids of the midship-house, inverted, and whale boats swung from davits on either quarter. Items of great importance for Cape Horners were the main bilge pumps and two wing bilge pumps carried in the ship waists.

There were many renowned New England ship-building firms—Flint and Chapman; Goss, Sawyer and Packard; the Sewalls, the Houghtons, Sam Watts, Ed O'Brien, N.L. Thompson, Titcomb & Thompson, C.F. Sargent and numerous others.

When the larger steel and iron hulled foreign flag sailing vessels and steamers reduced the role of the American Downeaster, many were relegated to other trades, and a large share of the fleet came under shipping firms based on the Pacific Coast. They found employment in the offshore lumber trade, Alaska cannery operations or in coastal trading. Though shorn of some of their rigging, scarred and mistreated, many lived to a ripe old age while others left their bones on the reefs and shoals of the hostile north Pacific shores.

The author, and Yachats fire chief Steve Hamilton, examine a portion of an old wreck uncovered after decades under the sand and gravel of the beach near China Creek, just north of Heceta Head. Brass and iron spikes, charred ribs and timbers, coal and ballast rocks marked the grave. Checking back in old Coast Survey records we learned that it was part of the four-masted ship **OCEAN KING,** Captain C.H. Sawyer, bound for San Pedro from Nanaimo in 1887, laden with 3,850 tons of coal. Buffeted by a gale off the Oregon coast between Cape Blanco and Cape Arago, she had to be abandoned in leaking condition. The crew was rescued by the schooner **ANGEL DOLLY.** Evidently the coal cargo must have caught fire as the wreckage drifted northward, a derelict. The 2,434 ton vessel was built on the east coast.

A miserable ending for the Columbia River Packers ship **JABEZ HOWES.** She was driven ashore near Chignik, Alaska in the spring of 1911 with 114 souls aboard. All reached shore safely but the 34 year old wooden-hulled vessel was a total loss below the snow-covered wastes of Alaska's rugged hills.

Wreck of the barge **AMERICA,** a former full-rigged ship and the tug **LORNE** on the outcrops of San Juan Island, Washington. The **LORNE,** towing the **AMERICA** from Seattle to Vancouver B.C. with a cargo of coal was a victim of fog on stranding August 30, 1914. The tug was salvaged, but the former semi-clipper ship became a total loss. She frequently raced the clipper **GLORY OF THE SEAS** when both vessels operated under sail in the California-Nanaimo run.

A toy ship on a mill pond? No, a real ship on a real sea—ship **JAMES DRUMMOND** on a peaceful bay on Puget Sound. *Courtesy Captain A. F. Raynaud*

This is the large classic four-masted bark **DONNA FRANCISCA** off the Strait of Juan de Fuca after the turn of the century. *Photo by H. H. Morrison, courtesy, Gordon Ross.*

Three-masted ship **TWO BROTHERS**, registered at San Francisco and under the ownership of Samuel Blair was cut down to a barge in 1903. *Courtesy Marine Digest.*

Final hour for the bark **JAMES CHESTON**, purposely grounded opposite Port Townsend and burned for her metal. Burned in the late 1890's her chronicale dated from 1855 when she was built at Baltimore, Maryland. She first visited Port Townsend in the 1860's and was for many years a lumber carrier in the service of Puget Sound Commercial Company. *From the collection of the late James McCurdy, later that of H. W. McCurdy.*

The hard working barkentine **ARCHER** did much of her trading from the West Coast. *Photo by O. Beaton (1912), courtesy Joe Williamson.*

Wreck of the barge **AMERICA** (left) and the tug **LORNE,** one mile west of Kanaka Bay, San Juan Island, Washington August 31, 1914. The tug was towing the barge in heavy fog when both went aground. The barge, formerly an American semi-clipper ship, laden with coal was a total loss. The vessel was built in 1874.

Grounded in the fog west of Port Angeles, Washington, the American brig **TANNER,** in 1903. She was later refloated. The trader was built in 1855.

Wreck of the British bark **PETER IREDALE** visited by horse and buggy in 1906 on Oregon's Clatsop Beach. *Coe photo.*

After stranding at the entrance to Willapa (Shoalwater Harbor), Washington, in 1901, the salvaged British bark **POLTALLOCH** eventually came under San Francisco owners. She is seen here in Pacific Northwest waters in a picture taken by O. Beaton probably off the Columbia River in the year 1913.

Like spiders in a web, crewmen of the stranded German bark **MIMI** tend the rigging 160 feet above the deck in the winter of 1913. The ship is aground near the Nehalem River in Oregon.

This is believed to be the French merchantman **FEUGOT** inbound to a West Coast port for a cargo of grain in the early 1900's.

Oops! Watch that camera. Big sea spray hits cameraman trying to take a photograph of the stranded British ship **GLENESSLIN** on the rocks below Neah-Kah-Nie mountain in Oregon in 1913.

Crew gathered on the fo'c'sle head after taking in the jibs aboard spritely bark **PERHYN CASTLE.**

Pride of the German merchant fleet serving the Pacific Coast was the **THEKLA,** seen here laden-down and outbound.

This fine looking steel ship is the German sailer **NIXE** of Bremen gathering wind as she moves toward a Northwest port in ballast. *Photo by H. H. Morrison.*

Thought provoking by its very presence is this fine steel three-masted bark, **MOLIERE,** which flew the French Tricolor, just after the turn of the century.

Sinking? No, only coasting in the trough of a great swell . . . Bark **STAR OF LAPLAND.**

Moving out of Seattle's Elliott Bay in 1913, the steam tug **GOLIAH** of Puget Sound Tug Boat Co. tows the barge **DASHING WAVE,** one of the last survivors of the clipper ship era. The Dashing Wave was built at Portsmouth, N.H. in 1853. Two decades later she came to the Pacific Coast and operated as a lumber drougher, coastwise, for C. Hanson & Co., Tacoma. In 1901 she was cut down to a barge for Taku Canning Co., and finally wrecked on Shelter Point, Vancouver Island in 1920. *O. Beaton photo.*

A unit of the Columbia River Packers Assn., the cannery supply ship **JABEZ HOWES** is pictured off Astoria about 1908. This three-masted ship was built at Newburyport, Mass., in 1877, and was driven ashore at Chignik, Alaska in April, 1911, with 114 persons on board, all reaching shore safely. *Woodfield photo.*

Four-mast Finnish bark **DUNDEE** berthed at Astoria, Oregon in 1911. The cro-jack yard is trimmed, the vessel discharging her ballast. The Dundee was registered at Mariehamn. *Courtesy E. A. Erickson.*

The five-masted steam auxiliary bark **R. C. RICKMERS,** flying the German flag, made history after her maiden arrival on the West Coast in 1908. She was one of the largest sailing vessels ever built, carrying 50,000 square feet of canvas, and was also the largest sailing vessel ever to enter the Columbia River. The vessel is pictured here off Astoria. Under Captain Bandelin, owned by Messrs. Rickmers & Co., she had a triple expansion auxiliary of 1,200 hp. The R. C. Rickmers was captured by the British during World War I.

"The beauty and mystery of ships, and the magic of the sea." The British steel bark **INVERCLYDE** at the end of the voyage in 1914. *Photo by Capt. G. E. Plummer*

German four-masted bark **THEKLA,** flying her signal flags.

"Oh, the times are hard and the wages low, Leave her, Johnny, leave her! I'll pack my bag and go below, It's time for us to leave her!" The big British sailing vessel **PINMORE** off Cape Flattery.

Like a painted ship on a painted sea—this big steel bark poses for her picture off the Columbia River in 1913. *Capt. O. Beaton photo*

Famous builder of clipper ships, **DONALD McKAY.**

A sight to behold—German four-mast ship **THEKLA** headed for northern Europe via Cape Horn.

Ready to tow in—the **W. J. ROTCH** and **HARRY MORSE** back in the early years of this century. *Capt. G. E. Plummer photo.*

Chapter Two

The Whaling Ship of Old Comes to Hawaii and Alaska

"The wonder is always new that any sane man can be a sailor."
—Emerson

Another romantic ear on the Pacific was the coming of the whaling ships. Though it may seem romantic to us today it was a rough, tough and often tragic experience for those who sailed under harsh masters on voyages that sometimes lasted up to three years. One of the few hopeful notes in the weary heary of the whalesman was when his ship dropped anchor off a Paradise isle and Jack was permitted to come ashore.

Both Hawaiian and Alaskan waters became major hunting grounds of the English and Yankee whaling ships.

Just as the swallows return each year to Capistrano, California, so does the Humpback whale return every November to the Lahaina Roadstead, the historic anchorage between the islands of Maui, Lanai and Molokai in the Hawaiian archipelago. In winter months there is nothing more intriguing than the sight of a playful 60 ton behemoth cavorting the azure Pacific. The whales arrive off the old royal capital of Lahaina today in mid-November just as they did more than a century ago. They romp with their young calves until May, when they begin the long swim back to the Bering Sea.

These great denizens of the deep, often over 50 feet in length are not fish but rather are great mammals. Like man and all other mammals, the whale breathes by means of lungs, not gills, and is a warm-blooded creature.

According to the *Encyclopaedia Britannica* one Alaska whale hunting settlement has dated back to AD 100 or 200.

There was a fishery started on the western side of the North Atlantic, centered at New England as early as 1645 to seek out the "right" whale. By 1880 it gave way to the great American sperm whale fishery begun in 1712 when a shore whaler blown off the coast in a storm, fastened on to a sperm whale and got it home safely.

New England whaling vessels sought the whale off the Azores in 1765, off Brazil in 1774 and in the Indian Ocean in 1788. Although Great Britain (in 1788) was first after sperm and humpback whales in the Pacific, the monopoly of this world-wide industry was American. In the peak year 1846 there were 729 Yankee whaleships at sea. A slow decline followed, though the last sperm whaling voyage was not made until 1925. The demise probably started by several causes, the foremost being the discovery of petroleum in Pennsylvania in 1859.

The sperm whale fishery was perhaps the only old style venture not ended by over fishing. As a consequence of the sperm whalers explorations, two further species were exploited. The Southern right whale, at first taken in great numbers around the southern Continents and sub-antarctic islands fared like its congener in the north and was greatly reduced by 1900. The Pacific gray whale, hugging the California coast on its winter migration suffered great depredations in the breeding lagoons from the boats both of whale ships and shore stations.

The warning shout of the old whalers, "Thar she blows!" refers to the powerful exhalation of breath which the whale makes when he rises to the surface from the ocean depths. As the heated breath strikes the open air, it condenses, forming a spume of vapor. Appearing like a column of water, this blast of expired air is still searched for by lookouts seeking out the leviathan. The whale is dependent on its great layer of blubber lying between its skin and flesh for warmth. The tail of a whale, called its flukes, spreads out in the horizontal, whereas the tail of a fish is vertical.

The whales come on a "honeymoon" and the waters off the island of Maui are a great breeding ground for the Humpbacks. For many years Lahaina Roads has been referred to as "The

Scenes taken aboard the old Bath-built Ship **ST. PAUL** at Ballard in the 1930's.

Whales Maternity Ward." Whales give birth not oftener than every two years. The young are born, live and nurse on their mother's milk. The whale mother is very loving and attentive and it is a memorable sight to see a mother and her calf playing in the warm, clear waters.

Occasionally a true decendant of "Moby Dick" himself may be seen—a pure white whale, swimming with his fellows, who are black with white undersides.

Though some whales have actual teeth, the Humpback has tusks of whalebone, also called baleen. To feed, the whale gulps a huge qauntity of seawater and then forces it back out through his baleen, trapping inside the tiny shrimp and crustaceans which provide its nourishment. During their stay off Maui the whales will often range as far as the tip of Oahu, sometimes even to Kauai. They also sweep along Maui's southern and eastern shores as far as Hana.

The whales can often be approached from downwind. Boats get within a few feet of the lazing mammals.

The arch enemy of the Humpback, the New England whalerman, also knew Lahaina Roadstead well. The town of Lahaina provided fun, frolic and food for the whaling crews after harsh, weary months in the Arctic. As many as 450 ships could be found anchored at Lahaina during the winters of the early 1800's. Maui's rum was greatly favored over that of the other islands, and the night saw much activity.

Whaling days in Hawaii are over, however, except for the yearly visit of the Humpback and the annual Lahaina Whaling Spree. The days of sail and harpoons are vividly recalled as are the whalermen who risked life and limb in their frail craft to subdue these behemoths to obtain a little oil for the lamps of the world. But the trail of adventures both at sea and ashore lives on.

The largest living thing on earth is the blue, or sulphur bottom whale which grows to a length of over 100 feet and weighs up to 125 tons. The world's fiercest animal is a killer whale—sometimes called the grampus—which reaches a top length of only 30 feet. Even larger whales flee from the ferocity of this creature because the species will attack in packs and bite huge chunks out of the victim, literally tearing it to pieces.

Though the Humpback was traditional off the Hawaiian Islands it was a formidable foe for the whalerman, just as the whalerman was often a formidable foe for the native populace of the islands.

It perhaps all started even before the American missionaries arrived in the islands. The crews of two whale ships, the *Balaena* of New Bedford and the *Equator* of Nantucket, killed a whale off Kealakekua Bay, Hawaii, in September 1819, and the next month two more whaleships visited the islands, the vanguard of a vast fleet to use the Hawaiian ports.

Lahaina, in its day, was a bustling, crowded place especially when the whaling fleet was in. An idea of its great activity is given by Dr. Dwight Baldwin, medical missionary, who wrote: "Ten days since we had two whaleships, next day ten came in and the next day six. From that time to this, scarce an hour but we have seen from one to half a dozen coming down the channel—50 ships now here."

During every spring and fall from the early 1820's through the 1860's the whale fleet repeated the operation. Lahaina Roads was considered the main anchorage of America's Pacific whaling fleet and the town became the crossroads between sea-weary, women-hungry, grog-thirsty whalermen and the ever accommodating Hawaiian natives.

Lahaina boasted as many as 429 whaling ships arriving in 1846, the peak year. Fledgling Honolulu could claim only 167 in that same year.

Lahaina boasted a population of 3,000 persons, who dwelled in 882 grass houses and 59 stone or wooden houses which in the outward sense left it still very much of a native settlement.

The anchorage was described by A. P. Taylor, pioneer:

"The anchorage being an open roadstead, vessels can always approach or leave it with any wind that blows. No pilot is needed here. Vessels generally approach through the channel between Maui and Molokai, standing well over to Lanai, as far as the trades will carry them, then take the sea breeze, which sets in during the forenoon, and heads for town. The anchorage is about ten miles in extent along the shore and from within a cable's length of the reef in seven fathoms of water, to a distance of three miles out with some twenty-five fathoms, affording abundant room for as large a fleet as can ever be collected here."

Each ship was boarded by the Harbor Master who presented the captain with a copy of the port regulations. Taylor continued:

"Every Master of a foreign vessel who desires the privilege of purchasing refreshments for his vessel at Lahaina, shall pay to the Harbor Master, ten dollars, in return for which said Master shall be entitled to receive five barrels of potatoes, with the privilege of purchasing at pleasure in the market, supplies for his ship, according to the rules of the place."

The records of Dr. Baldwin still remain and they tell that the chief food items supplied to the ships were "water, hogs, goats, bananas, melons, pumpkins, onions, squashes, sweet potatoes, young turkeys, ducks, fowls, and beef, of which can be had in abundance; but the greatest article for which they come is Irish potatoes which grow plentifully in the interior of this island."

The rancid, vermin-infested drinking water on the old whalers made it necessary that they put into the islands for water, and above all else fresh water was the number one item sought at Lahaina. Of course, to the seamen and whalermen, the chocolate-colored Polynesian maidens often took precedence over water and many whalermen jumped ship for the security of the easy living in the islands.

The process of procuring water was described by the whaling skippers as follows: "It was the custom for the whale ships to land the casks to be filled with water upon the beach, then the kanakas would roll them to the watering place, and after filling, roll them back to the beach and raft them off to the boats."

Lahaina offered the whalermen recreation, reveals the *Lahaina Historical Guide* (Maui Historical Society). It reveals that several whaling captains of old pointed out in a letter to the government, "The life of a whaler is one of hardship and toil, and upon his arrival at your port, he needs rest and relaxation. This is absolutely necessary to the lives of the sailors that they should have liberty days . . ." It was over what were considered the necessary ingredients of a sailor's "rest and relaxation" that the missionaries and government officials ashore, and the whalers afloat, carried on a continuing feud which burst into violence from time to time. The first serious Lahaina riot broke out in October 1825, when the crew of the English whaler *Daniel,* angered by a new law passed by the chief prohibiting women from visiting the ships, roamed the streets menacingly for three days. They twice threatened the home and lives of the Reverend William Richards and his wife, believing them to be instigators of the law.

The riot of 1827 was also started by an English whaler, this time under command of a Yankee, Captain Clark. Governor Hoapili, finding that some women had broken the tabu and gone aboard the whaler *John Palmer,* seized Captain Clark's boat and would not let him go back to his ship until the women had been returned. Captain Clark told his mate that if he had not been released within an hour, the ship should fire upon the town. After the Reverend Mr. Richards got Captain Clark's promise to return the women, he was released; but before he could reach his ship, the *John Palmer* began

firing. Apparently the muzzle-loaders were aimed directly at the mission house for the cannon balls landed in the yard. When Captain Clark boarded his ship, the firing ceased; but he sailed away to Honolulu without returning the women, and evidently the native belles were delighted by all of the fuss caused over them, and willingly took passage.

Naturally, as in all early day seaport towns, the control of liquor was the major problem. Lahaina was not without exception. It was a problem in which the whaling masters shared, as a letter from several of the captains to Governor Hoapili of Maui shows:

"We do not any of us like to go to Oahu, because bad men sell rum to our seamen. We like your island, because you have a good law preventing the sale of this poison. But now, after lying here in peace for some weeks, a vessel has come among us from Oahu with rum for sale. Our seamen are drinking it, and trouble is commencing. We now look to you for protection . . ."

In 1843, while the islands were temporarily ceded to England, grog shops were licensed and rioting flared up again. Dr. Baldwin describes an attack on Hawaiian royalty as follows:

"A party of half drunken sailors went to the King's to take him. The King's people returned the sailors' stones with great fury and one of his attendants knocked the leader senseless to the ground. After the riot was dispersed, he was taken to the fort—but the war went on. A

Ship **A. J. FULLER** locked in the Bering Sea ice. Built at Bath, Maine in 1881, by J. McDonald, the vessel was lost by collision in Seattle's Elliott Bay in 1918 on return from Bristol Bay with a $500,000 cargo of canned salmon.

chief on horseback was assailed by the sailors with stones—the natives flew to his aid, and stones flew on both sides—some skulls supposed to be broken—but none have yet proved fatal. Towards evening as the seamen gathered towards the landing—war, noise, oaths, obscenities, and hurled stones filled the air—but a party armed with swords by the authority, somewhat moderated the rage of the sailors."

The frustrating years rolled on and by 1845 Lahaina's constable complained, "There are so many beer shops here, and they have so many chances of selling spirits in their beer without detection that if I do all I can, and use all the means in my power, I cannot get a fair chance to find them . . ."

Though not considered so at the time, nor for many years after, the most renowned sailor to arrive at Lahaina was the immortal Herman Melville, who was to later write the book *Typee* and the classic literary gem, *Moby Dick*. He arrived at Lahaina on April 26, 1843 aboard the *Charles and Henry*, a Yankee whaler out of Nantucket, owned by Charles and Henry Coffin. He shipped aboard at Eimeo, after wandering in Tahiti with Long Ghost. Melville took his discharge at Lahaina, where he stayed until May 18, when he sailed on the *Star* for Honolulu. His departure was well timed, for the week following his departure, the *Achusnet,* which he had jumped in the Marquesas to hide out in Typee Valley, arrived at Lahaina Roadstead. The first thing the skipper, Captain Pease, did on coming ashore was to go to the U.S. Commercial agent to report, "Richard T. Greene and Herman Melville deserted at Nukehiva July 9, 1842."

Had they been at Lahaina they would have been placed behind bars for many months. But who can blame the likes of a whalerman for jumping ship for the solitude of a peaceful island?

The whaling ship men continued to play a dominant roll in the mid-1850's in lively old Lahaina. There, the waterfront was considered to have been a miniature of San Francisco's Barbary Coast, and the whalemen were determined to maintain its reputation. It was, to say the least, a wide open, hellish town of whiskey, easy women and whale oil.

As in most pioneer waterfront towns, the church goers carried on their crusade against the trends of evil. The two factions met head on. Vociferous efforts turned toward physical

From 1912 to 1923 the three-masted ship **ABNER COBURN** made annual voyages to the Bristol Bay area for Libby McNeill & Libby in their cannery operations. She is seen here in the frozen northland.

and often bloody conflict on the streets. The churchmen in their frustration even went so far as to extinguish the harbor navigation light to prevent whale ships from dropping anchor in the harbor by night. Again as before, to gain their revenge, during the Sunday service, the whale ships sometimes pointed their signal cannon in the direction of the church and lobbed cannon balls into the church yard. Though no direct hits were ever scored they sometimes came within whistling distance of the church bell and often kept parishioners minds off the spoken word.

A leading churchman in the town once labeled the settlement "one of the foulest breathing holes of hell."

It should be told that those protesting missionary leaders were instrumental in providing a seamen's rest home and reading room but most of the whalermen were more interested in other pursuits. This humanitarian act was literally overlooked in contrast with the sinful aspects of the old Hawaiian seaport.

Fortunately, disputings among rival factions faded slowly away, actually a victory for the Christians. The fleet of whale ships after 1865, began to take their trade to the island of Oahu, and fledgling Honolulu port became the leading

Idle in Lake Washington, ship **ST. PAUL** in the 1920's after roaming the seas of the Pacific and the Atlantic. *Webster & Stevens photo.*

mecca for the whale ships until the business began to wane.

Though Yankee whaling was solidly a New England institution, the growing presence of the whale ships on the Pacific gave them a close tie with the West. The first Yankee whaler to be insured by a West Coast underwriter was the old bark *Harrison,* in the year 1869. After a successful voyage to North Pacific waters, the *Harrison* sailed for the breeding grounds of Baja California. In a great storm she was smashed against the rocks near Pichilinque above La Paz, Mexico. When the tempest had stilled, the old whaler lay a hopeless wreck and about the only thing that kept her memory alive was the master's spyglass. It was kept on display at the Fireman's Fund insurance office in San Francisco until lost in the great 1906 earthquake and fire. Inasmuch as the telescope was the only thing of value from the wreck, it was referred to as the $3,000 spyglass, the amount for which the insurance policy had been written and which was paid in full.

The whaling men had a rugged life, for not only did they run the risk of death in harpooning and catching the whales from small boats, but worked long hours aboard, tending the needs of the ship, and cutting up the whales. The whale blubber was cut into chunks to be tried in the steaming vats. Once all the oil that could be cooked and squeezed from the blubber was barreled, what remained was used for fuel under the vats. The stench of a whaler is unforgettable—a thick, smoky, slightly fishy odor which is in a distinct class all its own.

Perhaps the greatest tragedy of all times among the New England whaling fleets occurred in the year 1871. Forty whalers bound for the rich grounds to the north, had entered the Arctic Ocean. Of the fleet, 33 of the vessels worked the waters off Point Belcher, some 60 miles south of Point Barrow, Alaska, where the seas abounded with leviathans. The catch was good and work continued around the clock.

On August 11, working to beat the early freeze up, trouble reared its ugly head. Driven by a persistent west wind, the ice floes threatened to trap the fleet against the shoreline. The immediate danger, however, passed, though the local Eskimos warned the whalermen that they should get out while they could. Failing to heed the warning the vessels remained, taking a bonanza of the great mammals. Weigh anchor they would not. They waited too long. On August 29, the ice commenced to drift again and this time great giant floes closed in, trapping the whale ships. With the long winter months ahead and crushing ice all about, the situation became perilous. The masters of the ships were forced to order abandonment. Failing to heed the words of the wise was to cost a fortune in ships and their valuable whale oil cargoes. The army of whalermen headed south in the hope of reaching seven of the whale ships working in safer waters. A total of 1,200 souls, including a few women and children, took off in one of the strangest armadas ever seen. Scores of whaleboats moving across 80 miles of ice-choked sea to gain safety. It was a cold chilling ordeal, and an amazing miracle that no lives were lost. The boats were rowed, sailed and pushed. Finally the survivors arrived at the anchorage of those ships which had wisely stayed behind in safer waters. All were packed aboard these vessels which quickly set sail. Such a downcast group of survivors have seldom been seen —many had lost all but the shirts on their backs.

Several underwriting companies failed after paying the losses, as all but one of the 33 trapped ships were totalled out as the ice completed its destruction throughout the severe winter. The strain on the underwriters was staggering and most shied away from further risk. Only one of the ships lost, the bark *Carlotta,* was insured by a West Coast firm. The $12,500 insurance carried on the ship was promptly paid.

Losses of whaling ships and those who manned them were staggering during that era, but no single whaling fleet demise ever eclipsed the financial tragedy of 1871, not even in the destructive raids on the whaling fleets in the Pacific during the Civil War.

The adventures of the old whaling ships are legion.

One of the bizarre dramas of the sea was enacted in the year 1860.

On September 22 of that year, the whaling ship *Hope* was nearly becalmed in the dangerous ice floes near Tierra del Fuego islands at the southernmost tip of South America when she came upon a huge ice mass that had drifted northward from the frozen wastes of the Antarctic.

All eyes were peering at the great wall of azure blue ice when suddenly Captain Brighton, master of the *Hope,* ordered the men to heave to. Then, in frightening astonishment they lined the railing. Before their very eyes the walls of the ice mass began to crack and split open, so that large hunks of ice parted and drifted away in the silent current. Then, as though peering through thick imperfect glass they saw the weird outline of a derelict ship. Indeed, they thought it only a strange appari-

tion. As their eyes remained glued to the indistinct shape inside the mass, more ice came crashing down. There, suddenly before them was the definite outline of a schooner. In silent awe they stood spellbound.

Hastily the captain ordered a boat lowered and he, with some volunteers rowed to the mystery ship. As they came close they were able to make out in faded letters across her counter, the name *Jenny.* On climbing aboard they walked on the moss-green decks and were immediately confronted with a lifelike scene of death.

In the main cabin were eight men, a woman and a dog, sitting or lying in the same positions as when they had perished, all perfectly preserved as if figures in a wax museum. The deep freeze had done its job well.

In the master's cabin the skipper was found still sitting in his chair. In his hand was clutched a quill pen and on his writing table in front of him lay the faded log of his vessel. In scratchy letters he had painfully penned the last entry, dated May 4, 1823. It read, "No food for 71 days. I am the only one left alive."

Thirty-seven freezing years had passed since the *Jenny's* master had made that final entry. The schooner had become trapped in the ice on January 17, 1823 the log revealed, and gradually became locked in. As the agonizing weeks rolled by, the vessel became encased in that frozen trap. The log showed that her de-

The **MERCURY** came to the Pacific Coast in the 1880's under ownership of Renton, Holmes & Co., and was registered at Port Townsend. Built at New York, as a Havre packet, the old bark is seen here, wrecked while serving as a barge for the Pacific Clipper Line, near Skagway, Alaska April 11, 1898. Standing by are the tugs **RESOLUTE** and the **CITY OF ASTORIA.** *Webster & Stevens photo.*

The golden age of whaling is depicted here by artist G. Johnson. The whaleships spent much of their time in the Pacific catching the big ones. One of the most successful was the staunch whaler **CHARLES W. MORGAN,** still afloat as a museum ship at Mystic, Conn. The photo here depicts one of the Morgan's whale boats hot after a leviathan. *Courtesy Atlantic Mutual Insurance Co.*

parture port had been Lima, Peru and her last port of call, a transparent coffin of ice.

The food on board had lasted for five weeks, and then came that terrible ordeal of exposure and starvation that teamed up to claim all hands—one after another. The ship's master had hung on, to the bitter end, until his feeble, frozen hands made that last entry before death.

The eerie, haunting scene prompted but a short visit by the crew of the *Hope.* They gathered up the log, the navigation instruments and a few pieces of equipment and then returned to their ship. They had elected not to bury the dead but to leave them at rest aboard the rotting derelict.

The very next morning the *Jenny* was almost fully released from the ice. Her seams opened up and she began to fall to pieces. As the crew of the *Hope* stood by, still in disbelief, they watched the *Jenny* sink beneath the surface and the sea swallow up her dead.

On arriving back in England, the *Hope's* master reported the facts of his discovery to the British Admiralty and presented the log as proof. In the archives today, that log still exists, relating one of the uncanny tales of the sea.

THE SECOND JONAH

"Now the Lord had prepared a great fish to swallow up Jonah. And Jonah was in the belly of the fish three days and three nights."

THE BIBLE
Book of Jonah 1:17

As has been stated, life in the whaleships of old was difficult, often three years at sea under the most trying conditions—long hours, hard work, privation, loneliness, sickness, shipwreck, starvation and death were often the menu. Little wonder that many jumped ship in remote but enticing South Pacific islands. Once in the frigid Arctic and Antarctic waters they were locked out from the rest of the world and their odoriferous prison was all that stood between them and extinction.

Many of these rugged whaling men met their deaths from the battering of an enraged mammal pocked with stinging harpoons. Imagine several tons of havoc smashing into a whaleboat tearing it asunder and pitching its contents into the vortex? Then the awful whiplash of the whale's tail which maimed and killed. Sometimes whales actually swallowed their victims.

In rare instances mammoth whales would attack the mother sailing vessels inflicting heavy

Auxiliary steam-powered schooner-rigged JEANIE, after 1887 operated out of San Francisco with the Pacific Steam Whaling Co. as a supply ship for their whaling vessels, making annual voyages to Alaska with coal and provisions. The rugged vessel, built in Bath, Maine in 1883 by Goss & Sawyer, in 1906 was in a collision with the steamer DIX off Seattle's Alki Point. The Dix sank with a loss of 39 lives. The Jeanie was originally four-masted, her mizzen doubling as an exhaust stack. She is seen here after alterations.

damage on massive hull timbers, much to the horror of those who watched helplessly. Sometimes they even sank large whalers.

To emulate the miraculous experience of Jonah of old, seems inconceivable in our time. That the Hebrew prophet emerged from the whale's belly after three days, by divine providence, alive, unharmed and much the wiser for his experience goes without saying. That such an act could be repeated seems highly remote but truth can be stranger than fiction.

David Gunston writing in the *Lookout,* the New York Seamen's Church Institute publication, tells of only one known incident of a modern sequel to the ancient story of Jonah.

In February, 1891, the British whaling vessel *Star of the East* returning from the Pacific was cruising near the far southern Falkland Islands, then a crossroads for ocean-roving whaling ships. The vessel was in search of sperm whales or cachalots, the huge barrel-headed 60-70 foot long kin of Moby Dick, which were at that time still the backbone of the industry.

The lookout, high on the mainmast suddenly bellowed, "Thar she blows!"

The deck jumped with activity. Less than three miles away a huge sperm was cavorting sending sizable geysers of water skyward. With great haste two whaleboats were dropped into the sea. Oars beat the water and harpooners stood like statues at the bows, weapons in hand. The first whaleboat to near the giant mammal came dangerously close and the harpooner flung his lance with precise accuracy. Writhing, the leviathan curved over to dive, its 12 foot wide forked tail flipping upward and catching the approaching second whale boat by surprise. There was massive turbulence. The

The Seattle waterfront in 1878, showing at left, the remains of the venerable old clipper ship WINDWARD. Three years earlier she stranded at Useless Bay, Whidbey Island. Refloated, the wreck was towed to Seattle and beached. Sold to J. M. Colman, the vessel was eventually covered over with waterfront fill and her remains now lie deep under the sod at Western Avenue between Columbia and Marion Streets in downtown Seattle. Built at Bath, Maine in 1854, the Windward stranded on Whidbey Island December 30, 1875, while carrying lumber to San Francisco from Puget Sound in command of Captain A. E. Williams.

Mammoth swell on the Columbia River bar. British ship **BATTLE ABBEY** tows to sea in 1911.

Arduous hours later the massive carcass of the whale was lying alongside the *Star of the East* waiting to be flensed. The crew set to work and spent the remainder of the day and part of the night dismembering their haul, rendering down into oil its thick underskin of blubber. The following morning they pursued their gory task, attaching lifting tackle to the whale's stomach, now fully exposed, and hoisted it on to the deck for cutting up. The men were suddenly startled by what appeared to be a spasmodic movement within the monster. Being well acquainted with the voracious appetites of the sperms, and doubtless expecting to see a large fish perhaps even a shark still alive, they immediately split open the great paunch. Inside to their horror, was the missing Bartley, doubled up, drenched, unconscious.

Not believing their eyes, the crew laid the still figure out on the deck and treated him with a crude but effective dousing of cold sea water. After several minutes of the shower, the man began to revive but was incoherent. Shivering, he was carried to the captain's cabin, placed in his bunk and bundled in blankets.

The ship's master down to the lowest seaman treated Bartley with kindness and solicitude rare among men of such rough exterior. For over two weeks Bartley remained under lock and key. His possible recovery had often been despaired. He was a half-human, gibbering lunatic. Gradually, however, he began to regain possession of his senses and by the end of the third week had virtually recovered from the psychic shock of the fantastic experience.

While housed in the whale's belly his unclothed parts were exposed to the terrible gastric juices which coated his face, neck and hands a ghastly white. The badly shrivelled appearance of his skin was akin to death itself. Those who saw him likened his looks to old parchment.

When at last the survivor could talk coherently of his ordeal he recalled the frightening sensation of being cast from the boat into the sea. Then followed a tremendous rushing sound which he thought to be the whale's tail slashing the water. Suddenly he was bound up in utter darkness. The sensation of slipping along a smooth passage that itself seemed to move him along and carry him onward, burned in his mind. This sensation lasted only a short while, and then he realized he had more room. As Bartley groped about in the blackness he

frail craft was split asunder and the men struggled to keep from going under. The other boat jockeyed in to pick up the survivors as the whale plunged, the lance still buried deep in its side. The survivors were picked up but one of their number had drowned and another was missing. The latter was a hardy young seaman named James Bartley.

Undaunted by this misfortune the whalesmen pursued the whale with added compulsion to kill the monster and avenge the death of their shipmates.

touched the walls of his slimy prison and then it dawned on his confused mind what had actually happened. Immediately he was filled with horror.

The air was difficult to get into his lungs and the heat was almost unbearable—a close oppressive heat that seemed to open up his pores and draw out his every ounce of vitality. In a short time he became desperately ill and extremely weak, haunted by the fact that there was no escape. Telling himself that he must face death calmly he was still very conscious of his predicament—the terrible darkness, the heat, the misery and the strange and eerie quiet.

Finally Bartley lapsed into unconsciousness and remembered nothing more until awakening in the master's cabin.

Little else is recorded of James Bartley's subsequent fate except that his terrible experience did not curtail his seagoing career. He shunned publicity concerning his experience, although after the *Star of the East* returned to her home port her officers and captain issued separate detailed accounts of the incident. The case was later taken up and investigated thoroughly by M. de Parville, scientific editor of the *Paris Journal des Debats*.

Numerous cases were reported through the years of whales in their dying agonies having swallowed human beings, but this is the first recorded case other than Jonah where the victim has come forth still alive. A number of natural history writers received accounts of Bartley's experience third and forth hand and insisted such a phenomenon could not have

A frequent visitor to San Francisco in days of yore was the ship **W. R. GRACE,** one of the progenitors of the Grace Line fleet. Bath built in 1873, this ship made 12 runs from New York to San Francisco via the Horn, her fastest time being 115 days—not as fast as the clippers but still creditable. She was 218 feet long and registered at 1,893 tons.

Steam auxiliary barkentine **BEAR** made Pacific Ocean history. She was launched in Greenock, Scotland in 1874 by A. Stephen as a Newfoundland sealer. A powerfully built wooden vessel she later became a famous Revenue Cutter under the Stars and Stripes, on Alaskan patrol. She served Admiral Byrd on two of his Antarctic expeditions and was still afloat until 1967 when she sank in the North Atlantic while being towed to New York to serve as a restaurant and museum ship. She is seen here on duty near Nome, Alaska as a Revenue Cutter.

occurred. It has been proven, however, that sperm whales can swallow a man with ease, and have in fact done so on several occasions.

One old whaling skipper asserted that he had caught a sperm with an "eight foot swallow" and instances of sharks both ten feet and 16 feet long have been reliably recorded as found in the stomachs of sperms when cut up on whaling ships. These massive creatures are known to have V-shaped trap door mouths lined with 18 to 28 conical teeth, eight inches long and this formidable equipment is mainly used for biting and eating large chunks of the giant squid that form their main food. However, complete, unbitten food is sometimes taken by whales, usually fish. There is also some evidence that when attacked, enraged and in pain, the mammals will attack man deliberately in self defense, occasionally swallowing their victims whole.

Gunston notes that the account of Bartley showed that he bore no teeth marks, and his unvarnished description of the swallowing and after, fits in with the known biological facts. The gullet would aid his progress stomach-

wards; the walls of the belly would be soft and mucous-covered and the insulation from outside sound would be complete. The heat he explained would come from the fact that the normal body heat of a sperm whale is about 104 degrees F., well above the body heat of a human being.

The main topic of dispute by scientists on the claims of Bartley is just how he was able to breath sufficient air during his incarceration. Life, however, could be sustained under the following conditions: the whale's belly was not full, nor indeed even partly full of gastric juices at the time, and as shortly afterward the mammal was in fact killed, its stomach secretions ceased altogether from that time. Bartley was never fully immersed in fluid and there was sufficient air within to retain life.

The entire incident remains a most remarkable occurrence—and lends complete credence in an age of skepticism that the ancient experiences of Jonah did actually happen. Jonah, through God's intervention must have fared far better than did Bartley, which perhaps goes without saying.

Activity on the San Francisco waterfront about the turn of the century. In foreground salmon is being unloaded in barrels. In background, left, British ship **BEACON ROCK** and at right, French ship **BAYONNE** at Howard Street Wharf. *Weidner photo, courtesy San Francisco Maritime Museum.*

The former ship **GLORY OF THE SEAS,** last ship to be built by Donald McKay (1869), is seen here at Seattle in 1911 serving as a barge, (floating cannery). *San Francisco Maritime Museum photo.*

Just in from the Far North, schooner **SALVATOR** unloads barrelled salmon on the San Francisco waterfront. *Courtesy San Francisco Maritime Museum.*

Early day picnickers come to view the remains of the bark **HARVEST HOME** wrecked on Washington's North Beach Peninsula January 18, 1882. Preston & McKinnon, San Francisco, owners of the vessel collected $14,000 in insurance on the old vessel. The age of the ship can be noted by her bow. She was originally registered at Stockton, Maine.

"Sicken again for the shouts and the slaughters, You steel away to the lapping waters . . . "*Kipling* Getting ready to go after more leviathans—the impressive auxiliary steam whaling bark **NARWHAL** at San Francisco in olden times. *Courtesy, San Francisco Maritime Museum.*

Unidentified four-masted bark under shortened sail pictured off the Washington Coast about 1912.

Whaling bark **GAY HEAD** wrecked at Chignik, Alaska June 27, 1914. The vessel was a total loss including her 9,000 barrels of sperm oil. She was the last of the square-rigged whalers under sail on the Pacific slopes.

The veteran wooden ship **SOOLOO** is seen sailing into harbor with the Stars and Stripes waving in the breeze.

Coast Guardsman comes ashore from steam barkentine **BEAR,** long operated by the Revenue Service and the U.S. Coast Guard on Alaska patrol duty.

Steam auxiliary barkentine **BEAR OF OAKLAND** with members of the Byrd Expedition aboard steams up the Potomac past Mount Vernon. She was formerly the **BEAR** built at Scotland in 1874.

Chilean ship **IVANHOE** made her last stand on the beach near Honolulu on December 30, 1915. Built in the United Kingdom in 1868, she was one of the iron clipper ships in the Australian emigrant trade.

Brigantine **TANNER** is seen ashore near Port Angeles after the fog lifted. This old trader dating from 1855, was one of the last of her breed on the West Coast when this mishap occurred about 1903. The Tanner was refloated.

Moving along under ballast, the **MOSAIPPA** prepares to take a towline.

Wreck of the ship **JABEZ HOWES,** victim of a gale at Chignik, Alaska April 7, 1911. Value of vessel and cargo was $105,000.

Note the unusual counter and slightly squared off stern of the bark **SANTA ROSA** as she awaits a tow after a long voyage.

Flensing a whale at an Alaskan whaling station about 1910. *Coutesy R. E. Mackay*

Rugged wood steam auxiliary whaling bark **BELVEDERE** pictured in bygone years at her homeport, Seattle. She was originally a New Bedford whaler turned out in Maine in 1880 for William Lewis. Later, coming to the West Coast the vessel made numerous voyages to the Bering, making good catches under her master and later owner, Captain S. F. Cottle. In 1919, under the Hibberd-Swenson Co. of Seattle, the Belvedere was crushed in the ice off Cape Serdze, Siberia.

Columbia River bar tug **ONEONTA** nosing into a mammoth swell on the Columbia River bar. She towed numerous tall sailing ships over the bar in olden days.

Three-masted ship **W. J. ROTCH,** entering the Strait of Juan de Fuca.

Auxiliary schooner **KAMCHATKA,** departing Elliott Bay, Seattle on her final voyage April 3, 1921. On this voyage she was destroyed by fire off the Aleutians while seeking whales, under the Hibbard-Swenson ownership. The Kamchatka was built as the wood steam auxiliary whaling bark **THRASHER** at Bath, for the Pacific Steam Whaling Co. of San Francisco.

The **BENJ. F. PACKARD** appears mighty tall in drydock about 1920. Built by Goss, Sawyer and Packard at Bath in 1883, she was purchased by the Northwestern Fisheries Co., Seattle in 1908.

Preserved for posterity as a tourist attraction on the Honolulu waterfront, the four-masted bark **FALLS OF CLYDE** had a long and successful career on the high seas. Among her many roles was service with Matson Navigation Company. She is pictured here under sail during her years with Matson. She was built at Port Glasgow, Scotland in 1878. Photo courtesy Matson Navigation Company.

Note the adornment on the counter of this big old bark named the **EMA LUISA** in the Strait of Juan de Fuca. She dated from 1851, and Lloyds Register had no builder listed. When the above photo was taken she was under the Chilean flag, and during her many years of service she served under several ownerships with alias names, **WILHELM, LITTLE WILLIE, LOUISA CANEVARO** and **NORTH AMERICA.**

Tranquil scene in Port Blakeley Harbor several decades back with two Yankee square-riggers, products of New England shipbuilders, lay at anchor awaiting loading orders. Joe Williamson collection.

Serving as a cannery vessel, the veteran wooden bark **CORYPHENE,** then registered at Anacortes, Washington is seen here in an interesting stern quarter view with sails set.

Towing in after a long voyage at sea—ship **ISAAC REED.** *Photo by Capt. H.H. Morrison*

"A full-rigged ship is a royal queen,
Way-hay for Boston town, oh!
A lady at court is a barquentine,
A barque is a gal with ringlets fair,
A brig is the same with shorter hair,
A topsail schooner's a racing mare,
But, a schooner, she's a clown-o!" (old shanty)
The schooner **SNOW & BURGESS**

U.S. Revenue Cutter **BEAR,** a steam barkentine-rigged vessel in the northern ice fields with the steamer **CORWIN.** *Courtesy Marine Digest.*

Bark **ANTOFAGASTA,** a 709 ton iron bark, built in 1875 by W. Doxford & Sons at Sunderland, England was a frequent West Coast visitor.

"With her starboard tacks aboard, my boys, she hung up to the breeze; It's time our good ship hauled her wind abreast of the old Saltees." Old Downeaster off the Columbia River bar, 65 years ago.

The Steam-Chest

Building a Yankee whaling ship in olden times. These old prints show the workers coppering the wooden hull; steaming the timbers in a steam chest and a view of the interior of the whaler as the various jobs are performed.

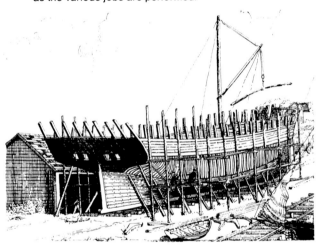

Coppering

Life ashore for the whaler man—tainted boarding houses, smutty saloons, houses of iniquity.

Chapter Three

The Transition

"A smooth sea never made a skillful mariner."

Seldom in the history of America was more cruelty shown to man's fellow man than on Yankee square-riggers. The lax laws and the low status of seamen put them in a category set apart from the rest of the world. They were grossly underpaid, underfed, often ill-clothed, uneducated. Shipmasters and officers frequently treated the seamen as though they were the lowest of scum, realizing that they could practice most any injustice upon them and receive no punishment for their foul deeds. Yet, if the fo'c'sle gang resisted or mutinied, they were placed in irons, flogged, beaten, kicked, molested, maimed and sometimes murdered.

Unfortunately, perpetrators of the cruel deeds often made news, but seldom the high-principled captains and mates.

The British ships were known for their poor food and because of it and due to the rash of scurvy-ridden crews, laws had to be passed to place limejuice on every English ship to prevent the awful disease. Thus the name "lime-juicer." English ships were sometimes labled "hell ships," where punishment was doled out for small offenses but generally the British officers stayed within the limits of the law, perhaps as a result of the infamous mutiny on the *Bounty*. Captain William Bligh, despite his miraculous open boat escape, was reprimanded at the subsequent hearing for the inhumane treatment of his crew. This renowned case had a profound effect on the latter day British officers in the merchant navy.

The Yankee shipowners from the time of the clipper were competition minded and prizes were offered masters for fast passages. This prompted them to drive their men, to press on all the canvas the ships could carry, and to use every breath of wind to its full advantage. The seamen often spent more time aloft than on deck. For the most part it was a hard, exacting life and the ill-treated crewmen, often mauled and clouted about by the mates and skippers, could neither defend themselves nor get legal council once ashore. Their meagre pay wasn't usually enough to last them a single night after weeks at sea.

Inasmuch as San Francisco was the cradle of West Coast commerce it was here also that a pioneer battle was fought for the rights of the seamen against overall mastery of shipowner, master and mate.

The nefarious crimps acting without restraint in the wake of the San Francisco goldrush, forced the shanghaiing of countless unfortunates against their will. In the saloons, flophouses, and abodes of prostitution, men were drugged, slugged, beaten, usually ending up on an outgoing wind ship sometimes after only a few hours on shore.

No man was safe on the streets at night regardless of his state, for when there were crew shortages even men of the cloth were not immune—men with no knowledge of ships, no experience going aloft or climbing out on a yardarm. The awkward position of green hands on sailing vessels is well portrayed (though in fiction) by Jack London's *Seawolf*. He knew the torment and anguish of unwary hands held aboard ship against their will, sometimes on long perilous voyages.

True sailors of old were a rough, tough lot, used to hardships. But in their ignorance most knew no other way of life. Though they often hated their lot and occupation, they kept going back again and again to subsist on a poor diet of salt pork, salt beef, hard tack, beans and potatoes, if they were lucky.

San Francisco's waterfront prior to the turn of the century was a cesspool of crime and inhumane acts. There was no justification for the righteous, and money flowed like water when times were good but slowed to a trickle when times were bad. The situation reached a low ebb in the 1870's and 1880's among seafaring men. They could muster no aid for their cause. They were wholly unorganized, and lacked funds or support until at last one, Sigismund Danielwicz, a member of the International Workmen's Association, not a seafaring man but a labor organizer, decided to take up the cause. He was present in a teaming crowd of seamen on East Street in 1885, protesting pay reductions about to be clamped on them by shipowners. Times were tough and to compensate for their lack of profits the owners, as usual, made up the difference by reducing the pay of the seamen.

The bulletin board on the central waterfront announced that offshore sailors would henceforth receive $25 per month and coastal and inland water sailors a mere $20. The date was March 5, 1885, and it was on that night that Danielwicz, either out of challenge or lust for notoriety, decided that the time had come for action. It was ironical that the frustrated seamen would accept the talk of a non-seafarer, but their lot had reached such a low ebb that they were ready to try most anyone. So they accepted the invitation of Danielwicz the following day to meet at Folsom Street Wharf, amid piles of Northwest lumber, to discuss their grievances. It was here that a union was formed under the title, Coast Seamen's Union. True, several other attempts had been made to organize the sailors through the 1860's and 70's but all had ended in tragic failure. Here, however, was a new twist and though skeptical, the seamen listened intently to talks of striking for better pay and treatment. They were determined this time to resist the infiltration of crimps and polished betrayers who would work their way into the ranks and sell the souls of

men — backed by false protective societies sometimes masked behind false religions, and humanitarian fronts.

This time, at last, hired professional organizers under Danielwicz had some backbone and a move was started to get additional pay for seamen with of course, a driving urge to extract a nice share to pad the pockets of the organizers. So the union got its start; its purpose was greatly aided by a sudden new avenue of maritime commerce—the growing coastwise trade created by timber needs from Northwest forests; the speed up in building fast, maneuverable windjammers and packets to supply the Hawaiian and South Sea islands—designed to bring back sugar or copra. At this period the steam schooner was also developed which opened up a whole new era of more dependable coastwise transit.

At last there were new searoads—San Francisco was no longer dependent alone on the square-riggers coming around from the East Coast. The demand for empty berths on ships was even greater.

So, along with the Coast Seamen's Union which began to flourish and grow, there came the rival Steamship-man's Union. This gave the shipowners and crimps another fulcrum and blood money was paid in ever increasing amounts to secure crews—the pay set by the size, experience and age of men delivered on board—sober, inebriated, out cold or semi-

Rare photo of the launching of the four-masted **OLYMPIC** at Bath, Maine in 1892. The 1,482 ton vessel was perhaps the only sailing vessel ever built with the foreward two masts square-rigged and the other two schooner-rigged. She was owned on the West Coast from 1899. Thomas Crowley of San Francisco converted her to a four-mast barkentine in 1917.

At rest in Seattle's Elliott Bay, the fine old bark **W. B. FLINT** is pictured. This 952 ton wooden vessel carried a crew of 12 men and here was owned by Libby, McNeill & Libby.

conscious. Even the unions were at odds and fought many pitched battles, weakening their own cause. Finally on July 29, 1891, the Sailors Union of the Pacific was formed, ending the head knocking and giving new power and prestige to a floundering endeavor. The membership grew to 4,000 strong and the treasury to $50,000. At last there was sufficient to fight for their cause against the Shipowners' and Coast Boarding Masters' Association.

Blood was to run red again in the dirt of the San Francisco waterfront. Both sides declared open war and ruthlessness was the order of the day. Every criminal in the whole of San Francisco jumped on whichever bandwagon suited his fancy and police were virtually helpless to stem the tide. Riots, murders, beatings and wanton destruction went totally unpunished and unionists often boarded ships to beat "scabs" senseless. Dead bodies, unidentified were frequently floating in the bay along the Barbary Coast. Mayhem broke loose in the saloons and houses of ill-repute. Ships' lines were cut, cargo stolen, rocks and bottles tossed at will at anything in sight. Crimps and their runners were having a field day, but whenever exposed by the unions were exterminated. San Francisco hung its head in shame once again.

The Sailors' Union finally appeared to be getting the upper hand for the first time and the battle-weary shipowners were ready to give in when the Manufacturers' and Employees' Association, a powerful group, took the side of the shipowners. This organization, notorious as union breakers, were enraged by the many hostile and outrageous acts of the sailors in wanton destruction of private property. They jumped in with a vengeance, so much so, that by the summer of 1893, the money pot of the Sailors' Union had tragically dwindled and the men were willing to settle for what they could get.

The screws were tightened. The SUP was undermined and wages sank to an even lower level than before the big strike—$15 per month.

The defeat was made even more bitter when in the early fall of the year a suitcase full of dynamite was ignited in front of Curtin's non-union saloon and boarding house. In an ear-shattering explosion, the front of the building was blown out and five men violently killed. A sailor was immediately tried and acquitted for lack of evidence, claiming it was the work of enemies trying to discredit his union. The guilty party was never found but the defunct Sailors' Union was labeled as the culprit and again was reduced to the lowest status.

The era was beginning to change slowly from sail to steam and the old crimps streamlined some of their methods in order to provide hands for the new steamships. Blood money, brutal treatment and the collection of seamen's ad-

69

vanced wages were still in vogue but the methods were updated and protected by criminal lawyers. The populace, however, was growing indignant about the blood-thirsty efforts to get men to sea against their wills. Still, the lot of the Sailors' Union appeared almost hopeless until a Norwegian sailor named Andrew Furuseth, came to the fore. Originally a Norwegian commercial fisherman, he had first come to San Francisco in a British ship from Calcutta and was incensed by the poor treatment of the sailor. He was a man of peculiar habits, but one who was basically honest. He was up on the Columbia River fishing when the Coast Seamen's Union got its start but the idea of joining appealed to him when he came back to San Francisco and he joined up with a genuine burden in his heart for the lot of the outcast seafarer.

A few months later, the rank and file who approved of his honest zeal, elected him secretary of the union and he was destined to hold that post until 1934, championing the cause of the sailor. The 30 year old Furuseth was not popular because of his personality—sometimes he was downright insulting. One thing that got him in was his obvious distaste for women. He hated them with a passion and was far more attracted to men. The fact that his predecessor was 'woman crazy" and that one of his belles had absconded with the union funds was perhaps a big factor in the election of Furuseth. The rumors about Furuseth being a woman hater were propogated by his fair skin and the fact that he never needed a shave. A rather poor speaker, his voice was high and shrill. All the odds physically were against him, but for some strange reason the union backed him in force and defended him. Some were even jealous of his long standing position. He wielded a powerful hand in the union. When things got bad he'd just take off on a commercial fishing junket and return when the air had cleared. He worked long hours and spent most of his spare time in solitude, not mixing it up in the grog shops with the other sailors. An obstinate man, he never laughed or joked.

Though his voice was not compelling he spoke words that got attention and this unusual man always got good coverage from the press. Indeed, the text of his speeches sometimes made the Congressional Record. San Francisco's populace took note of his crusade. When he spoke of the sailors as bondsmen, they listened. They listened harder when he labeled them "seamen in shackles." His famous words often reverberated down through the waterfront's dark alleys and along the wooden piersides where "We hold up our manacled hands."

With his sermons to the heart, Furuseth infuriated the shipowners. When debates occurred he had only to compare the life of a sailor with a landsman, and the heart was touched. He was determined, and in 1894 he went to the nation's capitol to take up the cause with the federal government. His efforts rekindled the writings of Richard Henry Dana which first awakened Americans to the brutal treatment of seamen. Immediately he began working on legislation to get a better deal for those before the mast. He found many in sympathy with his cause.

Perhaps even more than Furuseth's vocal persuasion was his brilliant effort in engaging a talented, youthful Scotch sailor named Walter Macarthur to start up a house organ publication for the Sailors' Union. Titled the *Coast Seamen's Journal,* it was to prove as in the past that the pen is mightier than the sword.

One of the featured articles in that publication was titled the *"Red Record"* and in this column in each edition were brief authentic records of the brutalites wrought upon seamen who had their cases brushed out of the hearing halls when they complained before the shipping commissioner. From a cubby hole on East Street under the shadow of the yardarms and bowsprits, Macarthur edited his publication. From the first issue in 1895, the journal got around San Francisco, and astonished citizenry were appalled by the records of unpunished brutality.

Macarthur became as famous as Furuseth. A handsome, well built individual he was a self-educated man. His parents taught him what little they knew and his keen mind absorbed much of what he read. From the time

On San Francisco Bay in bygone years, at left big square-rigger **ARRACAN,** freighter **VIRGINIAN** and steam schooner **SAMOA.** Courtesy Mike McGarvey.

Unloading carrera marble at San Francisco around the turn of the century. Note the use of A-frame on dockside and ship's yard to handle the marble. The bark arrived from Europe. *Courtesy San Francisco Maritime Museum.*

he left the Clyde he was constantly seeking knowledge and at last he had found his niche. He had dug deep in history back before the day of Christ to learn how the ancients treated those under their command. He even pointed out that the early Phoenicians had a law whereby a ship's master had the right to strike a man for not obeying an order, but when struck a second time the man had a right to defend himself. He pointed out this 3,000 year old law as just and fair alongside the incredible injustices of a so-called civilized world where a seaman could be kicked to death or maimed for life or made mentally incompetent from a belaying pin or capstan bar; where he could have his teeth knocked out, his nose broken, his ribs crushed, his organs inside or outside ruined without compensation, physically, financially or lawfully. If a seaman was a large man, a belaying pin was used instead of fists, and he was usually required to clean up his own blood afterwards.

The fact that the masters of sailing ships had sole authority once their commands cleared the harbor placed them in a totalitarian world. Those who possessed a devil, so to speak, ruled their little floating isles like gods whose commands were unquestionable. Many shipowners would have been horrified to know the conduct of their masters and mates aboard these tall ships but perhaps would not have protested

had they have known. The shipowner had no use for the underpaid seaman and would not hear his gripes once port was reached. It was always the seamen's word against those of the officers who had all the odds on their side. If, on the other hand, the officers brought accusations against their crew, the boom was often lowered. Even before the shipping commissioner, if a sailor bore a complaint, the master would merely counterbalance with a reverse accusation, frequently false, and the case was dismissed.

The power of Macarthur's *Red Record* had such an impact on the people of San Francisco that he bound his works together with a blood red cover showing a hand gripping a belaying pin, which became the mark of brutality. Within the covers of the *Red Record* were 63 cases of unpunished brutality and presented here are just a few of those cases:

———

(From the RED RECORD *of American "hell ships"—a brief resume of some of the cruelties perpetrated upon American seamen, 1888 to 1895.)*

Tam O' Shanter, Captain Peabody. Arrived in San Francisco, Sept. 6, 1888. First mate Swain arrested on three charges of cruelty preferred by seamen Fraser, Williams and Wilson. Captain defended his mate on the ground of incompetent crew; did not say how he came to sail with incompetent men. Mate released on $450 bond. Case still in courts.

* * *

Lewellyn J. Morse, Captain Lavary. Arrived in San Francisco February 1889. First mate Watski charged by seaman Arthur Connors with striking him on the head with a pair of handcuffs, imprisonment in the lazarette and gagging because complainant was singing. Captain was present during these inflictions, but refused to interfere. Watski released on a $500 bond. Case still pending.

* * *

Commodore T. H. Allen, Captain Merriam. Arrived in San Francisco, April 1889. A seaman MacDonald reported that while expostulating against the vile language of the third mate, he was struck several times by that officer, thrown against the rail with such violence that his shoulder was dislocated. The Captain remarked when appealed to "serves you damned well right," and ordered mate to confine McDonald in the carpenter's shop. As treatment for his wounds he was given a dose of salts. Another seaman fell sick and was confined with McDonald in the carpenter's shop—a combination of hospital and prison. There being only one bunk in the place, the weakest man had to sleep on deck. Diet for the sick man: common

ship's fare; medicine; salts. For four days he ate nothing. Finally he died. Interviewed about the matter, the third mate acknowledged McDonald was a good seaman but that he (the third mate) was down on him.

* * *

Standard, Captain Percy. Arrived in San Francisco, October 1889. Seaman E. Anderson went to the Marine Hospital and complained of ill-treatment from first mate Martin. One day out of Philadelphia, the first mate knocked Anderson down. Anderson got up and endeavored to expostulate, but was knocked down and kicked until he was insensible. Anderson since has suffered from intense pains in the head and chest and has been subject to fits for the first time in his life. Mate ordered him aloft contrary to the orders of the captain. Men had to lash him in the rigging to prevent his falling. Anderson was laid up and the mate endeavored to haul him on deck. Warrant sworn out for mate's arrest; mate disappeared and could not be found.

* * *

Reuce, Captain Adams. Arrived in San Francisco, November 1889. Seventeen seamen down with scurvy, one man died from some disease. Rotten and insufficient food was the cause. Every man was in a fearful condition as a result of the ravages of scurvy. Off the Horn

At anchor in San Francisco Bay at the turn of the century—the graceful ship **BALCLUTHA**. "O for a soft and gentle wind! I heard a fair one cry; But give to me the snoring breeze and white waves heaving high; And white waves heaving high, my lads." *A. Cunningham photo courtesy San Francisco Maritime Museum.*

This striking downeaster is the three-masted ship **HENRY FAILING** which was well known for many years on the West Coast. She was a dependable workaday square-rigger. *Photo loaned by Captain P. A. McDonald who once served aboard her as 2nd mate.*

men had to work through hail, wind and water on empty stomachs; while some of the men were holystoning the decks they were beaten by the second mate. The latter officer skipped as the *Reuce* was towing through the Golden Gate. Men will never recover from the disease. Case tried in District Courts and verdict of $3,600 damages awarded seamen.

* * *

Sterling, Captain Goodwin. Arrived in San Francisco, January 1890. Three seamen went to the Marine Hospital with scurvy. All hands had bad and insufficient food and brutal treatment from the officers.

* * *

Edward O'Brien, Captain Oliver. Arrived in San Francisco February 1890. First mate Gillespie charged with most inhumane conduct. He knocked down the second mate and jumped on his face. Struck one seaman on the head with a belaying pin, inflicting a ghastly wound, then kicked him on the head and ribs, inflictng life marks. He struck another man on the neck with a capstan bar, then kicked him into insensibility. He struck the boatswain in the face because the latter failed to hear an order. Gillespie charged and admitted to bail.

* * *

Henry B. Hyde, Captain Pendleton, arrived in San Francnsco, April 1893. First mate of the ship charged with breaking a seaman's wrist by a blow with a belaying pin, and otherwise ill-treating him. All hands tell a straightforward story in the courts, plainly proving his guilt. Case dismissed on ground of "justifiable discipline."

* * *

Tam O'Shanter (2), Captain Peabody. Arrived in San Francisco, July 1893. Charges of the grossest brutality made against second mate R. Crocker (late of the *Commodore T. H. Allen*). Crocker stands six feet, three inches in height and weighs 260 pounds. He assaulted several seamen. One in particular, Harry Hill, bore nine wounds, five of them still unhealed. A piece was bitten out of his left palm, a mouthful of flesh was bitten out of his arm, and his left nostril torn away as far as the bridge of the nose. Crocker is reported to have kicked a man from aloft; seaman hit down on deck, Crocker followed and administered a beating, marks of which showed in court. Crocker held on $500 bail. Case tried; usual verdict—acquittal.

* * *

M. P. Grace (2), Captain DeWinter. Arrived in San Francisco, July 1893. Captain DeWinter and second mate charged with cruelty. Case postponed until crew got to sea. Case called and dismissed for lack of evidence.

* * *

Shenandoah, Captain Murphy. Arrived in San Francisco, October 1893. One seaman, M. Bahr, fell overboard from the royal yard arm and no effort was made to save him. The captain acknowledged this but excused himself on the ground of rough weather. Ship had topgallant sails set. A passenger reports that the food was a revelation to him, being meager in quantity and bad in quality. Cruelty and constant abuse charged to the officers. The captain refused to see these goings on, or to interfere when complained to.

* * *

Francis, Captain Doane. Arrived in San Francisco, October 1893. First mate Crocker (late of the *Commodore T. H. Allen* and *Tam O'Shanter*), accused of gross brutalities to the crew. Seamen bore marks on their persons when they complained to the commissioner. Crocker arrested and admitted to bail; crew compelled to go to sea in meantime. Case dismissed for lack of evidence.

* * *

Hecla (2) Captain Cotton. Arrived in San Francisco, April 25, 1894, from Baltimore. Crew complained of brutality. Food scarce and of bad quality. Seaman E. J. Svendenberg charged that the first mate struck him on the head with a belaying pin. On other occasions the officers assaulted the crew, using hammers and marlinspikes. First mate John Cameron and second mate John St. Claire arrested. Case dismissed by U.S. Commissioner Hancock for lack of evidence.

* * *

May Flint, Captain Nickels. Arrived in San Francisco, August 1895, from Baltimore, Md. The crew charged that brutal treatment had begun before the vessel got underway on the Chesapeake. They asked Captain Nickels to send the police aboard. This the captain promised to do and instead he sent off a gang of crimps who beat and finally terrorized the seamen. During the passage one man, while kneeling at his work, was kicked in the testicles and permanently ruptured. Another man had his face laid bare with a holystone by Captain Nickels. One man was beaten for unavoidably spitting on deck while aloft and another was triced up to the spanker boom for some trifling fault. The seamen were frequently assaulted by

Captain Nickels, while at the wheel, and vile names were applied to them as a general thing. Captain Nickels and second mate Knight were examined by U.S. Commissioner Hancock and completely exonerated.

* * *

Benjamin F. Packard (2), Captain Allen. Arrived in San Francisco, October 24, 1895 from Swansea, England. Crew reported that trouble occurred on the vessel while lying in the stream at Swansea. Several seamen attempted to back out, but were terrorized into going aboard. "Cockney" Falconer, able seaman, was sworn at and assaulted while aloft by the second mate Turner. The man was afterwards put in irons and while in this helpless position was challenged to fight by Captain Allen, and was assaulted by the first mate and carpenter. William Ace, able seaman, was called on deck during his watch below and assaulted. Robert Lewis, able seaman, while clearing the main-topmast staysail dropped the clew on deck, and for this he was set upon and beaten by the second mate. Two boys who had shipped as ordinary seamen were constantly ill-treated by the second mate by having their ears pulled and clouted, etc. The second mate assaulted both quartermasters in their watch while they were at the wheel. The crew said they had never clewed up a sail in bad weather without having trouble of some sort. Two members of the crew swore to warrants for the arrest of the second mate and the carpenter. The former disappeared as usual, and the latter was dismissed by U.S. Commissioner Hancock on the ground of "lack of evidence."

* * *

Bohemia, Captain Hogan. Arrived in San

The ship **HENRY FAILING** at dockside in the golden years of sail. *Courtesy Captain P. A. McDonald.*

Francisco November 11, 1895, from Philadelphia via Rio de Janeiro. Reports the loss of spars and a mutiny of the crew, headed by second mate Eagan. Captain Hogan said that all hands, with the exception of the first mate, refused to work ship and compelled him to put into Rio. Second mate Eagan deserted in Rio, a fact which throws suspicion on the charge of mutiny, and Captain Hogan threatened to have his crew arrested, but did not. The crew on the other hand charged Captain Hogan with ill-treatment and said that he was responsible for the loss of seaman Frank M. Weston, who was drowned from the jibboom at the time of the vessel's dismasting. The steward recited a specific instance of cruelty when Captain Hogan clubbed him in Rio. Nothing done in the matter.

* * *

Susquehanna (2), Captain Sewall (late of the *Solitaire* (2)). Arrived in San Francisco November 12, 1895, from New York. The crew charged the usual ill-treatment against the captain. For the arrest of the first mate, Ross, on the charges of brutality, beating of seamen, etc. Captain Sewall threatend that if Ross were convicted he would have the crew arrested on a charge of mutiny. The case of Ross was heard before U.S. Commissioner Hancock and, as usual, dismissed. Captain Sewall is one of the most notorious brutes in charge of an American ship. This is his fourth appearance in the *"Red Record"* in less than seven years. He has openly boasted that he would beat his seamen whenever he felt inclined. Well sustained charges of murder have been made against him, but he has gone scot free every time, and once in Philadelphia in 1889, when he was in danger of conviction, he "disappeared" for a time and afterwards "healed the wounds" of the complainants with small considerations in cash. His case in the present case is simply a repetition of an old dodge to embarrass the officials.

* * *

The die had been cast and the ensuing newspaper stories in the wake of the *Red Record* aided greatly in the passing of the Maguire and White Acts in Congress. But still, though the lot of the sailor had greatly improved, there were rough times ahead. The pendulum was beginning to swing the other way. Times got better and in the year 1901 with the economy up, the Sailors' Union of the Pacific went on strike, forming picket lines to gain higher wages. They were joined by their counterparts, the City Front Federation.

San Francisco business ground to a halt and the waterfront once again was swept by brutal acts. Before a working agreement was forth-

Unfurling the sails to dry while idle in port—Downeast ship **CHARLES E. MOODY,** later well known on the West Coast. Courtesy of Captain P. A. McDonald, once second mate of the vessel.

The fine old ship **A. J. FULLER** while employed by Northwestern Fisheries Company as a cannery supply ship. *Courtesy Joe Williamson*

American bark **REAPER,** well known on Puget Sound in olden times ended her days on the shores of Port Ludlow harbor after being destroyed by fire there. *Courtesy Capt. A. F. Raynaud.*

Home from the Northland, the ship **ABNER COBURN,** an East Coast product converted for West Coast service—with homeport Seattle. Note signal flags flying. *Courtesy Joe Williamson.*

coming between the Union and shipowners, a year had slipped by with a rash of riots, gang fights, and murders.

Finally in 1904 Senator Alger of Michigan introduced a bill which was passed. It was entitled: "An Act to Prohibit Shanghaiing in the United States."

The crimps were outwardly through and their half century reign of terror could no longer flourish under the law. Though the law was frequently evaded thereafter, the seaman at least had the law on his side whenever complaints were registered.

Finally on March 4, 1915 as the sailing ship was in its sunset year, President Wilson signed an act to promote the welfare of "American Seamen in the Merchant Marine in the United States." It was the dawn of a new day, a day long overdue which has since seen the pendulum swing clear over in the opposite direction.

A chantey often sung aboard the bark **S. C. ALLEN** was called Tommy's Gone To Hilo. It went:

To Hilo town, we'll see her through,
For Tommy's gone with a ruling crew.
Oh, Tommy's gone from down below,
An up aloft this yard must go.

The Allen was wrecked off Diamond Head, October 13, 1913, but her crew of 12 reached shore safely, and were cared for by residents of Honolulu. *Courtesy Captain A. F. Raynaud*

Big German bark **POTRIMPOS** died a tormenting death on the North Beach Peninsula near Long Beach, Washington where she stranded December 19, 1896. Owned by Hamburg interests, she was later abandoned by the underwriters when salvage efforts failed.

Remains of the wreck of the American bark **AUSTRIA** at Cape Alava, Washington. The bark was wrecked January 30, 1887, but all hands reached shore safely. The now non-existent Ozette Indian village can be seen in the background. *Courtesy University of Washington Library.*

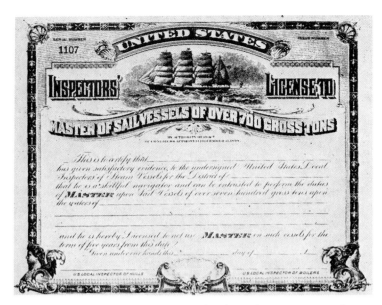

Inspectors' License-Master of sail vessels over 700 tons. *Courtesy U.S. Coast Guard.*

Only known photo of this ship under the name **GAINSBOROUGH**. She later became the **DIAMOND HEAD** after being wrecked off Diamond Head in 1896 and later salvaged. She was originally built in 1866 in London. *Courtesy Captain P. A. McDonald.*

In 1930, C. Arthur Foss, had the venerable old Maine built ship **ST. PAUL** towed to the Ballard locks in Seattle for preservation as a museum ship. She served in that capacity for some years under Puget Sound Academy of Science. Lack of funds caused her later sale to British Columbia interests who took her to Oyster Bay, B.C. for a breakwater. *Seattle Times photo.*

Yankee square-rigger heads for the Northland with Bristol Bay boats on deck. Several hands are gathered on the fo'c'sle head of the former Downeaster. This is the **SANTA CLARA**.

One of the last of the Yankee clippers to carry sail was the ship **DASHING WAVE,** seen here shortly after the turn of the century, registered at Port Townsend. She was built by Fernald & Pettigrew at Portsmouth, N. H. in 1853 and was wrecked at Shelter Point, Vancouver Island, March 16, 1920 while serving as a barge. *Edward S. Clark photo.*

The **OLYMPIC,** only vessel of her rig ever built—two square-rigged masts, two schooner-rigged masts—loading lumber at the Mukilteo Lumber Co. at Mukilteo, on Puget Sound. *Pete Hurd collection.*

Deplorable condition in the fo'c'sle's of sailing vessels, along with unpalatable food, and inhumane treatment brought about the publication of the *Red Record,* hell ships of the sail era.

A proud windship of yesteryear—the bark **DUNREGGAN** in calm waters off the Northwest Coast.

One of the most colorful of the lofty steel square-riggers was the bark **EDWARD SEWALL** out of Bath, Maine. Here she pitches into a lazy swell off the Pacific Coast.

Damp, smelly fo'c'sle's with make-shift bunks did little to cheer hands before the mast.

Nosing into a North Pacific swell—the British grain ship **GWYD-ER CASTLE** outbound for the United Kingdom. She was constructed at Dundee in 1893 as the **NEWFIELD.** Here she is owned by the Gwyder Shipping Company Ltd., and registered at St. John, New Foundland.

British four-masted steel bark **TWEEDSDALE,** built at Glasgow, Scotland in 1877 by Barclay, Curle & Company, was operated for several years by J. & A. Roxburgh.

Under shortened sail the ship OC-
CIDENTAL plunges into a nasty
sea off Cape Flattery. Built at
Bath, Maine in 1874 this staunch
wooden vessel was purchased by
Captain George Plummer in 1890
and operated out of San Francisco.

The 929 ton bark C. D. BRYANT came directly to the West
Coast after her construction at Searsport, Maine in 1878. She
was built by M. Dutch and sold to E. E. Kentfield of San Francisco. She is seen here ready to take a tow into the Strait of Juan
de Fuca.

Silouetted against a darkening sky—ship ST. FRANCES of the
California Shipping Co. Bought by the Alaska Fisherman's Pack-
ing Co. of Astoria in 1909 she was wrecked eight years later at
Unimak Pass, Alaska under the Libby, McNeill & Libby flag.

This vessel has been identified as the steel bark **BIDSTON HILL,** a frequent visitor to West Coast ports. This four-masted iron bark of 2,519 tons, was built by T. Royden & Sons at Liverpool in 1886.

Make fast that towline. The wood ship **W. J. ROTCH,** a veteran downeaster, about to tow in for a cargo of lumber.

German bark **MIMI** stranded on the beach near the entrance to Nehalem River bar, Oregon in February, 1913. A few weeks later she capsized during salvage operations drowing 17 men.

An innovation—windmills on sailing vessels—introduced before the turn of the century to cut down on the number of seamen. The windmills were used to pump the bilge, freeing the hands to tend the ship. The windmill is spinning fast here aboard the ship **LOUIS WALSH** in the North Pacific. This vessel was built at Belfast, Maine, in 1861, and was wrecked at Dutch Harbor, Alaska in 1902.

Here is seen another windmill in action aboard a big downeast ship. This vessel is believed to be the **ST. FRANCES** of 1,898 tons, which was well known in Pacific Coast ports.

Owned by A. P. Lorentzen, of San Francisco, the bark **REAPER** burned while at Port Ludlow, Washington to load lumber July 21, 1906. Her remains can still be seen across the bay from Port Ludlow where she was beached after the fatal fire. The coastal lumber drougher was built at Bath in 1876.

The iron bark **ARCHER** was dismasted off Cape Flattery in 1894 and sold to Capt. Rufus Calhoun who refitted her at Port Blakely as a barkentine, as seen in the photo below. Built at Sunderland as an English bark in 1876, she came under U.S. registry in 1895.

Full-rigged ship **BRABLOCH** bound for Astoria and Portland. The 2,026 ton vessel was built at Glasgow in 1889. Woodfield photo of painting, supplied by A.E. Erickson, Seattle.

On a port tack, high out of the water is the **HARRY MORSE** in the North Pacific. Built in 1871 by J. P. Morse, she was bought by John Rosenfeld at San Francisco who brought her to the Pacific in 1887. She went to the bottom after a collision with the schooner **EMMA LORD,** as a barge for the Texas Co. out of Port Arthur in 1916, taking eight persons to their deaths.

This vessel is believed to be the big wooden ship **CHARLES E. MOODY,** of 2,003 tons, a product of Goss & Sawyer in 1882, at Bath. She is seen here in a photo taken by Captain Orison Beaton in 1913. The ship burned at Naknek, Alaska June 28, 1920.

Captain Orison Beaton took this excellent photo of the steel bark **KAIULANI,** largest vessel of her rig ever built in the United States. Captain Beaton, a tugboat skipper of notoriety, kept a camera handy when his commands, such as the **SEA MONARCH** went out to Cape Flattery to take a sailing ship in tow. This photo was taken in 1913. The Kaiulani later became the **STAR OF FINLAND.** She was built at Bath in 1899, and her hull is still afloat at this writing, in Philippine waters. An endeavor is being made to bring her back to Washington, D.C. for restoration as a museum.

Nearly becalmed—this stately Limejuicer is identified as the **LINLITHGOWSHIRE.**

Coming about into the breeze—ship **SPARTAN**

86

This vessel ended her days when wrecked at Spreckelsville on the Island of Hawaii August 17, 1905. The **SPARTAN** was first owned on the Pacific Coast by P. B. Cornwall, of San Francisco. R. E. Jackson was her builder at Boston in 1874.

The **ABNER COBURN,** a wooden ship of 1,972 tons, seen here in the employ of Libby, McNeil & Libby who bought her in 1912. The vessel was built in Maine in 1882.

"A place of marvels and terrors," Joseph Conrad once said of the sea. Here is seen the ship **SPARTAN** plowing into a North Pacific swell.

The **ST. PAUL,** which like all of the old wooden downeasters has faded from the scene of American history. *O. Beaton photo, 1912.*

It's Christmas time aboard the **CORYPHENE.** Note tree abutting the bowsprit of the vessel.

"North and South and home again, Round the world and all." The wood bark **J. D. PETERS,** built in 1875, came to the West Coast to serve as a cannery ship in 1890.

This old photo is said to be the veteran ship **COLUMBIA,** built at Bath, Maine in 1871 by the Houghton Bros. While under charter to the Alaska Packers Assn. she was wrecked at Unimak Pass, Alaska April 30, 1909.

"As ships becalmed at eve that lay,
With canvas drooping—"
—Ship **SANTA CLARA**

Forest of tall masts—Alaska Packers Star fleet in winter quarters at Alameda, California in the 1920's. **STAR OF INDIA** at left, built at the Isle of Man in 1863, and still afloat at San Diego at this writing is the oldest commercial sailing ship afloat in American waters. *Tom White photo.*

Chapter Four

Of Fleets and Ships

*"To me the sea is a continual miracle,
The fishes that swim—the rocks—
the motion of the waves—the ships
that have men in them."*
—Walt Whitman

One of the truly grand sights of early century San Francisco were the tall square-riggers of the Alaska Packers Association. The fleet was formed about 1906 after the association purchased a quartet of ships which had once belonged to J. P. Corry's Irish Star Line, four iron Belfast-built ships that had acquired fame as fast sailers while under the Red Duster. These, among the last of the great West Coast-owned square-riggers, sailed north each year in April from San Francisco for Alaska canneries, as far as 2,500 miles, carrying Chinese and Japanese cannery hands, a variety of supplies and some passengers, usually connected with the canneries. The Orientals were employed because they worked for cheap wages and performed their simple tasks well. The entire Alaskan summer operation was carried out with the manpower and cargo brought by the company ships—aging sailing ships which could operate profitably in this trade but could no longer compete with the faster more reliable steamers on the high seas.

At the termination of the season the tall ships would be fully-loaded down in Alaska with crated canned salmon. The Orientals would reboard the vessels—little concerned by the cramped, miserable quarters—content with their meagre wages for the hard summer's work. The ships, if the weather cooperated, sailed home and were again tied up at their San Francisco winter quarters before late September.

The fleet eventually grew to eight of the largest square-riggers afloat.

After unloading, the ships wintered at Alameda, side by side, in a forest of masts, yardarms and miles of rigging. Acres of canvas were stored in sail lockers until the following season. This venerable fleet was composed of veterans of the Cape Horn trade, multiple rounders of the Cape of Good Hope, vessels that had been to virtually every port in the world before becoming cannery ships.

It was the tall square-riggers *Star of France, Star of Bengal, Star of Italy* and *Star of Russia* that initially formed the Packer fleet under the Stars and Stripes. To this handsome foursome the company added others until the Alaska Packers fleet reached an apex of 19 vessels.

It was a grand part of San Francisco Bay's marine heritage in the latter day of sail. The maritime-oriented folk loved their sailing ships and read with great interest the accounts of arrivals and departures. There were saddened hearts every time one was listed in the casualty section. Some were lost in their battle against the pounding and inhospitable northern Alaska seas. The terrible ordeal of the *Star of Bengal* on Coronation Island ranks with the worst disasters on the North Pacific from the standpoint of loss of life. *The Star of Falkland* ripped her hull open on Akun Head, victim of Alaska's jagged outcroppings.

As the sail era continued to die some of the vessels were idled and stripped of their wares to supply the needs of their counterparts, and to cut the rising costs of hard-to-get ships' hardware. Some eventually lost so much of their rigging that they were sold as barges, names eradicated and identity almost lost. Bare hulls were packed with coal or "perfumed" by the obnoxious smell of decayed copra. The demand for scrap by the Japanese sent others across the Pacific to be melted under the wreckers' torch.

Two of the AP fleet fortunately managed to live on to recall the rip-roaring days of sail. The *Star of Alaska,* as most know, has been restored under her original name, *Balclutha,* through the efforts of a spirited group of San Franciscans.

Of equal status is the earlier mentioned *Star of India,* a remarkable iron-hulled sailing vessel which dates from 1863, one of the oldest, if not the oldest commercially built iron sailing vessel still afloat. Berthed at the San Diego Embarcadero, she was purchased by the late James Wood Coffroth, who gave her to the Maritime Museum Association, San Diego, a non-profit community organization, which made her a maritime museum. Later she was rerigged and opened to the public in 1963, just a century after her construction in England.

But of the other units of the Alaska Packers "Star" Fleet, fate was not so kind. Those that eventually went for scrap were the *Star of Shetland, Star of Scotland, Star of Lapland, Star of Zealand, Star of Holland,* and *Star of Iceland.* The *Star of Greenland* became a Portuguese motor ship. Hulked were the *Star of Italy* in South America, the *Star of Peru* in the South Pacific and the *Star of Russia* in the New Hebrides. The *Star of England* became a barge in Canada while *Star of Poland* met a tragic end off the coast of Japan. The *Star of France* once escaping an Alaska stranding eventually was sunk by collision, and as has been mentioned the *Star of Bengal* and *Star of Falkland* were victims of the hostile shores of Alaska. Even the old *Star of Chile* was lost in B.C. waters as a barge after giving some service during World War II following many years as a lime storage ship at Roche Harbor, on San Juan Island. The *Star of Finland* too became a barge and is still afloat.

The most tragic of the Star fleet losses were those of the *Falkland* and *Bengal.*

The *Falkland* had made Unimak Pass in the spring of 1928 and was on a westerly tack before hauling eastward into Bristol Bay. Suddenly Akun Head, a rampart of one of the Aleutian Islands loomed ahead. There was not sufficient time to wear around and the ship would not come up to the wind. In a terrifying moment the vessel ground up on unrelenting rock. Her yardarms tumbled in a jumble of twisted rigging. The initial impact did much structural damage and the vessel's exposed position left little doubt that it was only a matter of time. The crew was rescued by the cutter *Haida* but the wreck left her bones on the barrier to redden and decay under the constant pounding of the sea.

Saddened San Franciscans read the following obituary in the shipping section of a San Francisco newspaper.

"This fall, when the prime old ladies of the deep remove their qauint white hats and shawls and foregather for another winter, their tales will be tempered with a note of sadness, at the loss of one of their sisters, the *Star of Falkland,* whose battered hulk, with tangled rigging, lies on the rocks of Unimak Pass. Better at that, 'they agree bitterly,' than to end her days as a coal barge."

The ship tragedy that shook the maritime

In October, 1927, the 308 foot barkentine **E. R. STERLING** is pictured dismasted at St. Thomas, Virgin Islands following a jinxed voyage from the Pacific Coast. She was an iron six-masted vessel and was built at Belfast in 1883. Pictured above, she was under the ownership of the Sterling Shipping Company of Blaine Washington. Under other rigs she served as the **LORD WOLSELEY, COLUMBIA** and **EVERETT G. GRIGGS.**

world, however, was that of the *Star of Bengal*. This vessel was originally built of iron at the Harland & Wolff yard at Belfast, Ireland in 1873. She measured 262 feet in length and was of 1,877 tons. After trading world-wide for several years she was transferred to the flag of Hawaii and from 1898 to 1900 traded between the Islands and California under the J. J. Smith house flag. In 1900 the *Bengal* received United States registry and six years later was purchased by the Alaska Packers Association. Her awful demise came on September 20, 1908.

Though the details surrounding the tragedy have never been completely made clear, it appears from the facts that there was a gross miscarriage of justice as an outcome of the hearing into the matter.

In Joan Lowell's (Joan Wagner) best selling but controversial book, *The Cradle of the Deep* (published in 1929), Captain Nicholas Wagner who was master of the *Star of Bengal* is believed by some to have used his daughter's book as a sounding board for his account of what actually happened. Though he took the full brunt of the blame and had his papers removed, a portion of justice was restored when he received amnesty several months later and returned to sea.

His cause, however, was not necessarily aided by the book; it was the story of the captain's daughter who was reputedly raised aboard her father's schooner from the time she was a baby until the full bloom of youth at age 17. So authentically was it written that no sailor could have initially denied that there could have been a possibility of deceit. But as it turned out, Joan Lowell like any other young lady, had spent most of her childhood in her hometown (Berkeley), receiving the usual education through high school. She must have sat at her dad's side for endless hours hearing of his experiences as master of the schooner *Minnie A. Caine* and the ship *Star of Bengal*. Based on fact but mixed with a generous seasoning of fiction, salty cuss words and sex, the book was released by the publishers as purely non-fiction and was sold with that understanding. When the author was exposed by local residents a few months later, the whole thing blew up like a firecracker, the book having already gone through several printings. The cry of "foul play" forced the publishers to offer the money back to any disillusioned purchaser. The added publicity only tended to promote the book more and it was the year's best seller.

The generally accepted true account of the wreck as told at the hearing follows:

The Alaska Packers Association bark *Star of Bengal* was en route back to San Francisco from Wrangell when the tragedy occurred on Coronation Island on September 20, 1908. She was commanded by Captain Nicholas Wagner, with Gus A. Johnson as mate. The iron-hulled vessel departed from Wrangell with about 50,-000 cases of salmon in her holds, and carried scores of cannery workers being brought home from the company canneries in Alaska. They were mostly Orientals.

The steam tenders *Hattie Gage* (Captain Dan Farrer) and the *Kayak* under a Captain Hamilton, handled the towing hausers as the vessel was led through the dangerous Alexander Archipelago toward the open sea where she was to drop her lines and spread her canvas.

Captain Farrer was in overall charge of the two tugs, which were actually cannery tenders owned by the Alaska Packers. As long as calm weather prevailed they encountered no difficulty with the *Bengal* but at midnight when a brisk wind arose and turned into a gale two hours later, the trouble began with a capital T. The *Kayak* which had little draft aft caused most of the strain to be placed on the other tender. The *Kayak* soon became completely unmanageable and the tugs were working against each other instead of together. Convinced that to keep up the strain would have meant outright disaster for all three vessels, the tug skippers ordered the lines cut and made a run for it, leaving the laboring *Bengal* at the mercy of the storm.

Before the tenders abandoned the scene, Captain Wagner, in desperation, had let the anchors go to thwart the drift toward the desolate island. The bark brought up in about ten fathoms, 50 feet from the beach. The tugs had sought shelter at Warren Island some 12 miles away, where temporary repairs were made, after which the *Hattie Gage* steamed back to Wrangell seeking assistance from the government cable ship *Burnside*.

In the terrible blow, the *Star of Bengal* and her terrified company waited in miserable solitude. Straining on her cables the ship was fully open to the storm off exposed Helm Point on a lee shore with precipitous cliffs.

Four courageous men, Henry Lewald, Olaf Hansen and Fred Matson, able seamen, and Frank Muir, a cannery cook, volunteered to get a line ashore. Their boat was smashed to bits in the surf but they succeeded in gaining the beach and making the line fast. In the interim the straining *Star of Bengal* parted her cables and struck the rocks. Within the hour the vessel broke up, only her mizzen topmast marking the spot of the grave. As the hull split open the steady flow of salmon cases and heavy steel drums were swept into the vortex interspersed with the bodies of struggling humans. The giant walls of water combed the devastating scene of man's losing battle against the sea. It was mayhem.

Later Captain Wagner who was among the handful of survivors, gave this official account:

"When the final shock came, the *Star of Bengal* appeared to heave up her entrails in three sections. As I was thrown into the water I saw the midships beams of solid iron come out in a tangled mass. The force necessary to produce this is scarcely conceivable. So strong had been preceding gusts that a five inch iron davit was snapped short off. After I was thrown into the water, any attempt to swim appeared ridiculous. As I struggled only to keep afloat, I was hurled toward shore among a thousand cases of salmon and hundreds of metal drums that constituted our cargo. I was practically unconscious when I reached the beach."

Though there has been some controversy as to how many were actually aboard the *Star of Bengal* most accounts placed the total at 132. Only 22 survived and they were picked up many hours later by the errant *Kayak* after the storm abated. There were reputedly 74 or 75 Orientals aboard and all but two perished. The Caucasians that drowned were mostly the ship's crew.

Captain Wagner was extremely bitter, charging criminal cowardice on the part of the tug skippers, who insisted that they would have accomplished nothing but the destruction of their own vessels and crews by hanging on longer. The inspectors of the Alaska district agreed with them apparently, for they were not censured, while Captain Wagner who was in no way responsible for the tragic episode had his license suspended, an unjustifiable act which was later rescinded by chief inspector Bermingham at San Francisco.

In 1914, ill-fortune continued to dog Captain Wagner while in command of the three-masted wooden cannery bark *Paramita* en route from San Francisco to Bristol Bay. For the three final days of the voyage the vessel was socked in by fog and no sights could be taken. Shortly after midnight on May 14, the fog lifted slightly, and the vessel found herself in a dangerous position just off Unimak Island. Both anchors were dropped, but the strong currents swept the vessel onto the outermost outcropping of rock. Captain Wagner worked her off and set a course for Unalaska but damage had been sustained and water gained on the pumps, igniting the cargo of lime in one of the holds. The pumps were halted, and the burning, sinking ship headed for Lost Harbor, Akun Island where she was run aground with 20 feet of water in her hold. There the fire was finally extinguished.

Inasmuch as the *Paramita* (built in 1879) was one of the few cannery vessels with no wireless, Captain Wagner and a few volunteers took a small boat to Unalaska to seek assistance from the revenue cutters *Tahoma* and *Unalga*. Unknown to him, the cutters were at anchor in a small cove a few miles from the wreck, and 15 hours were consumed in reaching Unalaska. The cutters were finally dispatched to the wreck but heavy seas had already prompted the crew to abandon ship and they had to be rescued from the beach. The survivors were taken to Unalaska where passage back home was arranged.

Meanwhile the 1,573 ton *Paramita* became a total loss, though there was some recovery of her cargo.

Hard-luck Captain Wagner, despite his misfortune, was considered one of the most able sea captains of his era.

It is like Joseph Conrad once penned:
"The most amazing wonder of the deep is its unfathomable cruelty."

Slack wind catches bark **STAR OF ICELAND** in solitary Pacific pose. She sailed the seas from 1896, when built at Glasgow, till coming under the scrappers hammer in 1929.

An impressive study in rigging—the big four-masted Standard Oil bark **ATLAS** towing into port in the early 1900's. In 1910 she became the Alaska Packers **STAR OF LAPLAND,** operating out of San Francisco to Alaskan cannery ports. She was built by Sewall in 1902.

Glory of the Seas

Requiem for the clipper ships that afforded maritime supremacy for the United States in the mid 19th century, was sounded in 1869 with the construction of the full-rigged *Glory of the Seas,* last of her type turned out by the renowned master-builder Donald McKay. To his credit were such famous record breakers as the clipper ships *Flying Cloud,* the *Great Republic* and others. The *Glory of the Seas,* though not as fully-rigged as some of the earlier clippers was McKay's last, and nothing was spared to make her one of the most handsome wooden sailing ships ever constructed. Beautifully appointed throughout, the ship featured hand-rubbed woods and interior panellings fit for a king's palace. Her lines were racy and she was a fast, efficient merchantman. Mr. McKay was justly proud of his last accomplishment.

In late 1873 the *Glory of the Seas* cast off from New York for San Francisco, via the Horn, and by the time she passed through the Golden Gate only 96 days had elapsed, a standing record, only seven days less than the all-time record. This was a route that often required twice that long for run-of-the-mill sailers. But not for the *Glory of the Seas,* which in 1875 added to her laurels with a passage from San Francisco to Sydney, Australia in 35 days, which averaged out to eight knots, far faster than the steamers of that era.

95

The *Glory of the Seas* was a large vessel in her day, and her size coupled with her speed made her a reputable money maker. She measured 240 feet in length, with a tonnage of 2,103, enabling her to pack bulk cargoes up to 3,600 tons. Her mainmast was 175 feet from keel to truck and she carried royals on all three masts. Her keel, floor timbers and keelsons were all bolted together giving her great strength. 'Tween deck beams were 16 inches square and her sides were two feet thick.

As has already been mentioned, the West Coast ports were a repository for many of the queenly square-riggers of yesteryear. The *Glory of the Seas,* like many others of her type, came West to stay. She came earlier than most, 1886 to be exact. After being in the coastwise coal trade out of San Francisco for 18 years, her appearance had indeed wilted, and she never left the North Pacific in all that time. Her days of rounding the Horn were long gone. She was bought by Barneson & Hibbard, of San Francisco in 1906. She next made her homeport at Port Townsend, and became a lumber drougher. But, aging fast and no longer competitive, by 1908 she was laid up at Eagle Harbor on Bainbridge Island.

A slight reprieve came in 1911 when she was sold for conversion to a floating cannery out of Seattle, an ignominious role for a once acclaimed clipper. She was later operated by the Glacier Fish Co. of Tacoma as a cold storage barge, reducing her status to an even lower degree. But still, though shorn to her lower masts, she had a remarkable grace and still carried her original figurehead, a Greek goddess protruding from the trailboards of the ship.

Though the figure's right arm had been rudely broken off at the elbow, her left hand still clutched flowing Grecian draperies. It was a lovely carving.

Salty stories that blew out of the near forgotten clipper ship days prompted a move to preserve the *Glory of the Seas* as a maritime relic. Several efforts were started after the Glacier people announced that they would have to burn the old ship for her metal, but when it actually came to footing the bill, the pot was bare. So the owners ran the vessel up on the beach at Endolyne, near Fauntleroy, south of Seattle and she went up in a blaze of "glory" on May 13, 1923. For many years her charred bones protruded from the sands and were once visited by Donald McKay's son and grandson who recalled the lusty days of tall windships and the shipbuilding genius of another generation.

Diamond Head ex *Gainsborough*

It was indeed a nostalgic day in 1950 when this writer rode the fabled old barge *Diamond Head* on her final trip to the sand spit at Everett on Puget Sound. There she was soaked with oil and the torch touched to her interior. The tug *Lea Moe* herded the *Diamond Head* to the spit and then shoved her aground without fanfare.

A short time later the grand old ex-sailing ship went up in a choking, smokey blaze aided by the long accumulation of bilge oil in her tanks. So hot did she get during the fire, that her plates bulged out and almost necessitated her being scrapped on the spot.

At the termination of the blaze after her inwards had been gutted, what remained was

Death agonies of the American ship **LUCILLE** wrecked at Ugashik Alaska, August 19, 1908. Her crew and cannery workers aboard, 160 strong, all reached shore safely. The ship and cargo were valued at $186,000. The Lucille was built at Freeport, Maine in 1874.

The derelict British ship **MELANOPE** was picked up abandoned, except for a starving dog, in 1906. The crew abandoned thinking the vessel would sink. The Melanope was towed in for salvage. She dated from 1876, when built by Potter at Liverpool, England.

'MELANOPE'

Four-masted bark **RED JACKET** at a Pacific Coast port in 1917. She was built as the British flag **BALASORE.** A few weeks after receiving the name **RED JACKET,** at San Francisco she had it changed to **MONONGAHELA,** the name she held until the end of her career. She was built at Glasgow, Scotland in 1892.

towed back to the Puget Sound Bridge and Dredging Co. shipyard in Seattle to be cut up for scrap.

The *Diamond Head,* a living legend in her agonies as a fuel storage barge for a power company at Seattle's Lake Union, had an interesting past. She was built by C. Lungley as the *Gainsborough* in 1866 at London. Amid considerable fanfare, the beautifully constructed wrought iron vessel, rare in that day of wooden ships, caused a considerable stir. She was a full-rigged ship, crossing single topgallants and royals over double topsails. The Red Duster flew smartly from her gaff. Of 1,000 registered tons, the *Gainsborough* bore an effigy of Lady Gainsborough or the Duchess of Devonshire under her bowsprit, a symbol that was to guide her over countless miles of sea on an adventurous career.

The vessel on her early passages spent much of her time in the South Pacific sailing out to New Zealand from England carrying freight and immigrants, and it was not unusual to have as many as 300 persons aboard. Often she carried livestock, which presented complicated problems on 100-day voyages.

Later the *Gainsborough* served as a troop vessel from England to India and in addition, carried small horses used by the British army, from Australia to India. Though she operated with considerable success, much of the *Gainsborough's* early history is hidden in obscurity.

The second phase of her history, however, began in 1896, when she took on a cargo of coal for San Francisco at Westport, N.Z. Plagued by a miserable voyage with provisions running low, in a constant battle against adverse winds and stormy seas, she was forced to alter course for Honolulu. Coming in, the vessel missed stays and ran up on a reef off Diamond Head. Unfortunately, there was virtually no insurance on the ship. As she lay on the reef under the constant pounding of the Pacific, there was little to do but to sell, where is, as is. Her dis-

97

consolate skipper and principal owner, Captain Alexander McPhail, at auction was able to get only $1,825 for the wreck, which left him virtually penniless after paying his debts.

A major salvage effort removed the cargo of coal and then refloated the vessel in early 1897; she was resold to Allen & Robinson for $5,000 and oddly enough was renamed for the great Hawaiian landmark, Diamond Head. Under command of Captain Ward, and flying the Hawaiian flag, the vessel continued her interrupted voyage to the Golden Gate.

After an overhaul at San Francisco, the *Diamond Head* operated offshore and coastwise, coming under American registry in 1900. In 1910 she was sold out of the lumber trade (from the Pacific Northwest to Hawaii) and shorn to her lower masts to serve as a barge for the Tyee Company of Seattle, who used her in conjunction with their Alaska whaling station. In 1913 she was sold to the General Petroleum Company as an oil storage hulk in Seattle's Lake Union. The lake had become a repository for sailing ships that had outlived their usefulness, especially during the depression years. But the *Diamond Head,* though a miserable old green painted hull, still had the lines of a queen of the seas, and eager newspaper men anxious to make good reading, told many tall tales about her that always sparked interest. True, she was old, built in 1866, but not true was the fact that she was the first iron ship ever built and that 100,000 persons turned out at London "to watch her sink." She was christened *Gainsborough,* not Lady Gainsbor-

One of the gallant units of the Alaska Packers cannery fleet was the four-masted bark **STAR OF SCOTLAND.** She was built as the **KENILWORTH** in Scotland in 1887, and almost bowed out under the ignominious role of a gambling ship named **REX,** until the war demands saved her. In 1941 she was re-rigged as a six-masted schooner and went back to sea for limited trading.

ough as was so often written. Nor was she a pirate ship, a treasure ship, a convict ship or a hoodoo ship, as various marine editors had tabbed her. In her day, however, she was a "Shipshape and Bristol fashion" type vessel, handsome in appearance, a far cry from her state when she reached the end of the line.

Though Puget Sounders would liked to have believed that the *Diamond Head* was actually the world's first iron ship, she was only one of about 250 ships built of iron in the British Isles, when delivered in 1866. To be sure she was one of the larger commercial sailing ships of her day but again by no means the largest.

In fact, the *Star of India* which is still afloat today as a live museum ship at San Diego, California, was built as the full-rigged *Euterpe* at the Isle of Man in 1863 and still in fine shape is visited by thousands of persons annually. She weighed in at 1,240 tons, compared to 1,012 for the *Gainsborough*. Another well known iron ship that spent many of her years on the West Coast was the *Star of Peru,* of 975 tons, built at Sunderland, England, in 1863 as the *Himalaya.*

Actually very little is known about the history of the *Gainsborough* before becoming the *Diamond Head.*

It has been recorded that on January 25, 1868 she sailed from London with 96 passengers for New Zealand and being buffeted by terrific gales, put back to Plymouth from where she again departed February 8; and after a fairly good passage, arrived at Lyttelton, May 2, 1869.

Again on October 23, 1877, she is known to have left London with cargo and 232 immigrants, New Zealand-bound; again she met with gales, causing the loss of the jibboom, fore-topmast and main topgallant masts as well as suffering considerable damage to rigging and sails.

Repairs were made at sea and after a passage of 125 days, she arrived at Wellington, N.Z. During that passage she experienced much heavy weather, and so said her logbook, she reeled off 300 or more miles per day at times. More voyages were then made to New Zealand at intervals of years during which she tramped the sea lanes of both hemispheres.

Facts are lacking, however, that she ever became a convict ship transporting prisoners to Van Diemens Land (Tasmania), though it is possible that she did carry an occasional cargo of coolies to areas in need of cheap labor or even forced labor to the Guano Islands. Of this her chronicle remains forever silent.

The James Griffiths Story

James Griffiths & Sons is a name that has been synonymous with water transportation on Puget Sound, British Columbia and the Pacific Coast for several decades. The founder of that company, Captain James Griffiths, played a dominant role in the history of the old square-rigged sailing vessels. He made a fortune in the maritime industry in coastal towing, and the nucleus of his pioneer fleet were old sailing vessels which he converted to barges.

Briefly, Captain James Griffiths was born in Monmouthshire, England in 1861, arriving at Tacoma in 1885. He organized a company at Tacoma to build a tugboat, as he saw a definite need for such a vessel in those pioneer years on Puget Sound. With the backing of Tacoma's top banker, Gen. L. W. Sprague, the Tacoma Steam Navigation Co. was formed. The stockholders, six in all, hired Hiran Doncaster to design the tug, and Boole & Co. of San Francisco to build it. The result was the *Mogul*. The Tacoma Steam Navigation Co. was dissolved in 1888 and the *Mogul* was taken over by Griffiths, Stetson & Bridges until 1891 when sold to the Puget Sound Tug Boat Co. for operation by its Canadian subsidiary, the British Columbia Tug Boat Co. On May 4, 1895 the *Mogul* was rammed by the British bark *Darra* off Cape Flattery and became a total loss.

Captain Griffiths' firm became shipping agents in various Puget Sound ports, and as Northwest manager for the NYK-Great Northern Railroad shipping interests, Captain Griffiths was instrumental in gaining the first berthline service between Seattle and Japan. A contract was signed between NYK and Great Northern on July 11, 1896 and the initial vessel, the *Miike Maru,* arrived in Seattle to a tumultuous welcome on August 31 of that year.

Griffiths later organized important steamship, barge, stevedoring and shipbuilding enterprises some of which have been continued down to the present day by his sons and later by his grandsons.

Though the late Captain James Griffiths was an empire builder in his own right, amassing a fortune in the maritime industry, much of his foresight was his ability to buy up old sailing ships bogged down because of depressed rates, financial problems, through salvage or steam competition. He purchased at low prices, sold

Now enshrined as a museum ship at Honolulu the famed ship **FALLS OF CLYDE** is one of Hawaii's most visited and photographed attractions. Built by Russell at Port Glasgow, Scotland in 1878 she was rescued from her role as an oil storage vessel in Alaska in her final years of active service and restored to her former splender as one of the illustrious square-riggers. The above painting depicts her when under the Matson houseflag as a tank sailing vessel delivering oil to the Hawaiian Islands and returning to the mainland with molasses.

at high prices and often converted these square-riggers to lowly barges using his own ships to tow them. He was actually the grandfather of long distance West Coast commercial towing, using jumbo-sized barges, an updated business that flourishes today despite the many fast modes of land transportation.

Many of the most famous sailing ships owned on the Pacific Coast were under the Griffiths house flag at sometime during their careers. They included the ship *America,* bark *Amy Turner,* bark *Baroda,* bark *Big Bonanza,* ship *Charger,* bark *Carondelet,* bark *Daylight,* bark *General Fairchild,* bark *Gerald C. Tobey,* bark *Henry Villard,* bark *Haydn Brown,* bark *John C. Potter,* ship *James Drummond,* bark *Louisiana,* bark *Lord Templetown,* bark *Melanope,* bark *Palmyra,* ship *Riversdale,* bark *Rufus E. Wood,* bark *Quatsino,* bark *St. James,* bark *St. David* and bark *William T. Lewis.*

Many of these tall ships were cut down to barges and paid for themselves many times over despite an ignominious departure from their originally intended purposes.

Of all of the sailing vessels that passed through the ownership of James Griffiths' interests, none had a more colorful or notorious history than the *Melanope.*

The Curse of the Melanope

The strange history of the full-rigged ship *Melanope* placed her in a discarded chapter of maritime history. Probably there was no more handsome ship in her day, but ships like people despite their appearance, are often relegated to cursed lives.

The *Melanope* was built in 1876 by W. H. Pot-

Six decades later—the **BALCLUTHA**, like a breath out of the past moves through San Francisco Bay, with a tugboat escort. Restored through the efforts of the citizens of San Francisco, backed by the San Francisco Maritime Museum and the State of California, the vessel lives on as a memorial to the lusty past. *Photo by Karl Kortum, director, San Francisco Maritime Museum.*

ter and Company of Liverpool, England and was troubled from the start, for her very name is derived from the Greek "melanos" which means black or belonging to a dark or black class. That name was born out when the ship in her waning years as a barge was painted black and coated with the dust of coal and the slime of oil.

It all started on her maiden voyage when being towed to sea with a full load of passengers and cargo. The 256 foot vessel had been designed for the emigrant traffic from England to Australia. But on that initial voyage after casting off, a haggy old woman was found selling apples to the passengers. The ship's officers had earlier asked her to leave the ship and were astonished to find her still at her chores as the ship was towing to sea. Enraged by the incident, the captain demanded that she leave the ship and go ashore on the tug. Appearing much like an old witch the adamant woman stoutly refused to leave the ship and finally had to be removed forcibly. The air turned blue with her profanity much to the amusement of the passengers and crew. It was funny

to the onlookers but dead serious to the struggling old woman who vented her wrath with a vengeance. They finally lowered her to the tug which had been hailed to stand by. Once aboard, leaning over the railing she continued to curse the master, the officers, the crew, the passengers and the ship. "To you, ship *Melanope,* I curse you forever." Her words were still reverberating as the two vessels parted company.

On that maiden voyage while crossing the Bay of Biscay the *Melanope* was hampered by a succession of storms which seemed to grow in intensity. The passengers were confined to their bunks, many desperately seasick, and their plight turned to fear when the ship was dismasted. The officers and crew went without sleep for hours and the master paced the poop, constantly shouting orders. It was at this time that mumblings started aboard about the curse placed on the lofty three-masted vessel by the old hag.

The crew set about to install a temporary jury rig which was the means of getting the ship to port for urgently needed repairs. Though the tars blamed the curse, the more practical officers believed the ship to be over-rigged, and in re-rigging her, the sail plan was altered and nearly ten feet subtracted from the height of each mast.

On every succeeding voyage, however, the *Melanope* seemed to have a misfortune. Some of the incidents were slightly seasoned with an additional portion of salt, but most were based on fact and all were to the detriment of the ship.

One well documented tale tells of a master of the ship in the 1880's becoming involved with an attractive lady passenger who unfortunately was a married woman of considerable means. She became infatuated with the ship's master who was inclined to have a bit of a flirtatious eye with any striking bit of femininity. This woman, however, was insistent, and after the ship landed in Australia she booked passage for the return trip in order to be near her captain. The skipper on the other hand had tired of the designing female and tried to prevent

her return to England aboard his ship. According to the story, she persisted and he resisted. Defiantly, the woman purchased the controlling interest in the ship and took passage, much to the chagrin of the irate captain. His desperate predicament played on his mind at sea. Then one dismal day the mate heard shots ring out, and on investigating the cabin found the prostrate bodies of the woman and the captain. The ship's master had reputedly shot her and then taken his own life.

Also, in the grisly lines of the ship's log was once recorded a knife fight to the death between two of the ship's crewmen. They stabbed each other fatally and died in a mutual pool of blood.

Perhaps the most widely circulated story of agony aboard the *Melanope* revolved about a certain skipper, a bounder of sorts, who had married the daughter of a rich Indian merchant. Much to the sadness of her parents, the two eloped aboard the ship departing Antwerp

"They mark our passage as a race of men
    Earth will not see such ships as those again" . . . Masefield.
Alaska Packers yard and fleet—a forest of masts—Alameda, California. *Courtesy San Francisco Maritime Museum.*

for Panama, but the honeymoon which started out as an adventure turned to revelry and wild drinking parties. The ship's master became inebriated day and night. Sometimes in his rage he would beat those under his command, causing near mutiny.

As the ship was nearing Panama the attractive bride suddenly died, a victim of alcohol and malaria, and the skipper who sobered up enough for her burial at sea, himself, became so remorseful that he leaped overboard and drowned.

The first officer then took command and sailed the ship to San Francisco, where, in order to pay the crew the vessel had to be sold. It was rumored about the ship that the mate had been seen counting piles of gold in the former master's cabin. It was even claimed that inasmuch as nobody had seen the skipper leap overboard that the mate may have conspired to murder him.

Alaska Packers Association's ship **STAR OF FALKLAND** was wrecked in adverse weather in Unimak Pass on Akun Head, near Pinnacle Rocks, Alaska, May 22, 1928. The crew reached shore safely. The 2,163 ton vessel was built originally at Glasgow in 1892 as the **DURBRIDGE**.

J. J. Moore and Company purchased the *Melanope* in 1900 at the end of that infamous voyage. She was placed in command of Captain Nicolls K. Wills, who had a fine reputation as a ship's master. He probably did better with the *Melanope* than any other, but he, too, had his problems. In fact it was during his years in command of the vessel that (in 1902) she posted a most unusual record passage. Sailing from Puget Sound for Cape Town with lumber, she logged an average passage half way to destination. Then the trouble started. For steering an erratic course, Captain Wills confronted the helmsman, and following a heated argument the helmsman ended up in irons. Several other crewmen protested and refused to go back to work until their shipmate was released. Despite the threat of the captain's gun and the officers' belaying pins, the fo'c'sle gang still refused to work and finally all were placed in irons, leaving only two mates, the sailmaker, cook, steward, the carpenter and two apprentices. With this skeleton crew, Captain Wills sailed the *Melanope* across the South Atlantic with favorable following winds, logging 5,000 miles in the record time of 19 days, and a total passage of 72 days.

At Cape Town, the mutineers were taken into custody but were placed back aboard at sailing time because the authorities did not want to be burdened with the dissident men.

Then Captain Wills sailed to Australia but the troublesome seamen eagerly quit the ship there without pay. Even the mates were docked some of their wages for declining to report certain incidents during the voyage.

Virtually an entire new crew was signed on.

The old apple lady's curse stuck to the *Melanope* like glue. Three years later, in 1906, the ship was sailing under ballast off the mouth of the Columbia River, still in command of Captain Wills. Aboard was his wife, and young son. A howling storm contorted the ocean's face and the vessel took the same kind of a beating that she had on her maiden voyage. The topmasts went by the board, water slopped deep in the bilge. All but one of the ship's boats were damaged and the *Melanope* began to heel over on her beam ends. Navigation was impossible. Fearing for his family and the safety of his crew, the captain, in desperation, ordered abandonment. All 22 persons on the vessel piled into the remaining ship's boat and with great effort after almost capsizing, got clear. The *Melanope's* mascot, Queenie, was left behind in

The role of a barge befell many a proud sailing ship such as the **ST. DAVID** seen here aground in Yakatat Bay, Alaska after the tug **DANIEL KERN,** which was towing her became disabled October 30, 1917. The barge was being towed from Cordova to Anyox, B.C. at the time of her grounding. It was said that the tug crew did not know how to handle the old wooden-stocked anchors on the St. David which would have kept her from going aground and becoming a total loss.

The first sailing vessel on which Captain P. A. McDonald served as an officer was the **WM. H. MACY,** which he considered an exceptional vessel. She is seen here in a waterfront scene, yards canted for handling cargo.

the frantic evacuation, and a sad departure it was. It was assumed that the dog would go down with the ship.

After bobbing up and down on a pulsating sea for many hours, the miserable survivors were sighted by the schooner *William H. Smith* which promptly took them aboard and discharged them at Port Townsend.

But the story did not end here, for a few days later the *Melanope* was picked up by a small coastal freighter and claimed as a salvage prize. She had refused to go down and Queenie, whining, cold and starving, had waited patiently for her master's return. The ship was towed into Astoria, a wreck.

The Wills family were eventually reunited with the delighted mascot, but found that most of their possessions left aboard in abandonment of the ship were lost, either in the storm or by light-fingered salvagers. Captain Wills and his family moved to Seattle and he became a pilot in British Columbia and Puget Sound waters.

The *Melanope* was then purchased by the well known Captain James Griffiths, who took her over after the salvage money was paid. Under his supervision she was converted to a barge, afterward being sold to Canadian Pacific. She spent most of her latter years coaling merchant ships in Vancouver harbor. Still afloat during World War II, the aging old hull reminded one of the hag that had placed the hex many years before. On occasion during the war years, the *Melanope* at the working end of a towline carried coal from Ladysmith, B.C. to the Aleutian Islands for the war effort.

A young lady who lived on the *Melanope* when she was a barge at Vancouver once found a gold bracelet in the rotting upholstery in the ship's main cabin. It is believed to have belonged to the unfortunate bride who had died aboard ship many years before.

Yes, indeed, the once beautiful trim-lined *Melanope* boasting double topgallant and royal yards, ended her days in sad disarray, just as the old hag had prophesied.

The end of the jinxed ship came in the 1940's. As a coal barge, she was towed to Royston, B. C., in Comox Bay, to a wharf owned by the Comox Logging Co. Near there, she was sunk to a shallow depth and left to the mercy of the sea, as a breakwater. Only traces of the hulk now remain. Winter storms have demolished the upperworks, and rusted metal and decayed wood are a sad reminder of the lusty past. A gaping hole in her hull allows the tide to ebb and flow through her musty holds, an eerie, haunting sight, though a delight to curious fish and nesting birds.

And so the *Melanope* died on the mudflats at Royston, not a fitting death for a great square-rigger. For certain, the old apple lady had her revenge.

* * *

There is a letter in existence in Vancouver, B.C. that plays down the one facet of the *Melanope's* notorious history.

Captain Creighton Robinson, once master of the *Melanope*, wrote:

"Now as to the old *Melanope,* books and news accounts give some of her early history and latter day usage with a lot of bunk in between,

Reproduction of a painting of the great bark **MOSHULU** one of the largest square-riggers ever to sail under the Stars and Stripes.

particularly that pertaining to the purchase at Antwerp, etc. I took charge of her in 'Frisco in late 1900 and took my wife, Kate, with me on a voyage to Sydney, Australia.

"The *Melanope* was then rigged as a bark and poorly rigged in the way of running gear, at that—they wanted a man with British license to take command.

"The story I got first hand from Green, who was mate, was that the captain and his wife had purchased the vessel at Antwerp, intending to cruise around the world.

"On reaching Panama she died of fever. The captain also contracted fever of which he died en route to S.F.

"I made a fast trip, 45 days to Sydney and 65 days back, then loaded for Adelaide where my son Lance was born, and left her on return to San Francisco. A man named Wills, a Penzance man who had been master of the SS *Arab,* Dollar Company, took her."

Buckingham, Vessel of Many Names

Captain P. A. McDonald, former master of the largest square-rigged sailing vessels under the U.S. flag, and a historical writer on old sailing ships, recalls in his reminiscences, the history of the bark *Buckingham* (and her lovely figurehead), on which he served as chief mate and master during World War II. The vessel then bore the names *Ottawa* and *Flying Cloud.*

(I call you Buckingham, a fit name for a royal ship. May all your voyages be fortunate and prosperous.) So launched by Queen Victoria, Liverpool, 1888, was this sailing vessel, McDonald records.

McDonald wrote that "sailors reckon it bad luck to change a ship's name, but under the flags of Great Britain, Germany and the United States, the *Buckingham* changed her name five times and her luck held. From *Buckingham* to *Bertha,* then *Muscoota, Ottawa, Flying Cloud* and back to *Muscoota.* Names and owners, captains and crews they all changed, but the image of the dead Queen (ship's figurehead) remained, bleached and scarred and cracked it is true, but still showing evidence of the skill lavished on her by a forgotten figurehead carver.

"On Christmas Eve, 1922, as the *Muscoota,* she left Melbourne for Sydney on what was to be her last voyage. The next night, Christmas Day, she collided in Bass Strait with the Norwegian steamer *Yarra,* bound for Melbourne. She struck the *Yarra* amidships, her bowsprit twisting the steamer's funnel out of shape, then as she drew clear and swung around, her lower yards swept the steamer, bringing the top of her aftermast and wireless crashing to the deck.

"The bow of the *Muscoota* cut through the *Yarra's* steel plates like a great knife. The cook of the *Yarra* was in the galley, and to his amazement he beheld the effigy of Queen Vic-

Two great square-riggers—the **WILLIAM DOLLAR** and the **JAMES DOLLAR** idle in Lake Union in Seattle after the call for ships had died in the wake of World War I. *Photo courtesy Captain P. A. McDonald, who once commanded the William Dollar.*

toria come sailing in, to drop at his feet on the galley floor. Both ships reached their respective ports, but the famous figurehead remained in the galley of the steamer, and formed an important part in the hearing of the claim for damages, which the *Muscoota* finally won. She was awarded 5,267 pounds and 150 pounds for the disappearance of the figurehead.

"The *Muscoota* was converted into a hulk in Sydney, from a royal vessel, launched by the Queen of England. The figurehead was almost ruined in Melbourne when souvenir hunters chipped off pieces. It was later offered for sale and eventually disappeared and where it got to no one seems to know. After years of service as a fuel barge in Sydney harbor, this once proud ship, while performing the humble service of fueling two allied ships in Milne Bay, New Guinea, 1942, was crushed and sent to the bottom."

* * *

Captain McDonald recalls that at the entry of the United States into the war against Germany early in 1917, the demand for tonnage for overseas trade grew to such fantastic proportions that everything that could float was pressed into service; old wooden crates long past their days of usefulness were yanked off the mudflats, drydocked and refitted and sent out with the blessings of all concerned, so that the owners could take advantage of the fabulous freights that kept mounting as the war progressed.

The United States sail tonnage, particularly square-riggers in the offshore trade, had at this time reached a low ebb, but with the entry into the war and the necessity for bottoms many restrictive tariff laws were swept aside and ships of other flags in American waters automatically received American papers and later, full registry. Up to that date practically all the square-riggers on the Pacific were owned and operated by the Alaska salmon packers, who had something like 18 square-riggers of wood and steel, including the remnant of the original "Stars" —*Star of Italy, Star of France, Star of Russia.* These ships and their running mates operated seasonally only, and were not usually available for overseas service.

In addition to these square-riggers there was quite a number of ships formerly British, but which, though U.S. owned, still flew the British (Canadian) flag. Amongst them were such ships as the *British Yeoman, Lord Templetown, Howard D. Troop, Lord Shaftesbury,*

Dunsyre and *Robert Duncan,* and still others which, as the war progressed, were given complete American papers and in some cases changes of name. To swell this fleet of sailing ships came a number of German vessels which had sought refuge in American harbors when America was still neutral. In 1917 these ships were seized and immediately overhauled without regard for expense, and loaded with valuable cargoes for the various allied countries. These German ships were in most cases formerly British, and all except one were British built. At first these ships were given the names of former American clippers, but these were later changed to Indian names—*Arapahoe* ex *Northern Light,* ex *Steinbek,* ex *Durbridge* of 2,160 gross tons; *Muscoota,* ex *Flying Cloud,* ex *Ottawa,* ex *Bertha,* ex *Buckingham* of 2,665 gross tons; *Moshulu,* ex *Dreadnaught,* ex *Kurt* of 3,116 gross tons; *Chillicothe,* ex *Gamecock,* ex *Arnoldus Vinnen,* ex *Flotow,* of 1,862 tons; *Tonawanda,* ex *Indra,* of 1,745 tons; *Monongahela,* ex *Red Jacket,* ex *Dalbeck,* ex *Balasore,* of 2,780 gross tons. These were all steel ships and in addition, there was a wooden bark *Montauk,* ex *Matador,* built in Germany, of 1,500 tons. Some of these ships sailed on a Pacific voyage or two while under clipper ships names; others had names changed to the Indian versions before leaving port.

There was nothing in the past, nor in the subsequent performance of these ships, to justify the extravagant optimism of giving them names once held by the world's famous clipper ships. The outstanding ship in this fleet was the *Moshulu,* built in Scotland, 1904, for German owners and for the nitrate trade. As for the *Kurt* she made some splendid passages to the nitrate ports in 68, 76, 79 days, and on one occasion, deep laden with 5,000 tons of coal from Newcastle, N.S.W. to Chile, made the passage in 31 days. This is within reach of the record of 29 days, 15 hours, set by the British ship *Wendur.*

The *Moshulu* was strictly a 20th century ship of the most modern design, all yards and spars of steel, steered and conned from midship, a fine arrangement for a ship nearly 350 feet long. She was a good performer, and though no clipper, packed a good payload. Having commanded this fine ship as well as the former *Buckingham,* Captain McDonald spoke of both ships with authority as well as with some affection.

In 1917 he joined the bark *Ottawa* in San

Francisco as chief mate, having charge of her while she was given a complete overhauling, new rigging, sails and gear; and after drydocking, the vessel loaded a valuable cargo of varied items from lumber to oil and paint, for Wellington, N.Z. She was an all-round fine, even handsome ship, McDonald recalled, with a fine sheer and lines, but as to sailing quality he was soon disillusioned and so settled for a rather comfortable ship that would in God's own time arrive at port of destination, winds being willing. He recalled a passage of 67 days to Wellington where after discharging cargo, they loaded for Melbourne a part cargo which consisted chiefly of New Zealand flax and lumber. After a slow passage of 27 days across the Tasman Sea they arrived at Melbourne about the middle of December, 1917.

As the *Flying Cloud,* few if any, recognized the four-master as the one-time *Buckingham* even with her famous figurehead and the legendary launching in the presence of Queen Victoria. Captain McDonald had a large and very thirsty crew and, like many another American ship of that period, plenty of money to spend; the old ship became quite notorious, if not unpopular, at least with the police. After discharging their cargo at South Wharf and taking on 1,100 tons of ballast preparatory to proceeding to Newcastle, the question of finding an available powerful enough tug for the purpose, became it seems, something of a problem.

Finally there arrived upon the scene a craft of such shape and design as to defy any coherent description as to date or origin. Her name was something like *Koputai,* but better known as "Cup-of-tea" in local waters. She was an odd and venerable thing with enormous side paddle-wheel boxes, low in the water with a high smokestack. Just how this ancient looking tug could expect to tow the sizable *Flying Cloud* filled Captain McDonald with some apprehension, and since he was the mate, details were of course his concern.

The captain of the tug was something of a character and evidently part owner of the turtle-like monster. From his sanguine talk as to the thousands of powerful horses comprising *Koputai's* engine, he soon dispelled any fear Captain McDonald had previously harbored; his worry then was the fear that this veritable Paul Bunyan would pull the keelson up through the fore hatch or otherwise tow the ship apart. He forgot how many thousand the horsepower was but the past prodigious feats of performance of the boat was such as to leave them all ashamed for having doubted the tug skipper and so they accepted his towline shackled on to their anchor cable and proceeded in tow toward Newcastle.

*　　*　　*

(Captain P. A. McDonald went to sea at an early age and after several years before the mast in British and American deepwater square-riggers, made his first voyage as second mate in 1905 on the full-rigged ship *William H. Macy.* Afterwards he served as second mate and later as chief mate of such vessels as the bark *Carondelet,* the ships *Charles E. Moody, Henry Failing* and *William H. Smith;* the schooners *Oceania Vance, Melrose, Crescent, Carrier Dove, F.M. Slade, Edward R. West* and

Six-masted barkentine **EVERETT G. GRIGGS,** originally built in 1883, was perhaps better known under the name **E. R. STERLING.** She was built as the **LORD WOLSELEY.** As a six-masted barkentine, she was the first of her rig ever to sail the seas.

One of the foreign built three-masted ships well known on the coast was the **HOMEWARD BOUND**, which later became the **STAR OF HOLLAND**.

the barkentine *Lahaina*. Later he was master of the four-masted bark *Flying Cloud*, ex *Buckingham;* the schooner *Corona*, the barkentine *Jane L. Stanford*, the ship *Dunsyre*, the four-masted bark *William Dollar* and the four-masted bark *Moshulu*.)

Tale of the Robert Kerr

A miserable old sailing bark known as the *Robert Kerr* which ended her days in ignominy as a coaling barge on the Vancouver, B.C. waterfront, once won a humanitarian reprieve. But let us go back to the start.

The *Robert Kerr* was built in Quebec City in 1866. Unfortunately her sailing days ended prematurely. On September 6, 1885 in a heavy fog she hit the outcroppings of San Juan Island, seriously damaging her forefoot on the rocks, ending a troublesome ocean voyage which started in Liverpool, September 30, 1884. Pummeled by one storm after another, sickness, plague and quarrelsome, almost mutinous hands, the vessel was jinxed from the start of that voyage. Her rigging and hull were badly damaged by the heavy seas that constantly swept her decks. Much of her canvas was ripped to shreds and then to make matters worse, her master, Capt. Edward Edwards died at sea after the ship had rounded the Horn en route to British Columbia.

First officer John Richardson then took command, and with his responsibilities inherited the crew troubles. The most unsavory crewman was William Anderson who was involved in arguments or fights with nearly every man aboard. For these assaults he was

marked in the log-book almost as much as the weather. Once he stuck a cotton hook deep in the cheek of his shipmate Seraphim Fortes. (Fortes was a genial colored man who later became one of Vancouver, B.C.'s most beloved personalities as the lifeguard of English Bay.) Till his death he always said he was glad when the *Kerr* struck San Juan Island for he felt the vessel was jinxed.

Getting back to that last voyage, however, the slow-to-anger Richardson finally had all he could take and must have barged into the troublesome AB with a vengeance, as the log lists Anderson as being confined to Sick Bay for an indefinite period.

The ill-fated *Robert Kerr* after her stranding was towed to Vancouver Harbor and was at anchor there when the great Vancouver fire of June, 1886 broke out. "Joe" Seraphim Fortes, deep scar still in his cheek and still attached to the vessel, emerged as a hero, alone responsible for saving scores of lives in that disaster by directing people to the ship.

When Fortes died in 1922 he was highly honored, and a drinking fountain stands in his memory today in the park at English Bay.

Shortly after the fire, Captain William Soule purchased and beached the *Kerr* alongside the Hastings mill and there careened and repaired her. Having lost his family home in the fire, the Soules took up residence on the ship till a time when a charter could be secured and the vessel sent back to sea.

When Vancouver was incorporated as a city, the old bark, then a waterfront landmark, was gayly decorated with all of her flags flying. Her role in the great fire had gained her a place of prominence in the hearts of the local citizenry.

Canadian historical writer B. A. McKelvie further relates the vessel's role in the great fire.

"When the residents of Vancouver fled from the red holocaust that was sweeping down upon them that Sunday in June of 1886, many of them turned towards a battered old sailing ship that was anchored off the burning community. It was the *Robert Kerr*, damaged on the rocks of San Juan Island, brought to Vancouver and sold by the underwriters to Captain William Soule, who superintended the loading of ships at Hastings Mill.

"The *Robert Kerr* was invaded by men and women in rowboats, in Indian canoes and on rafts and logs, seeking sanctuary from the flames. At first the watchman hesitated to allow them aboard, but all objections were overcome and some 150 to 200 persons found safety on the decks of the vessel."

Captain Soule and his family took refuge on the German bark *von Moltke* loading at Hastings Mill during the fire. After the *Robert Kerr* became the Soule's home, the joy of living aboard a sailing vessel never diminished for the two children. But Mrs. Soule had to call upon her reserve many times to keep her floating home "Shipshape and Bristol fashion." One dark, stormy night while she and her children were left alone on the vessel, it began to drag anchor and was in grave danger of slamming into other sailing vessels moored at the lumber mill. She and the two children, in a herculean effort, readied a second anchor and managed to get it over the side, which was just the grip needed to prevent a collision.

The *Robert Kerr* became known as the "greeter ship" in the harbor and the skippers and officers of vessels calling at the mill often came aboard to dine or to take afternoon tea, much to the credit of the gracious hostess, Mrs. Soule.

When the Soules decided that shoreside living might be more convenient, Captain Soule decided to get rid of his charge in a unique way. He sold chances on her at $100 each in the local saloons and water front establishments. Tickets were printed and circulated with the words, "Grand Raffle of the good ship *Robert Kerr*." The response was amazing. He sold 80 chances, but whether by law or by chance, the raffle failed to come off. Instead, the vessel was sold to Canadian Pacific Steamship Company, then in dire need of a coal tender to supply its great Empress liner fleet in Transpacific service. The *Kerr* was the only hull around large enough and strong enough to meet their needs. She measured 190.5 feet in length and was rated at 1,123 tons. Her holds were spacious and she could more than pack her weight in coal. Thus the vessel was purchased for $7,000 on October 3, 1888 and reduced to the role of a coal hulk. She, however, played a vital role in supplying the celebrated liners that put Vancouver Harbor on world maps everywhere.

After hard usage, the *Robert Kerr* was placed in drydock to tighten up the seams in her wooden hull, and in 1891 was sold by Canadian Pacific Steamship Company to Canadian Pacific Railroad. For 20 years she carried coal between Ladysmith and Burrard Inlet, at the far end of a towline.

It was a sad day for the maritime sentimentalists of Vancouver, B.C. when word reached the city that the familiar grubby humanitarian ship would no longer be seen traveling through Canadian waters. In a heavy fog, under tow of the Union Steamship's tug *Coutli*, the *Kerr* slammed into Danger Reef off Thetis Island on March 4, 1911, and there stuck fast.

She died hard, however, and for years her bones lay bleached in dismal disarray for all to see. Termed by many a "black drudge" she nevertheless had kept company with Empresses. As late as 1927, the *Kerr's* bell was presented to the Vancouver City Museum and still tolls the memories of the past.

Balclutha Lives On

The State of California and the staff of the San Francisco Maritime Museum had great foresight in preserving the old *Balclutha*, perhaps the finest example afloat today of the once great fleet of British square-rigged merchantmen of the late 1900's. Restored to her original splendor, the majestic relic of the days of sail has been visited by scores of eager tourists, school children and local citizenry of all ages, who can thrill at the sight of tall masts, lofty yardarms, and miles of rigging. They can frequently rediscover the fo'c'sle, the captain's cabin and the main saloon. They can see the deep cargo holds and the instruments of navigation.

The *Balclutha* was built in Scotland in 1886.

Her first 13 years were spent wandering the world in the typical ocean trades of her day; coal from Cardiff, wheat from San Francisco, case oil from New York, rice from Rangoon, nitrates from Iquique, guano from Lobos de Tierra, wool from New Zealand, wire and window glass from Antwerp, jute gunny bags from Calcutta, wine and spirits from London. During this period of her career, which lasted until 1899, she rounded Cape Horn 17 times.

In 1899, the *Balclutha* came under the Hawaiian flag and made three voyages from Puget Sound to Australia with lumber. She was the last ship to fly the Hawaiian flag at sea. In 1901 she obtained United States registry by special Act of Congress.

After shipwreck and repairs, in 1906 her name was changed to *Star of Alaska,* and under the banner of the Alaska Packers, for the next 24 years the ship made a voyage each year to Alaska, carrying fishermen north and canned salmon home. She was the last square-rigger engaged in the trade. In the 1920's the *Star of Alaska* and the bark *Star of England* cleared from San Francisco on the same tide and raced to Chirikof Island, Alaska. It was a grudge battle to claim the title of the fastest windship on the Pacific Coast. The *Star of Alaska* won the race. Her final voyage under sail was made as late as 1930. After three years of idleness, the ship was sold to Southern California owners in 1933, and renamed *Pacific Queen.* For nearly 20 years following, she was used as an exhibition ship and on a few occasions as a background for harbor scenes in motion pictures. Slowly deteriorating, the old ship was towed to San Francisco in 1952 and laid up on the mud flats.

When plans were afoot in 1954 to dismantle the aging vessel, she was purchased by the San Francisco Maritime Museum Association and given her original name. Restoration of the *Balclutha* to her original state as a Cape Horn square-rigger was a remarkable year-long community effort in which some 18 Bay Area labor unions and other volunteers donated 13,000 hours of work, and more than 90 business firms contributed $100,000 in supplies and services.

The steel-hulled *Balclutha* is a typical British merchant ship of the late Victorian period. In the year 1897, for instance, there were 515 of these steel sailing ships (as well as 936 built of iron) under British registry. Britain in those days still ruled the seas. A majority of these square-riggers were familiar to San Francisco because of the California and Northwest grain trade from the 1880's until after the turn of the century.

The *Balclutha* is 256.5 feet in length; breadth 38.6 feet; depth 22.7 feet and she is registered at 1,716 gross tons. The ship has on occasion, carried as much as 2,660 tons of cargo, and so laden was capable of making about 300 miles per day before a fair wind.

The vessel's mainmast is 144 feet from deck level to masthead. The standing rigging now on board represents almost a mile and one half of wire cable. Additionally there are some three miles of manila running rigging now aloft. Underway, the *Balclutha* set 25 sails with an average crew of 26 men. Her name is the ancient Gaelic word for the town of Dumbarton, home of Robert McMillan, her original Scotch owner.

Perhaps the most perilous moment in the life of the *Balclutha* has been aptly captured on canvas in an excellent painting by Oswald Brett.

One of the most dreaded mishaps that could overtake a sailing ship is to have the cargo shift, pinning the vessel over on her side. The *Balclutha* escaped a near disaster in 1894, when, outward bound from Wales to Iquique, Chile, her cargo of coal shifted in Bristol Channel. In the words of Captain Alfred H. Durkee, who was in command of the ship:

". . . We had the men aloft making fast some of the sails, as it was by now blowing a heavy gale. The ship was rolling badly and shipping great quantities of water, washing overboard everything movable around us, including our chickens and two pigs. While the men were still aloft, the sea suddenly gathered and a huge roller struck the ship, and with a great roll she went over on her side, shifting

The British four-mast bark **HINEMOA** is pictured here anchored off Astoria in the Columbia River. This vessel had a jinxed career and a short life. *Photo courtesy Pete Hurd.*

the coal cargo, and there she lay with her lee deck full of water.

"The men aloft had great difficulty in holding on and getting the sails fast, but eventually we got them down and began trying to get the ship around. But, as we were lying over so far the men could not stand on deck without holding on to something, so ropes were stretched across the ship and made fast. In our case, we very nearly lost two of the men, which rather took the heart out of all of us. However, after much difficulty and danger we got the ship around and began running back for anchorage."

Falls of Clyde

The vessel *Falls of Clyde,* now fully restored for preservation by the Bernice P. Bishop Museum, Honolulu, is unique in American maritime history.

She is the only former four-masted full-rigged ship whose hull is still afloat. Additionally she is.perhaps the only sailing oil tanker still in existence.

The *Falls of Clyde* is an iron vessel 266 feet long. Her beam is 40 feet. She was built in 1878 by Russell and Company, Port Glasgow, Scotland, on the River Clyde.

Her first years were spent in the India trade under the British flag. In 1898 she was purchased by Captain William Matson, temporarily registered under the Hawaiian flag, and placed in the California-Hawaii trade. For nine years she carried passengers and general cargo from the mainland to the islands, returning with sugar.

When Hawaii was admitted as a territory of the United States in 1900, the *Falls of Clyde* came under American registry. During the time of Matson's ownership, the vessel's rig was changed from a ship to a bark. This meant that her aftermost, or jigger mast was changed from square sails to fore-and-aft sails.

In 1907 the bark was sold to the Associated Oil Company. With the installation of ten bulk fuel tanks, she was converted to a sailing oil tanker. She continued in the California-Hawaii trade carrying as much as 17,500 barrels of bulk oil, opening up a new era in petroleum supply to the paradise islands.

Twenty years later she was sold to the General Petroleum Company. With her masts cut down, she served as a floating fuel depot in Alaska until 1959. A private buyer then towed the *Falls of Clyde* to Seattle expecting to sell her for a handsome price to a preservation group. When no buyer came she was destined to become a part of a breakwater on Vancouver Island, but was saved from this fate by interested parties in Honolulu who, with contributions of citizens of Hawaii, raised funds to purchase the hulk. After a 20-day tow, the *Falls of Clyde* arrived in Honolulu on November 18, 1963.

Work was immediately begun to preserve what was left of the vessel. In May, 1968, the *Falls of Clyde* was formally acquired by the Bishop Museum, and an active program of restoration is now underway.

Bark Daylight

One of the finest sailing vessels to grace the waters of the Pacific Coast was the bark *Daylight,* a huge, strongly constructed steel vessel and a sister ship to the *Brilliant.* These two vessels were the largest four-masted barks ever built.

It was the demand for kerosene to light the lamps of China and other sectors of the Orient that prompted the building of such large ships. The oil came from many sectors of the globe and California was not without exception.

By the turn of the century the demand had increased to such an extent that a fleet of kerosene clippers—four-masted steel barks—were built to carry the flammable liquid. Some of these great sail ships were equipped with ballast tanks but all had ample cargo space for stowing special packages of two five-gallon cans in a wooden crate.

One of the most handsome ships designed for the trade was the *Daylight.* She was built in 1901 for Anglo American, a Standard Oil subsidiary, at Russell's in Greenock, Scotland and was the second of two sisterships. Costing more than $150,000, she was a mammoth sailing ship measuring 353 feet in length with a 49 foot beam and a keel to main deck draft of 28 feet. Unlike many steel ships, the *Daylight* carried wooden topgallant masts and royal yards, fashioned of Oregon pine.

The *Daylight* could pack 152,000 cases of oil. Her gross registered tonnage was 3,756. She sailed westbound in the kerosene trade and took on tea from Hong Kong for the backhaul, or when tea was unavailable, coal from Australia or manganese ore from Vizagapatam.

For five years she operated successfully in this trade, and then tragedy struck when she caught on fire while at Yokkaichi, Japan. She had to be scuttled in order to extinguish the flames. Fortunately she did not go down in excessively deep water and salvage was immediately undertaken. After all, she was considered one of the finest vessels of her day and with only a few years of service behind her there was no hesitation on the salvage decision. After being raised and refitted at a local yard she was returned to her trade. Because of her ballast tanks, later converted to carry cargo, the *Daylight* managed to hold her own with the transition to bulk haulage that was begun in 1910.

Still flying the British flag at the dissolution of Standard Oil Company in 1911, the *Daylight* came under the ownership of the Standard Oil Company of New York, along with another kerosene clipper, the *Drumeltan*.

In 1914 the *Daylight* and the rest of the ships in that British flag fleet were transferred to Socony's subsidiary, Standard Transportation Company of Hong Kong. While under Hong Kong registry, she continued in the kerosene trade between San Francisco and the Far East until the early 1920's. Though not a fast sailer, she was dependable and packed a good payload even in the waning days of sail.

On her final voyage under Standard Transportation's burgee she sailed proudly through the Golden Gate for Manila with 150,235 cases of kerosene and returned with 1,428 tons of copra.

In 1921, the Charles Nelson Co. of San Francisco purchased the *Daylight* for a meager sum, as the post-war shipping slump had set in. The giant square-rigger brought only $22,500. The sailing days of the *Daylight* were waning. There just wasn't enough business to keep her going. Three years later, James Griffiths & Sons purchased her and stripped her to the lower masts for use as a barge for hauling gypsum rock from San Marcos Island off Lower California to Long Beach, California. The *Daylight* was one of the largest barges then in operation. James Griffiths & Sons (Seattle) interests made good profits by purchasing large sailing ships for paltry sums in the 1920's and converting them to barges.

When the depression hit, the *Daylight* was laid up at Eagle Harbor on Bainbridge Island, still usable as a sailing vessel except for her stumped masts. Her beautiful saloon, skipper's and officers' quarters were still intact, but hope of ever spreading her sails again had all but vanished.

Four-masted bark **ECUADOR** steps along off the Columbia River.

But then came the war clouds of the World War II era, and again idle ships began finding employment. The demand was great. James Griffiths who had last been using the *Daylight* as a gypsum barge between British Columbia and Puget Sound was offered a good price for the vessel and sold her. She left for Vancouver to fit out with a pair of 400 horsepower diesel engines augmented by a peculiar barkentine rig, utilizing her old lowermasts with topmasts fitted to them, with the addition of huge staysails. The highly unorthodox rig (labeled leg-of-mutton) was appalling to windship men, but strangely enough it worked rather well and the vessel carried a cargo of lumber from British Columbia to South Africa in 86 days. Subsequently the *Daylight* passed to Brazilian owners and was still operating after the war ended.

The Ship With Many Lives

They called her many names, and like a cat she had many lives, not to mention many faces. She caught the imagination of the West Coast maritime world.

But let us go back to the beginning, back to a bustling shipyard in industrial Belfast, Ireland, in 1883. There the Harland & Wolff yard launched one of the big sailing vessels of that day—the four-masted ship *Lord Wolseley*, a beautiful vessel with an overall length of 308 feet and of well over 2,500 tons. Hundreds were on hand to see the great windship take to the water. That was the beginning of a long and eventful but sometimes checkered career. Sailing in many world routes, the *Lord Wolseley* in 1902 became the German four-masted bark *Columbia* and it seemed then that the colorful sometimes frustrating chapters of her career began. Shortly after, she was dismasted and mauled by huge seas coming across the Pacific from Japan in ballast. The vessel was towed in from Cape Flattery by the *SS Hyades* and brought into Esquimalt in a sad state. In her wrecked condition she was sold to British Columbia interests for the role of a ballast lighter—a lowly assignment for a handsome iron-hulled sailer. The Vancouver owners did, however, restore her original name which added to her lost prestige.

During this period, Everett G. Griggs, prominent lumberman and civic leader of Tacoma, Washington had his attention called to the *Wolseley* as an investment. Though Griggs put up the money, actual ownership of the vessel was at first in the name of Walter Oakes as trustee, who was also an executive with Northern Pacific Railway. The new owners had the dismasted vessel towed from British Columbia waters to the Moran Shipyard in Seattle for a conversion job that commanded the attention of shipbuilders in many corners of the globe.

By prevailing standards, she was a freak windjammer, on that fall morning in 1905 when she departed the rigging dock at the yard; seamen gathered on the waterfront to look at her and to ponder with tongue in cheek. She was the first of her rig the world had ever known—the former four-masted *Lord Wolseley* was now a six-masted barkentine. Towering above her deck was a veritable forest of masts fore-and-aft rigged except for her square-rigged foremast. Across her counter was the new name *Everett G. Griggs* of Vancouver, B.C. and she flew the flag of Canada. Although the vessel was owned by Griggs, president of St. Paul & Tacoma Lumber Co., along with other investors, she had been registered in Canada to allow the new owners more freedom in her operation.

At age 22, the vessel embarked on a new career course. The cost of refitting was about $65,000, a small sum in our day, but a whopping big expenditure back then. She had already sailed under the British and German flags, and now, paint gleaming and brass work polished she was ready in the fall of 1905 to begin her role as a lumber carrier—an assignment which was to produce handsome dividends.

The bark **ABBY PALMER,** was originally the **BLAIRMORE** and as such capsized and sank in Mission Bay, San Francisco Harbor April 8, 1896. She later became Alaska Packers' **STAR OF ENGLAND.**

Another view of the stately **ABBY PALMER,** a vessel built by Mc Millan at Dumbarton, Scotland in 1893.

On her initial voyage as the *Everett G. Griggs,* the ship still bearing her colorful figurehead, departed Puget Sound with a cargo of lumber for the Antipodes under command of master mariner Captain G. E. Delano.

She was a photographic sight as she dropped the tug and raised her canvas on all six masts just off Cape Flattery. Her new rig required a smaller crew than when she was a four-mast bark despite the fact that she now had two additional masts. As the first of her kind she reacted well in the Pacific tradewinds. The square sails on the foremast bellied out and the fore-and-aft sails on the other masts followed suit like sheep after their shepherd. She was a gorgeous sailer, when packed down with 2.4 million board feet of lumber, more than twice the payload of the average coastal schooner.

The St. Paul lumber facility in Tacoma in those early years had become the largest softwood lumber producer in the world and it was this mill that supplied the cargoes for the *Griggs,* much of which went to Australia.

The *Griggs* became a favorite on Puget Sound and though she most frequently berthed at Tacoma, she also occasionally berthed at other local ports of call. Horse-drawn wagons hauled full loads of lumber from the mill across 11th Street and out to the St. Paul pier to where the barkentine lay at dockside. Longshoremen sweated with block and tackle and steam winches, as sling load after sling load went aboard.

In the months to follow, the owners of the vessel lined up cargoes of lumber not only for Australia but for Latin American ports as well, and when lumber was scarce loaded her with wheat, coal or nitrates. In the fall of 1908 the *Griggs* made a voyage from San Francisco with a cargo of barley for Europe and returned with general cargo. Loading there for Puget Sound with a cargo of pig iron for Alaska Junk Company of Seattle, she was at last plagued by hard times. Freight rates had hit the bottom of the barrel; her crew had been paid off and through the bleak Christmas season of 1909, the vessel swung idle at her anchor in Seattle's Elliott Bay. Rumors persisted that she was up for sale for a mere $35,000.

That rumor interested enterprising Captain E. R. Sterling and in the spring of 1910 he purchased the barkentine for a song, spruced her up and put her back to work. His new acquisition had her ups and downs for the first few years but when the dark clouds of war draped themselves over Europe, the now renamed *E. R. Sterling* was no longer considerd a freak sailing vessel but an iron-hulled pot of gold. With this and his interest in other ships, Captain Sterling became a millionaire, and is reliably reported to have turned down a $300,000 cash offer for his aging windjammer. Captain Sterling's ship, along with just about any vessel that was capable of traveling through deepwater with cargo, was at a premium and despite the new ships being turned out in droves, the demand continued. The *E. R. Sterling* continued plying the Pacific, often blacked out, carefully plotting her course to avoid U-boats and German raiders. It was hard to hide a vessel like the *Sterling* with all sails set, in fact she was visible for miles at sea, so tall were her sticks.

Captain Sterling who both owned and commanded this, his "favorite ship," made her a veritable home at sea. He had her fitted out with every convenience, completely foreign to the oft-deprived hands who sailed before the mast. The *E. R. Sterling* boasted electric lighting and a telephone system, a high speed motor boat and even an automobile for the skipper's use ashore.

But the days of sail declined fast after the war ended. The steamers pushed the tall ships off the seas as the competition tightened in the post-war shipping slump. Cargoes for the slower undependable windships were hard to secure and sometimes months of idleness passed before the windjammers could find something to fill their hungry holds. Experienced hands drifted into freighters. Still, the *E. R. Sterling* when idle or employed always captured the imagination of her many admirers.

Her adventures made good reading in 1925 when returning from a transpacific voyage. The Cary-Davis tug *Douglas* of Seattle, commanded by Captain Russell E. Davis, went out to pick up the *E. R. Sterling* somewhere off Cape Flattery. Visibility was none too good and though the two vessels were in constant touch by wireless they had difficulty locating each other. Finally the tug's skipper at nightfall turned his powerful searchlight straight up in the air. From 35 miles away the watch high aloft on the *Sterling* picked up the beam and the two vessels were drawn together like a magnate. The tug promptly towed the vessel into Puget Sound.

Captain E. R. Sterling was justly proud of his command and even though a millionaire, he continued to skipper his ship. As one of the most experienced sailing ship masters, he had earlier had long tours of mastery over the square-riggers *Patrician, Great Admiral, W. F. Babcock* and other fine sailing vessels.

Then came the final voyage of the *E. R. Sterling,* and such a hectic voyage it was that even skipper Sterling would later reluctantly agree to give up his beloved ship. He had difficulty securing a cargo as the vessel lay idle at Adelaide for several months. Then she, along with 18 other windjammers, was commissioned to carry wheat to England. She departed Adelaide on April 16, 1927, beginning the long voyage around Cape Horn. After rounding the stormy cape, the *E. R. Sterling* ran squarely into a frightening blow on July 4 off the bleak Falkland Islands. The wind zoomed up to the top of the Beaufort scale, and the sea was whipped into great acclivities. The vessel was wallowing with bare poles, taking an unprecedented beating. Despite all Captain Sterling and his exhausted crew could do, they were but a plaything in the grasp of the gale. Finally the main and mizzenmast went by the board. For days the gale continued and the seas were irascible. The pumps were going constantly.

Temporary repairs were made as best as possible and the vessel with her rather unorthodox rig, missing and damaged masts plus oft-patched canvas began moving along, responding poorly to the helm.

After two months, supplies ran low and water became polluted. Then, as if the devil himself was trying to put an end to the ill-fated voyage another storm struck. The vessel was streaked with rust, her deck a shambles and her fo'c'sle gang exhausted and grumbling. Captain Sterling never had such a voyage in his many years at sea.

Now several miles off Cape Verdes, the full fury of the gale slammed into the vessel and

Once described as the ugliest sailing vessel in the world, the **MAY FLINT** as an iron four-mast bark was converted from the English steamer **PERSIAN MONARCH.** Built originally at Scotland in 1880, she became a sailing vessel under U.S. registry and was renamed **MAY FLINT** in 1895. As a unit of the California Shipping Co. who purchased her from the Flint interests in 1899, she carried coal cargoes out of Seattle to San Francisco. At 3,576 tons, she was one of the world's largest sailing vessels when she was sunk in a collision in San Francisco Bay in 1900. This photo was taken a few weeks before her loss.

ripped out the remainder of her foremast, seriously injuring the mate, Roderick Mackenzie.

The captain took the best care he could of the officer and faithfully treated the many bruises and cuts inflicted on his men. The ship did everything but sink and only three damaged masts were still standing.

Under a jury rig the vessel finally made the Virgin Islands in deplorable condition, ending a 286 day uncompleted voyage from Adelaide. The discouraged and disgruntled former millionaire skipper, couldn't raise enough money to refit his battered ship and was forced to sell her to Sunderland shipbreakers for a pittance.

With tears in his eyes he watched his big ship towed away to England by the big Dutch tug *Indus*.

Taken to the Thames—she was scrapped in 1928—ending a 45 year career. The so-called freak windjammer of Puget Sound at last passed into the realm of memory and memory is fragile stuff.

Nova Scotian born Captain Sterling lived on, crossing the bar in California in 1943, a true old salt to the sea.

—"All were glad,
And laughed and shouted, as she darted on,
And plunged amid the foam, and tossed it high
Over the deck"—

Bark **ACME**, built by A. Sewall in 1901 for Standard Oil Co., later became Alaska Packers' **STAR OF POLAND.** She was wrecked in Japan in 1918.

"The way of a ship in the midst of the sea" . . .
Owned by the Alaska Packers when this photo was taken, the ship **SANTA CLARA,** built in 1876, operated out of San Francisco after 1896. Her hull was afloat till 1939, at Los Angeles.

What a story this salty old wheel could tell. This photo was taken while the barge **FALLS OF CLYDE** was moored at Kennydale on Lake Washington in 1959, prior to being towed to Honolulu for restoration to a museum ship. The Falls of Clyde was built as a full-rigged ship at Glasgow in 1878.

The author stands at the wheel of the barge **DIAMOND HEAD,** ex bark **DIAMOND HEAD,** ex **GAINSBOROUGH** just before the historic old iron hulk was towed to the Everett sandspit and burned out before scrapping at the Puget Sound Bridge & Dredging Co. in Seattle 1949-50. The vessel was built at London in 1866.

"The way of a ship . . . it is too wonderful for me," wrote Solomon 3000 years ago. (This is the bark **ANTIGONE**). She was built at Kiel, Germany in 1889. The 236 foot iron bark was of 1,490 tons and operated out of Hamburg for many years under the ownership of M.G. Amsinck.

Main saloon aboard the classic **FALLS OF CLYDE,** was typical of the British sailing ships.

A volominous swell off Cape Flattery is forded by the great **STAR OF LAPLAND,** 3,381 tons, built in 1902, as the **ATLAS,** for the case oil trade to the Far East. Here she is a unit of the Alaska Packers.

Home is the sailor, home from the sea. In comes the towline for the haul to Puget Sound. The handsome square-rigger is the **BRYNHILDA.**

The main cabin aboard the **FALLS OF CLYDE** was both spacious and comfortable.

"And the wheel's kick and the wind's song and the white sails shaking."
—John Masefield

This is the British bark **JUTEOPOLIS** one of the best known foreign square-riggers on the West Coast around the turn of the century. Measuring 310 feet in length, the vessel was built by W.B. Thompson & Company at Dundee in 1891.

First of her rig—six-masted barkentine **EVERETT G. GRIGGS,** was perhaps the best known of all Puget Sound sailing vessels. She later was renamed **E. R. STERLING,** for her skipper-owner. The Griggs is pictured here in 1912 in a photo by Captain Orison Beaton. The vessel was built as the **LORD WOLSELEY,** a four-masted ship at Belfast, Ireland in 1883, at the Harland & Wolff yard.

Count Felix von Luckner, commander of the sailing ship raider **SEEADLER,** sent this beautiful hunk of sailing vessel (the **PINMORE**) to the bottom, with regret, February 19, 1917. She is pictured here off the West Coast about four years earlier. Luckner's reluctance came from the fact that he once served on the vessel and had carved his initials in the ship's wheel. The Pinmore was launched as the **PASS OF BALMAHA.** She was sunk by a bomb placed within her hull.

Iron ship **STAR OF FRANCE,** Irish-built in 1877 for J. P. Corry, came under Hawaiian registry in 1898, and in 1905 was bought by the Alaska Packers from the Puget Sound Commercial Co. As the fishing barge **OLYMPIC II,** she was sunk off Los Angeles in 1940 with the loss of six lives, when struck by the Japanese steamer **SAKITO MARU.** *H. H. Morrison photo.*

Beautifully carved figurehead of the Prince of Balasore gracing the bow of the steel four-masted bark **MONONGAHELA.** The Monongahela was built as the **BALASORE** at the Barclay, Curle yard at Glasgow, Scotland in 1892. She also served as the German bark **DALBEK** and the American flag **RED JACKET.**

Chapter Five

Ships' Figureheads

Poets of ancient times have sung . . .
"the beauty and mystery of ships, And the magic of the sea."

Fabulous, grotesque, graceful and tantalizing figures—like something washed ashore by the sea, they stand and hang—only head and torsos, smooth and motionless as if each had a story to tell. On the walls of maritime museums from Stockholm to San Francisco, from Spain to Seattle they hang, all that is left of the schooners, brigs, the barks and the ships of old whose magnanimous projecting adornment they had been once upon a time. Each had its own salty tale, an individuality, uniqueness that has already been built into them by the hand of the carver, that makes us still today look at these old figureheads, long deprived of their native element, with such a naive interest.

No reminder of the sea so smacks of the romantic era of sail as do these colorful images that adorned the prows of near forgotten ships.

Already in antiquity, carved, molded or painted emblems and symbolic figures were fixed to the prows of ships. And not for aesthetic reasons alone either, in those far away times when the gods still passed their time with human kind, was the most prominent part of th vessel decorated specially with an ornament. The ancient pagans sometimes slew beautiful young maidens, used their blood to grease the shipways and attached their heads to the ships' bows to appease the gods of the sea. Above all, evil spells were supposed to be warded off and good luck attracted by the decoration on the bows, and it is in this way that the lion and the ram's head of the old Egyptian craft and the horse's head of the Phoenician ships are to be explained.

Greeks and Romans transformed the forward ram of the ship into ram's and boar's heads or placed their galleys under the protection of their mythical goddesses Hera and Aphrodite, Venus and Minerva whose voluptuous figures hovered as stem decorations above the waves of the blue Mediterranean.

Nor can the Vikings' part be ignored. While they were making unsafe all the large rivers of Europe by their plundering and ravaging in the early Middle Ages they succeeded in striking fear and terror into the inhabitants wherever they appeared with the help of the fantastic grotesque heads of dragons and sea serpents which were fixed to the bows of their longboats.

Only in the 16th century when the cumbersome beamy ships with their generous castlelike superstructures at bow and stern were replaced by slimmer, faster and more trim designs was there sufficient room at the long and firmly constructed stem for the figures which one called so aptly "Neptune's wooden angels."

During the course of about 300 years they have personified, visible to everybody, the name of their ships. On the Seven Seas of the world one came across unicorns and salamanders, lions and seahorses, and in every port a Hermes and Hercules, Circe and Calypso lay peacefully side by side.

Apart from the figures of ancient mythology, amongst which mermaids and water nymphs were always to be seen in the baroque-like generosity of their figures, it was mainly the allegorical personifications of luck—Fortuna and Providence—which enjoyed the special affection of sailors as figureheads. Up to the 19th century they still maintained their significance as patron saints whose protection was invoked by captain and crew alike when the unfathomable power of the sea threatened their ship. The figureheads still kept a residue of the magic power attributed to them when, towards the end of the last century, they often became only decorative symbols of the ship's name when shipowners were struck by the idea of having themselves carved full life-sized and fastened to the ship as a figurehead, as for instance the Liverpool owner, James Baines.

In his frock coat buttoned up to the neck, a silk hat on his head, he was always present to the crew of the ship which carried his name.

Such a figure's popularity depended on many things—how well the ship fed, pay and treatment. Perhaps few sailors took the pride in painting up of a shipowner's figure that they did in dolling up the curvacious torso and face of a raven-haired maiden. The more buxom the feminine figure the more delight the sailor took in the task of maintaining her and boasting of her charming qualities.

Many renowned sculptors, artists and carvers made great names for themselves fashioning figureheads for ships. Unfortunately their works were not always viewed by potentates of the arts but more so by the rougher element —the hardy breed who went down to the sea in ships and whose basic knowledge of art was somewhat restricted.

Two of the great sculptors of old both got their start carving figureheads for ships of their time — the Frenchman, Pierre Puget (1620-1694) and the Dane, Bertel Thorvaldsen (1768-1844).

Figurehead of the British ship **GLENMORAG** wrecked north of Ocean Park, Washington March 19, 1896. Figurehead represents Ceres, goddess of Agriculture. *Chas. H. Fitzpatrick photo.*

In general it was the clever artisans who, following traditional designs as prototypes, carved their figures in such a way that in their solid realism they were understandable to the simple sailor, and were given no scope in their strict circumscribed orders to put anything of their own into the work. Their names are forgotten but their works belong to the fine products of European and American folklore.

Apparent and also internal reasons were responsible for the figureheads disappearing more and more from the ships' stems by the turn of the century. There was no longer room for them at the straight and steep bow of the steamers, and when the constructors later adapted the bow to the old design of the clipper ship stems, the desire to fix allegories and symbols had only remained with very few shipowners conscious of tradition. Thus the few figureheads that remain today belong to the realm of culture cultivation in the museums. And there for a long time yet they will find their interested and affectionate beholders as long as everything that tells of the past times of seafaring is still embalmed in the fragile realm of memory.

It has often been said if something basic is outmoded it will sometime come back in vogue again.

Credit the Norwegians for a revival of the figurehead on modern ships. Perhaps one of the earliest type of vessel to carry a figurehead was the ancient Norse longboat or Viking ship, and again it is the Norwegians that have revived use of the bow decorations.

Fred. Olsen Line which operated one of the finest and most modern merchant fleets afloat has had more than a half a hundred figureheads cast in the past four decades, thus giving Norwegian sculptors a ready made opportunity for world-wide exhibition. Attractive and skillfully sculptured half-ton bronze figures they are—not carved of wood like their more ancient counterparts but just as beautiful in every sense of the word. Thanks to the clipper bow replacing the straight stem on modern freighters, a suitable spot now exists to emblazen the bronze figures.

Fred. Olsen Line revived the practice of mounting figureheads on their vessels in 1936 and many of these ships have been seen in Pacific Coast ports with such bow adornments as a Philippine maiden, a Nordic nude, an Indian Chief, Buffalo Bill and others.

But somehow, the figurehead belongs to the sailing vessel and the best remaining examples are beneath the bowsprits of some of the sail training ships still in service today. The Coast Guard's three-masted sail training ship *Eagle,* taken as a prize from Germany after World War II, has an imposing figurehead of a golden eagle and the sail training vessels of such nations as Japan, Norway, Germany, Italy, Chile and Spain also have beautiful bow adornments or scrolled billetheads.

Unfortunately, only a handful of West Coast-built commercial sailing vessels carried figureheads — most had fancy scrolled billetheads. But West Coast ports were privileged to have an endless fleet of ships from virtually every maritime nation in the late 19th century and the early part of this century boasting a great assortment of figureheads.

Many times when these ships were wrecked along hostile Pacific shores their figureheads were found drifting about at sea or heaped in the driftwood on the shore, a grim reminder of tragedy.

The skillful wood carvers of the last century have all but vanished. Their talent is almost a lost art, and the maritime world is the loser.

The English probably reached the greatest heights in the art of figurehead carving and more ships flying the Union Jack carried ornamental carvings beneath their bowsprits than any other merchant navy in maritime history.

The American-built ships that carried figureheads were limited compared to the British and other European maritime nations. Most of the American sailing ships of the late 19th century settled for scrolled billet heads, though there were some fine examples of figureheads on Yankee vessels.

Elm and oak were the preferred woods used by the English carvers for fashioning figureheads. These woods were hard and very durable. Many times they outlasted the ships which carried them and were then transferred to newer ships.

American carvers preferred the softer more workable woods such as white pine. The pine carvings were often splendid specimens of work but frequently had to be replaced due to rot or damage.

The early American whaling ships nearly all carried figureheads of dragons, sea serpents, fish or sea maidens. One carver, of New Bedford, Mass., carved a six foot dragon for a whaler.

Ancient figurehead from unknown square-rigger, carved of oak. Courtesy *Karl F. Wede Inc.*

The first clipper ships carried allegorical figures.

Many figureheads of old had double lives with slight alterations. Take the case of the figurehead that got a shave—on the bark *Robert Duncan,* a large 2,500 ton steel four-mast bark built at Port Glasgow, Scotland by R. Duncan in 1891. She bore a life-sized figure of her builder. In 1910 she was purchased by the Hind Rolph & Co. of San Francisco and renamed *William T. Lewis,* for their port captain. The Duncan figure had a beard and in order to make it more closely resemble Mr. Lewis, the beard was literally eradicated without the aid of shaving cream.

This famous figurehead is now housed in the Maritime Wing of the Museum of History and Industry in Seattle, part of the H. W. McCurdy collection.

On December 1, 1887, the British bark *Sir Jamsetjee Family* was wrecked near the Quinault River on the lonely Washington Coast. The ship was named for a Parsee nobleman, member of a sun worshipping sect of India, descended from the Persians who first settled there in the eighth century A.D. For a figurehead the vessel carried the bust of a Parsee, head of the Sir Jamsetjee family, but this sun worshipping emblem must have been an evil omen as the ship was wrecked in one of the rainiest spots in America.

Longfellow once said: "Ah! what pleasant visions haunt me as I gaze upon the sea! All the old romantic legends, all my dreams, come back to me." Such lines come to mind in this photo of the bow of the old **STAR OF CHILE** taken at Roche Harbor, Washington on San Juan Island. Her beautiful figurehead guided the ship from the day she was built in 1868 as the **LA ESCOCESA** at Dundee, Scotland.

A breath of the past—bowsprit and figurehead of the **GLORY OF THE SEAS** at berth in Seattle in bygone days.

The elegantly carved figurehead of the British bark **TORRISDALE** wrecked off the Grays Harbor bar December 28, 1912. The figurehead later drifted ashore and was found by G. W. Elliott of Westport. The figure was later destroyed in a fire.

Old sailing ship figureheads preserved aboard the famous British clipper ship **CUTTY SARK** in England.

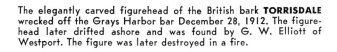

Survivor of the wrecked British ship **GLENMORAG,** wrecked near Ocean Park, Washington March 19, 1896 stands alongside ship's figurehead (1944). William Begg, a seaman on the ship, settled in the area and married a local belle. The figurehead now belongs to his offspring living in Vancouver, Washington.

Figurehead of the ship **AMERICA** on the grounds of the old Moran Estate in 1932 (now Rosario Estate), Orcas Island. The vessel was wrecked on San Juan Island August 31, 1914 while under tow of the tug **LORNE.**

Figurehead of the historic iron bark **STAR OF INDIA,** now a museum ship, restored and re-rigged at San Diego Harbor. As the oldest commercial sailing ship hull on the West Coast, the Star of India is a real breath of the past. She was built as the British vessel **EUTERPE** at Ramsey, Isle of Man in 1863, by Gibson & Co.

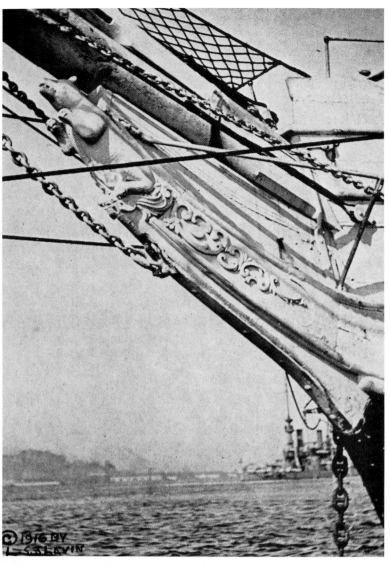

With a Napoleon-like pose this figure is seen on the bow of the ship **McLAURIN** of Boston. The bow adornment was evidently a likeness of the ship's owner Mr. McLaurin. The ship was built at Newburyport, Mass., in 1878 and was of 1,374 tons. *Photo taken in 1916 by L. S. Slevin, courtesy Pete Hurd.*

A cub when this vessel was launched at Greenock in 1873, this figurehead grew to maturity on the classic bow of the **REVENUE CUTTER BEAR.** The vessel's bow adornment was photographed by L. S. Slevin in Seattle harbor in 1916. The Bear sank off the East Coast March 19, 1967. Lat. 42° 25' N Long. 65° 35' W. *Courtesy Pete Hurd.*

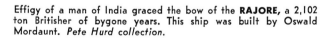

Effigy of a man of India graced the bow of the **RAJORE,** a 2,102 ton Britisher of bygone years. This ship was built by Oswald Mordaunt. *Pete Hurd collection.*

The British ship **LORD CAIRNS** carried an effigy of Cairns in formal attire. Needless to say, seamen were much happier with figures of lovely maidens; men's figures often gracing the bows of ships created thoughts of vanity. *Pete Hurd collection.*

Nostalgic scenes like this are seen no more. This photo from an old glass negative, courtesy Pete Hurd (shipwright), shows the bow of the old wooden bark **SONOMA** of 1,061 tons, built at Chelsea, Mass. in 1868 by Pierce & McMichael. Seen in her latter years here, one can note the starboard anchor tied off and the anchor chain used to moor the vessel; also mooring ports on each side of the stem which could be opened for loading lumber. The Sonoma was typical of the old Downeasters. The buxon figurehead and artistic scrollwork were typical of the ships of her day.

A roaring lion was the figurehead carried by the big four-mast steel bark **JAMES KERR** of Liverpool. The 294 foot vessel was built by Royden but in later years was owned by J. A. Vance of San Francisco who added his name to the bow adornment. *Photo by L. S. Slevin (1915), courtesy Pete Hurd.*

This kingly figure appearing like one from King Arthur's round table, was the bow adornment on the British sailing vessel **HADDON HALL,** built by Royden in 1868 and long engaged in the West Coast-European grain and lumber trade. *Photo by L. S. Slevin, 1915, from Pete Hurd* collection.

Completely garbed in battle arraignment, this gallant spartan graced the bow of the ship **SPARTAN** of Boston, a vessel well known on the West Coast. Built in 1874 by R. E. Jackson the vessel stranded in the Hawaiian Islands in 1905 becoming a total loss, the figurehead along with her. *Pete Hurd collection, taken in 1915 by L. S. Slevin.*

Donald McKay's last shipbuilding effort was the **GLORY OF THE SEAS** in 1869. It is understandable that this graceful ship would carry a beautiful figurehead of a woman, as did most New England built clipper ships. *Pete Hurd collection.*

Handsome figurehead of a lovely lady gracing the bow of the ship **BUCKINGHAM.** This appealing lady ended her days of sailing the seas when as a result of a collision she was left detached inside another ship. Captain P. A. McDonald, now living at Santa Monica, once served as both chief mate and master of the Buckingham, a vessel which had several names during her career.

She probably wouldn't win any beauty contest by today's standards, but this is the figurehead of the ship **RIVERSDALE**, at Marine Garden, Victoria, B.C. Ship last served as a barge for Island Tug & Barge Ltd. As a sailing vessel, she first served under the Red Duster and later became the German ship **HARVESTHUDE** and then **REINBEK**.

Beautifully carved figurehead of the ship **AMERICA** is still on display at a resort on Orcas Island. The vessel was wrecked on San Juan Island while serving as a barge in 1914. The ship was built at Quincy, Mass., in 1874.

It was a sad step down for a great square-rigger to the role of a lowly petroleum barge. Here is seen the **FALLS OF CLYDE** at Ketchikan in the early 1950's, still displaying her lovely figurehead.

Lack of wind, inexperienced crew, incompetent officers and a hint of drunkeness were the ingredients that caused the wreck of the British ship **GLENESSLIN** below Mt. Neah-kah-nie near Oregon's Manzanita Beach October 1, 1913. When barratry was hinted a lengthy court trial was held in England. The iron vessel was built at Liverpool in 1885.

Chapter Six

Grain Fleet

"I thought I heard our chief mate say . . .
Give one more pull and then belay."

The late years of the past century and the early years of this century was an era of the great steel sailing ships that carried wheat from the Pacific Coast to the United Kingdom and European ports.

In addition to San Francisco, Portland was the mecca on the Columbia River and Tacoma on Puget Sound. Tacoma docks and Commencement Bay were often full of these lofty square-riggers, including some of the finest and largest steel and iron vessels of sail ever constructed.

The route of these sailing ships was generally the same. From European ports they headed west in ballast for New York where they loaded kerosene oil in five gallon cans, two to a crate, bound for the Orient. A side stop was sometimes made at Rio de Janeiro but mostly the vessels sailed around the Cape of Good Hope and through the Indian Ocean, passing below the East Indies, through the Strait and the Timor Sea, but usually sailing around Australia and then north through the Tasman Sea and on to China and Japan with oil for the lamps of the Orient. After discharging the oil the vessels then loaded rock or sand ballast and skirted across the North Pacific with favorable currents and winds to Pacific Coast ports to load grain for Europe.

This circumnavigation of the earth often required a year to complete and when rates were depressed layups could sometimes mean that officers and crew might be away from home for up to two years.

At Tacoma's bustling port these tall ships took on full cargoes of bagged wheat, and the long layovers awaiting a berth of repairs afforded considerable business for the riggers, yard workers, supply and chandlery houses. On departing Tacoma, the vessels beat their way down the coast to the southern climes and the often awesome track around the Horn. Then once around the grim headland they set sail for Queenstown in southwest Ireland or on to Falmouth for orders.

Among the best known of the grain and sometimes lumber fleet frequenting Tacoma's portals were the *Cressington, Claverdon, Prince Robert, Wellington, Pass of Killiecrankie, Falkirk, Agnes Oswald, Whitlieburn, Chelmsford, Jordon Hill, Senator, Earl of Dalhousie, Atalanta, Imberhorne, Andelana, Walter H. Wilson, Levenbank, Invernesshire, Montgomeryshire, Frankiston, Iranian, Falls of Halladale, Osborne, City of Florence, Lynton, King Edward, Dachna, William Renton, G. W. Watson, Glendale, Kilmallie, Springbank, Port Elgin, Grenada, Heathfield, Belford, Cabul, Mount Stuart, Queen Margaret, Arracan, Carnedd, Lewelyn, Clan McPherson, Sofia, Adderly, Yola, Durham, Dunstaffnage, Andromeda, Penguin, Miranda, Scottish Glen, Cordova, Alice of Leigh, Howth, Clan Galbraith, Peter Iredale, Wynnstag, Celtic Chief, Carnarvon Bay, County of Caithness, Arctic Stream, Gwydyr Castle, Tamar, Marechal Tucket, Oceano, Scottish Locks, Iverna, Dandrath Castle, Garsdale, Dirigo,* and many more which filled the shipping pages of the Tacoma newspapers.

These represented the pride of the British merchant fleet, with an occasional American, German, French, and Norwegian square-rigger thrown in. A polyglot mixture of sailors from every corner of the world rubbed elbows on Tacoma's waterfront, and captains and officers often entertained each other aboard their respective ships. The entire waterfront was a riproaring, wide open frontier where gambling, drinking and prostitution abounded, though by no means as notorious as San Francisco's Barbary Coast nor as dangerous as Port Townsend's little Barbary Coast.

Respective masters of full-rigged ships, four-masted barks, and barkentines often made bets as to who had the fastest vessel. Wagers were made when ships left for the same destination. Perhaps the most tragic outcome involved the ship *Atalanta.*

On a reef four miles south of Alsea Bay,

Oregon, on November 17, 1898, one of the tragic episodes in West Coast maritime history was enacted. The handsome British semi-clipper ship *Atalanta,* one of the finest sailing vessels under the Red Duster was the victim of a grisly wreck that claimed all but three of her crew of 27.

The drama started at the Puget Sound grain port of Tacoma. The *Atalanta,* in command of Captain Charles McBride, a hard skipper and a speed merchant, was loading a $65,000 cargo of grain for the United Kingdom. While in port in conversation with the masters of other square-riggers, the usual argument arose as to which had the faster ship. The prideful Captain McBride was quick to take any challenge and wagered that he could lick two other vessels traveling over the same route to the Dark Continent. One of the ships departed a good two weeks ahead of the *Atalanta,* and the other a week earlier. The wager was who could make the fastest passage, but in the mind of McBride, he not only wanted the fastest passage but the thrill of beating the others to port, despite the handicap.

On November 14, the *Atalanta* departed Tacoma, towing out to Cape Flattery and then hastily hoisted every piece of canvas her yards could hold. The vessel breezed down the coast with favorable winds making a remarkable show until she encountered nasty seas off the Oregon coast. The ship was on a southeast tack, about November 16, and Cape Foulweather (Yaquina Head) Light was obscured by fog and heavy sheets of rain. It was during the dark early morning hours of November 17, the *Atalanta* struck a breaker-washed reef 1½ miles offshore.

All hands were called on deck, the men jumping from their bunks not stopping to get dressed; and a futile attempt was made to save the ship which was lurching and grinding. Combers lashed at the vessel mercilessly raising it up and then letting it slam down on the jagged reef. The ship's hull was no match for the solid rock which sliced through, severing her in half. Half-crazed crewmen were thrown into the vortex amid a wild array of wreckage. Others aboard tried to lower the ship's boats from the after section but each craft was tossed unceremoniously into the water unmanned. Only by chance one of them floated past a seaman named George Fraser, a Yankee, who managed to latch on to the gunwhales and struggle into its confines. He was able to rescue John Webber who was clinging to the other side. They in turn were able to save Irishman Frances McMahon from the tempestuous seas. But without oars, the trio was unable to go to the rescue of the others. Captain McBride, ironically, was unable to swim and along with the others was hopelessly abandoned.

Hopelessly lost—German bark **POTRIMPOS** on the beach north of Long Beach, Washington. Salvage attempts failed and the Potrimpos rolled over on her side, a total loss. The year was 1896. Built at Hamburg, Germany in 1887, by Blohm & Voss, the 228 foot vessel was under the ownership of F. Laeisz. *Courtesy Chas. H. Fitzpatrick.*

In that dramatic episode of tragedy, that one usable boat drifted away from the drowning crewmen into the murk of the stormy night until the mournful cries of despair were carried away on the wings of the wind. Driven at the mercy of the elements the boat was carried farther away from the wreck as the three numbed survivors bailed with their hands to keep from swamping. For hours they drifted but the set of the wind kept them from being carried out to sea.

Tossed to and fro, jostled up and down and constantly soaked with sloshing seawater and driving rain, the men were almost senseless when they heard the increasing crescendo of mammoth breakers. Suddenly, their boat was driven toward the hostile shore. Terrified, they could do nothing but hang on and pray. With no oars they could not steer and a sharp comber raised the craft to a voluminous watery summit. Following seas spun it wildly; then it hit the bottom and split open, throwing the occupants into the churning maelstrom. With what strength they could muster they thrashed in the water until able to claw the sand with their fingers in a thin film of liquid. By an act of God all managed to gain the beach, hardly believing they had been spared. They lay on the cold sands almost too weak to move. Finally crawling up to the driftwood line they lay there virtually motionless as the rain beat down on them without let up. There was no sign of life anywhere and it appeared but a matter of time until their lives would be snuffed out. Later they managed to build a crude shelter about them. Finally with that last great effort that comes in time of despair, one of the three exhausted individuals stumbled down the beach to find help. In the pale dawn, he eventually sighted an old farmhouse, back from the beach, and there he found the help so urgently needed. All three were cared for by the sympathetic farm folk and eventually the survivors managed to get transportation back to Portland.

Interviewed, they told how the ship struck the reef and at once broke in two; that the bow was totally crushed and sank. The stern section also foundered, but as the crew had been ordered on deck, no one was trapped in the forecastle as an Oregon newspaper had surmised as a rub against the reputed cowardice of the Yaquina Bay Lifesaving crew. In every disaster somebody becomes the target of blame and in this case it was the lifesaving aggregation. The newspaper in question had insisted

End of the line for the German bark **POTRIMPOS,** stranded on North Beach Peninsula on December 19, 1896 inbound to the Columbia River from Manzanillo in ballast. She was a unit of the Flying P Line. *Courtesy Chas. H. Fitzpatrick.*

that the lifesaving crew was powerless to give assistance due to lack of equipment and know-how.

The Yaquina crew was only two years old at the time and was the pride of the local area. Its main purpose was to rescue the perishing, and Captain Clark, who headed the well-disciplined crew was a capable leader. Most of their rescues had been in and around Yaquina Bay which was the reason for the station being located there. The news of the *Atalanta* disaster was very late in coming and the wreck was located a considerable distance away from the station.

In fact it was at 6 p.m., 16 hours after the ship struck the reef, that the station received the first news of the disaster.

Draft horses, which had already put in a day's work hauling wood, were borrowed and an attempt was made to haul the line-throwing cannon and rescue gear along the beach 20 miles to the scene of the wreck. The horses

High and dry on the North Beach Peninsula, south of Willapa Bay, the British ship **GLENMORAG** as seen in 1896. *Photo courtesy Mabel Thompson.*

drifting up on the beach south of the Siuslaw River, but it was not until December 9 while on his way from Gardiner to Florence that the mail delivery man, H. H. Barrett, found the body of a man near Ten Mile Creek. Three days later this mailman found two more bodies on the beach two miles below Ten Mile.

All were believed to be sailors from the ill-fated *Atalanta,* which would have meant that the sea currents and driving winds carried the deceased about 40 miles from the locale of the wreck.

Still later, the mutilated bodies of others were found between the two creeks and by early January 1899, one half of the dead were accounted for.

Meanwhile those aboard the two ships that had accepted the race challenge with Captain McBride had no way of knowing of the disaster that befell the *Atalanta* until long after they reached their African destination.

Even more shocked by the tragedy was the Tacoma waterfront where the men of the *Atalanta* had become so well known. The townsfolk refused to believe that the capable and reputable Captain McBride would have used reckless and unorthodox methods to win his race, as the survivors had charged. All three claimed that the vessel, trying to save time, broke off from her course and ran on the reef in the black of night when she should have been well off the notorious Oregon coast. Though many shore dwellers took the side of the deceased skipper, the testifying survivors to a man charged reckless navigation. Thus the combination of a dark, stormy night and poor navigational judgment was declared responsible for one of the most regrettable wrecks along the central Oregon coast during the era of sail.

Another tragedy that old Tacoma never forgot, happened right at her front doorstep. On January 6, 1899, the *Andelana,* a masterpiece of naval architecture, flying the Red Duster, arrived to load wheat for the United Kingdom. In command of the lofty steel bark was Captain G. W. Staling of Nova Scotia. The second and third mates and eight crewmen were reportedly discontented with their ship and had asked to be paid off in favor of berths on the *Dirigo* and the *Henry Failing,* two well known American sailing vessels in port at the time.

There had been much grumbling aboard the *Andelana* and the master cancelled shore leave for the remaining crewmen and turned them to

gave out about six miles south of the station, at Surflands, and the men themselves dragged as much equipment as they could the rest of the way. Exhausted, they were disheartened to find that the cannon could not shoot a lifeline to the wreckage and that they could not launch the surfboat in the rough water along the reef. Nor did it seem likely that there was anyone left to rescue. And there wasn't. The survivors backed the lifesaving crew by revealing that no one was trapped inside the wreckage. All were swept overboard immediately after the ship *Atalanta* broke up.

The ship's logbook eventually was washed up on the beach, and contained within was the November 17 entry which read: "Cape Foulweather is concealed by fog and there are heavy sheets of rain." One short hour later the vessel met her fate.

During the following weeks, wreckage began

swabbing down the deck and scraping rust.

The *Andelana* lay at anchor about 300 yards off the St. Paul & Tacoma Lumber dock and all her ballast had been removed within a week after her arrival. She rode high in the water, supported on either side by chained logs.

On January 14, she was to be towed by the tug *Fairfield* to the grain dock to load out for England. Meanwhile Foss launches brought out supplies of food and staples for the long voyage to England.

The fickle finger of fate then intervened, for Captain Staling was visited that afternoon by Christine Funnemark, guiding light at the Tacoma Seamen's Rest. She invited him and the crew of the *Andelana* to an evening at the mission. The master told her that he would come, but not that evening, nor would he allow the crew to leave the ship at that time.

Before the day was out, a second invitation to dinner was accorded Captain Staling, this from the master of the sailing vessel *Walter H. Wilson* at anchor in the bay only a short distance from the *Andelana*. Captain Doty of the *Wilson* was a long time friend of Staling, the two having known each other in Nova Scotia. But Staling, perhaps because of the state of his crew was in rather low spirits and declined this invitation as well. But he did spend part of the afternoon aboard the *Wilson*. Doty was alarmed by his friend's attitude, for during the course of the conversation Staling told Doty that he had had a premonition that he would die on his ship. He stated that his wife had been urging him to retire from the sea and come home to settle down in Nova Scotia. Staling said that he was planning to do just that after the ship delivered her grain cargo.

It was about 4:00 p.m. when Doty left the *Andelana's* skipper off and rowed back to his ship.

A young apprentice seaman aboard the *Andelana* named Percy B. Buck had asked permission of the skipper to leave the ship as he was suffering from an abscessed tooth. Permission was granted. Staling decided about the same time that he would go ashore also, but on feeling ill decided to remain aboard.

Shortly before the midnight hour the wind began to blow across Tacoma's harbor and within two hours became a near gale. When dawn cast its pale hue over the leaden waters, as was his custom, Captain Doty came up on the after deck of the *Wilson* and peered about

the harbor. To his amazement he noted that the *Andelana* was not at her anchorage. Thinking that the vessel must have slipped her anchor chains in the blow, he summoned Captain Kenny, Lloyd's agent and surveyor for Tacoma. The two hastily boarded the tug *Fairfield* to search for the missing vessel. On their way out of the harbor they noted an overturned ship's boat, broken oars and mattresses. Then came the horrible reality that the ship had foundered during the night. The town was alarmed.

Immediate dragging operations were begun and the *Andelana* was located on her side in 23 fathoms near the spot where she had been anchored. Except for the apprentice with the toothache, Captain Staling, first officer E. H. Crowe and the entire crew were entombed inside the massive steel hull in one of Puget Sound's most regrettable ship tragedies. It must have happened in a matter of seconds.

The supporting logs along the hull of the *Andelana* were only chained, not spiked. They had broken loose in the high wind, allowing the high riding vessel to turn broadside and capsize. All attempts to salvage the *Andelana* failed and only her anchor was brought to the surface.

Captain Staling's weird premonition had come true.

Crewmen of stranded British ship **GLENMORAG** discuss the grounding of their vessel after the mishap in 1896. They are seen on the ship's deck as it lay aground on Washington's North Beach Peninsula. Two perished. *Courtesy Mabel E. Thompson.*

As if lifting her arms to pray—the remains of the British ship **GLENMORAG** well down in the sands of North Beach Peninsula, a few years after she stranded in 1896.

Another view of the ship **GLENMORAG** ashore (1896) near Oysterville beach approach. Two of her crew perished in rescue operations and the ship became a total loss. *Supplied by Chas. H. Fitzpatrick.*

French ship **ALICE** wrecked on the North Beach Peninsula January 15, 1909. One of the big French steel square-riggers, she was built at Bordeaux in 1901, and was buried just eight years later in the cargo of cement she was carrying.

Ship overloaded with sand—British bark **CAIRNSMORE** sucked down until only her masts protrude. She stranded on Clatsop Beach, Oregon September 23, 1883 and became a total loss.

Driven ashore in a gale off the entrance of Willapa Bay, November 26, 1900, the proud four-masted bark **POLTALLOCH** defied the destructive forces of nature for several months and became one of the few ships to be salvaged from that sandy prison.

The Norwegian ship **STRAUN,** was abandoned in sinking condition off the Oregon Coast in 1890, en route to Melbourne from Port Discovery, Washington with lumber. Picked up for salvage by another vessel, the Straun finally foundered off Nestucca Beach, Oregon, after her dog mascot was rescued.

French bark **HENRIETTE,** sank in the Columbia River near Astoria, Oregon December 27, 1901 when she settled on her anchor in shallow water. Salvage operations were undertaken by Daniel Kern of Portland. After several weeks he succeeded in raising the vessel after which the hull was sold to McKenzie Brothers of Vancouver, B.C. and cut down to a barge. In 1905, the vessel was rebuilt as a screw steamer and placed in service between northwest ports and Skagway, Alaska. In 1918, the vessel was purchased by Captain Woodside of San Francisco and converted to a four-masted schooner for service to Fiji and the South Pacific where she was wrecked in 1922.

Sailing vessels loading lumber at Tacoma—schooners, ships and barks. Note bow loading ports on each side of ship just left of the schooner. Long pieces of lumber were loaded through these and also through stern ports. Loading ports were all sealed before departure. *(Oregon Historical Society collection.)*

Sailing vessels at Everett, Washington on Puget Sound about 1900. *Pete Hurd collection.*

WILLIAM DOLLAR, left, ex German bark **ALSTERBERG,** ex **WALKURE,** 3,238 tons, and the **JAMES DOLLAR,** ex **COMET,** 3,017 tons, idle in Seattle's Lake Union. *Courtesy Captain P. A. McDonald, former master of the William Dollar.*

Hungry holds are in search of cargo as this picturesque square-rigger, the **EMILIE** moves into the misty Strait of Juan de Fuca a century ago. This vessel was built as the **BRITISH AMBASSADOR** at Liverpool in 1873 and later sold to German owners. Pictured under the German flag and the houseflag of E.C. Schramm & Company she homeported at Bremen.

Laden deep with grain for the United Kingdom, the British sailing vessel **DECCAN** departs a Pacific Coast port in the bygones. She was owned by the British & Eastern Shipping Co., of Liverpool.

Speaking another ship, the British bark **CLAN GRAHAM** displays her call letter flags off the Northwest coast. Out of Glasgow, she was owned by the Scotch shipping house of T. Dunlop & Sons and was a distinguished unit of the "Clan Line."

"The good ship tight and free
    The world of waters is our home,
       And merry men are we . . ."

Barkentine **JAMES TUFT** towing up San Francisco Bay. She was built on the waters of Puget Sound and had a full life. *Courtesy San Francisco Maritime Museum.*

Like a legendary monster rising from the sands is the forlorn remains of the wreck of the British bark **PETER IREDALE** as they appeared south of the Columbia River entrance in 1947. The vessel stranded on October 25, 1906.

Dry land tack—British ship **GLENESSLIN** hard aground at the base of Mt. Neah-kah-nie, Oregon, October 1, 1913.

Grays Harbor was a thriving port (Hoquiam-Aberdeen) when this photo was taken in 1922. As one of the chief exporters of lumber, a host of wooden and steel steam schooners are pictured, and the big square-rigger at the far right is the **JOSEPH DOLLAR.** *Jones photo, courtesy Marine Digest.*

The Chilean ship **CARELMAPU** foundering in a pulsating sea off the West Coast of Vancouver Island November 23, 1915. Nineteen of her crew of 24 were lost in the tragedy. Distress flags are flying and sails have been torn to ribbons.

A gallant ship the **WILLIAM T. LEWIS,** built at Port Glasgow, Scotland in 1891 as the **ROBERT DUNCAN.**

British ship **KILBRANNAN** ashore near Point Wilson, at the entrance to Puget Sound in February, 1896. She was salvaged in December of the same year and later renamed **MARION CHILCOTT.**

142

Chapter Seven

Irish Pennants

"The ocean has no compassion, no law, no memory."
—Joseph Conrad

One of the longest battles in rounding old Cape Horn was logged by the bark *Edward Sewall* in 1914. She took 67 days to round the Horn on one of the last westward passages around the tip of South America by an American square-rigged sailing ship, March 7 to May 13, 1914.

The *Edward Sewall's* passage in the winter of 1913-14 seemed ill-fated from the time the ship, two months out, reached the latitude of the Horn. Twice her bowsprit was broken off in heavy seas, forcing the ship to put back for repairs. When finally she got off to her third attempt to round Cape Horn she met with such unfavorable winds that it took 67 days to sail from 50 degrees South latitude in the Atlantic to 50 degrees South latitude in the Pacific. The usual entry in the ship's log read: "Strong gale and heavy seas: wind W.N.W. to W.S.W.: ship under water." Having sailed from Philadelphia on October 18, 1913, the *Sewall* arrived on August 5, 1914 at Seattle, marking a passage of 293 days.

* * *

An exciting race took place during the year 1910, between two of the best known Yankee square-riggers on the Pacific. It was watched with great interest by shipping men along the West Coast.

It involved a race from the Pacific to the Atlantic seaboard between the *Erskine M. Phelps* and the *Shenandoah,* two of the largest sailing ships then afloat. The *Phelps,* a frequent visitor to the Pacific Northwest was commanded by Captain Robert Graham, whose wife always sailed with her husband, and many people declared that she was quite capable of taking charge of the ship herself should the occasion arise. In those days, when motors were in their infancy, the Grahams always carried a motor car aboard the vessel which they found very useful during their stays in port.

The *Shenandoah* was in command of Captain William Murphy, and on account of it being the ship's last voyage under canvas, he tried to get all he could out of her, as the vessel was to be sold and converted into a barge upon arrival at New York. She sailed from San Francisco February 16, and was regarded as having about an equal start with the *Phelps* which sailed from Honolulu February 12, with the new season's sugar aboard.

The race was won by the *Erskine M. Phelps* which arrived at the Delaware breakwater June 7, 115 days out from Honolulu. The *Shenandoah* arrived at New York three weeks later, on June 24, 128 days out from San Francisco. (courtesy A. O. Anderson, Washington D. C.)

* * *

One of the favorites among the last of the clipper ships was the ship *Dashing Wave* which had a long and illustrious career. Her ten best runs around Cape Horn averaged 127 days. She was once sunk for seven months, but was raised and continued in the clipper trade. Later, as a coaster on the West Coast, she made one 54 hour run from San Francisco to Cape Flattery, despite more than a half century of hard service. The aging queen was finally cut down to a barge and as such, stranded in Seymour Narrows in 1920 while in service between Puget Sound and Alaska.

* * *

Captain P. J. R. Mathieson, master of the *Antiope* once revealed a wierd incident told him when his ship reached San Francisco. He was informed of the death of Captain Jensen of the four-masted barkentine *James Johnson.*

Captain Jensen succumbed while still in the prime of life of a heart attack while the barkentine was bound for San Francisco from Newcastle, N.S.W. The incident occurred in the doldrums just north of the equator. The ship's carpenter made a coffin, but when the remains were committed to the deep the next morning, without any ceremony whatever, the necessity of putting a weight in the coffin to sink it was overlooked. The vessel lay in a calm for two days with the coffin floating in sight nearby, the entire time. Whenever the captain's widow came on deck she saw the casket gently rocking in the distance.

To further aggravate the situation, the grieving lady was subjected to the unfortunate behavior of the mates and crew who emptied the liquor cabinet and proceeded to get drunk, boisterous and obnoxious for days, until the last drop of liquor was gone. The dead captain had been the only navigator on the *Johnson*, and the mate, now trying to find the Hawaiian Islands, was hopelessly befuddled in his dead reckoning. For weeks he followed one course and then another hunting the empty sea for a landfall.

As fate would have it, a steamer eventually passed close by and its master afforded them the course and distance to Honolulu where they arrived a few days later. There the distraught widow cabled the owners. A master was secured for the barkentine, and Mrs. Jensen was sent to San Francisco by steamer.

* * *

One of the most storied, dependable, persistent and swift of the "hangers-on" in the latter days of West Coast sail was the iron bark *Antiope*. Well ahead of her time, this 242 foot long, 1,508 ton vessel was built in 1866 by J. Reid & Co. at Port Glasgow, Scotland for J. Heap & Sons of Liverpool. She was a sister to the *Marpesia*. Much of the *Antiope's* career was spent trading in the Pacific and she made many fine passages. One of her finest, made in 1902, is a record which still stands. After many years of hard usage, the venerable *Antiope* made a crossing with a full cargo of lumber from Eureka, California to Sydney, N.S.W., a distance of 7,130 miles in 44 days flat, anchor to anchor. That record was never surpassed.

Though the *Antiope* was a hot number when it came to speed she was a cold number when it came to heat. Employed in the Southern trades for many of her years the vessel had no heating facilities. Whenever she got in North Pacific waters north of the 40th Parallel in the winter months or down around the roaring Forties of Cape Horn, the crew suffered much. With not a single stove for heat on board the only warm places on the bark were the galley and the donkey room.

Many of the old square-riggers lacked heating facilities and the ship's cook was often the most envied man aboard in bitter weather when the sides of a ship iced up.

In the year 1916, the *Antiope*, under Captain Telleck got ashore in a gale on the New Zealand coast at Bluff Harbor. The mishap occurred while the bark was under tow and the towline parted. There she lay awash, on her side, exposed to the seas for 96 days. After several futile attempts she was at last refloated and repaired, little the worse for the experience. Finally in December 1920, she caught fire at Lourenco Marques, Portuguese East Africa, while discharging a cargo of lumber loaded in Sweden. She was then condemned and sold, becoming a refrigeration hulk at Beira.

* * *

British sailing ships as well as those of other flags suffered from a grave problem when they ran their "easting down." They ran the risk of "poopers," those massive seas that could and often did sweep a ship's poop. Many a helmsman was killed by these devil seas. Frequently steersmen ran from the wheel when they saw

British bark **GALENA** hard aground on Clatsop Beach, where she stranded the night of November 13, 1906 inbound from Chile, in ballast to load grain at Portland. She was in command of Captain Howell, and owned by S. Galena & Co. of Liverpool. The Galena, following unsuccessful salvage attempts, became a total loss. The 2,294 ton bark was built at Dundee in 1890. *Photo courtesy of Charles H. Fitzpatrick.*

This is believed to be the bark **DAYLIGHT,** of 3,756 tons, sistership of the **BRILLIANT,** built at Glasgow in 1902 to haul case oil.

Freighter **JAMES GRIFFITHS** tows the bark **MAE DOLLAR** into San Francisco Bay about 1925. The bark was built as the **SOMALI** and was the largest British bark afloat on her completion at Port Glasgow in 1892. She was of 3,410 tons. The vessel ended her days as the barge **PACIFIC CARRIER** for Island Tug & Barge Ltd. of Victoria, B.C. *Courtesy Mike McGarvey.*

one coming, placing the ship in danger as it broached to. This grave fear prompted many builders to construct wheelhouses or similar protections for those at the helm.

Basil Lubbock in his classic book, *The Last of the Windjammers,* mentioned two typical sailing ship log entries.

June 21—9 a.m. A large sea came aboard, flooded the cabin and gutted the officers' rooms out.

June 22—3 a.m. This morning an A.B. ran away from the wheel on noticing a big sea coming along.

Such giant poopers packed enough wallop to demolish a wheel and frequently left the steering apparatus in such a sad state that a jury had to be rigged to steer the ship.

The four-masted ship *County of Linlithgow,* well known on the Pacific, (in latter years under the name *Katherine*), was pooped on March 11, 1905, when bound from Frederickstadt to Melbourne. Every spoke in her wheel was broken off at the hub. Besides doing other damage, that sea carried a great part of the deck cargo of timber overboard.

Another Limejuicer, the *Beecroft,* in 1910, had her skipper washed overboard by a pooper. The avalanche of water swept the two men at the wheel down on to the maindeck, the binnacle was taken over the side and the boats broken up.

Such mishaps were legion in the day of the windship.

*   *   *

Lubbock has also recorded much about the dangers apparent on square-riggers. One incident that stands out involved the ship *Inverclyde,* another Britisher well known in the Pacific. It shows the incredible ability of a vessel to recover herself. Confirmed by her master, the *Inverclyde* had rolled over so far in a contrary sea that her topsail yardarms were actually in the water.

Quoting from the master's abstract log:

November 23, 1914—Left Seattle for Queenstown.

January 20, 1915—Lat. 41° 21′ S., long. 126° 01′ E. Course S. 29 E. Distance 154 miles. Winds S.W., West, N.N.E., N.W., force 5 to 11. Noon, wind veering from south towards S.W. and ugly appearance. Barometer falling rapidly. Put ship under lower topsails and full foresail.

8 p.m., reefed the foresail, wind veering towards west. Kept ship off to course.

Midnight, wind N.W. and remained there to 4 a.m. Weather improved a little and barometer steady to a slight rise.

Hugh W. Frith, of Vancouver, B.C., took this photo of the bark **PAMIR** in a 55 knot gale off Cape Flattery January 6, 1946. She had just cast off from the tug **SNOHOMISH,** under way for Australia from Vancouver, B.C., flying the New Zealand flag. Pamir was lost under the German flag in a hurricane in the North Atlantic in 1958, that claimed her entire crew.

5:30 a.m., wind began to haul more North and increase to hurricane force. Called all hands on deck and hove to on port tack with fore and main lower topsails set. When brought to the wind, the vessel listed over heavy and several sails blew adrift out of the gaskets. They were the foresail, the upper topsails and the fore lower topgallant sail. The foresail and main upper topsail could not be secured by the crew and the foresail split to ribbons. The lower topsail, of course, was split to pieces in a few minutes. We had to leave them to jettison cargo. Whilst attempting to secure the sails, W. Gronbeg was beaten off the main upper topsail yard and landed on deck. We were not able to examine him owing to the critical condition of the ship.

She was listing heavier and getting worse all the time. She laid down until several feet of the lee side of the main hatch were in the water. The lee side of tarpaulin got adrift through wedges and battens being knocked out and water began to go down through the hatches.

The lower topsail sheets were let go, and after getting two three inch planks spiked on the hatch all hands except the carpenter and two men were called to the cabin to jettison cargo up from the lee side of after 'tween deck through the lazarette and cabin companion. This was carried up on to noon. The foresail and upper topsails had to be left battering about to get all possible men to jettison cargo.

January 21—Lat. 43° 06' S., long. 125° 34' W. No canvas set. All hands working as hard as possible trimming cargo over from starboard to port, but vessel did not upright any as there was a great amount of sea water getting down the lee side of main hatch.

Jettisoned cargo until able to get the main hatch battened down, which was done about 11 a.m.—a lower topgallant sail being used—the hatch having been burst from 8 a.m. of yesterday. After getting main hatch closed watertight again, found one cleat drawn on the lee or starboard side of the rivet.

All hands employed up to dark clearing up and getting gear in place, and had a hard job to get davit in place as it had been jammed hard on the deck.

January 22—Lat. 43° 47', long. 125° 15' W. Course S. 50 E. Distance 27 miles. No observations. Winds N.N.W. to North. Hands trimming cargo and getting ship cleared up. When the ship was upright the crew refused to proceed as all cargo in the 'tween decks except amidships was on the port side. I told them I would not put the ship back but would jettison the wet cargo in the main hatch which was all on the starboard side. This would let a quantity of sacks come over from the port side.

They then agreed to proceed. Mr. Cotton, the first mate, assisted me in every way to talk the crew over. Hands jettison cargo to bring vessel upright and relieve stanchions in main hatch broken. Most all the wheat thrown over was that damaged around main hatch down to below the 'tween decks. Main hatch center ladder in 'tween decks bent and the stanchion at fore end of hatch had the bolts cut out. Battened down main hatch at noon—crew could not stand in water longer. No canvas set except storm mizzen.

January 23—All hands trimming cargo up to dark. At daybreak set fore and main topmast staysails, shifted foresail and topsails and set the sails. 9 a.m., kept ship off to course.

* * *

Similar problems faced many Pacific square-riggers. The beautiful four-masted bark *Torrisdale* lay on her beam ends for two days with the sea making a clean breach over her; her sails were blown to ribbons, boats stove, topgallant rail and poop stanchions gone and cabin flooded. She recovered, however, and kept on sailing under the Red Duster until 1912 when she crashed ashore near Grays Harbor on the Washington Coast.

Likewise, in 1908, under Captain P. J. R. Mathieson, the *Antiope* while crossing from Newcastle, N.S.W. to San Francisco, had a similiar experience. After four days of driving gales, her cargo shifted in lat. 33° 5', long. 174° E. and she went over on her beam ends. The entire crew trimmed coal for their lives but before they could get the vessel upright the seas had breached the decks clean, the sails were blown out of their gaskets and left in rags.

* * *

One of the most tragic episodes on the San Francisco waterfront concerned the British bark *Blairmore* in the year 1896. She was anchored in Mission Bay without any ballast, when a sudden gusty wind struck causing the vessel to capsize, buoyed up only by the air imprisoned inside her hull. Entrapped in the hold were seven men who had been chipping and painting when the bark rolled over. A few others managed to scramble on deck and jump overboard, but the unfortunates below were buried or half buried in the ballast.

The ship's master who was on the poop when the vessel capsized was not a good swimmer and was kept afloat by his faithful dog.

The suddeness of the incident caused utter confusion. After tapping sounds were heard inside the hull the port authorities were alerted, and instead of sending a diver down with spare diving suits for the imprisoned men, called for a gang of steel workers from the Union Iron Works to cut a piece out of the bottom or side plates, large enough for the men to crawl through. As soon as a few holes were drilled, the pent up air escaped with the result that the vessel sank like a rock, drowning the seven still inside.

The incident caused much agitation on the waterfront and the blame was passed freely about. But this did not restore the lives of the unfortunate victims.

The *Blairmore* was eventually raised and rebuilt as the *Abby Palmer*, flying the Stars and Stripes.

* * *

Many of the tall sailing ships that plied the Pacific were deprived of much faster passages by the collection of sea grass and barnacles that clung to the submerged part of their hulls.

The big case oil sailer *Daylight* on her arrival at Philadelphia in 1908, after a passage of 145 days from Vizagapatam, had 40 tons of barnacles scraped off her bottom. Many of these barnacles ranged to five inches in length and most had a base larger than a dollar.

When the *Halewood* was drydocked at the Winslow Marine Railway and Shipbuilding yard on Eagle Harbor, Puget Sound she had not been scrubbed down for three years and

some 30 tons of barnacles, mussels and seaweed were scraped from her underwater plates before a new coat of bottom paint could be applied.

The lengthy wanderings of tramp sailing vessels made it hard to find time or ports that had facilities for drydocking. Frequently big square-riggers had to be careened on a sandy beach or at dockside by shifting ballast and rolling them way over on their beam-ends while the crew applied a scrub job. Needless to say, scrubbing down a 250 foot steel sailing vessel with hand tools was no easy job.

* * *

The strange case of a sailing vessel that refused to give up, was that of the 997 ton ship *Ada Iredale,* an iron-hulled, strongly built Britisher. Under a heavy cargo of coal, this vessel caught on fire in the South Pacific on October 15, 1876, in a lonely spot in the open ocean some 2,000 miles east of the Marquesas.

The severity of the fire, producing red hot decks, prompted the ship's master to order abandonment. All the survivors eventually reached land, without the slightest doubt that the *Ada Iredale* had long before gone to Davy Jones' Locker. But such was not the case. Eight long months later, a French cruiser sighted the derelict and towed her into Papeete with her cargo still burning—a self contained seagoing furnace. Even after reaching the South Pacific port the fire was still not fully extinguished. In fact, it was not until May, 1878, when the *Ada Iredale* was purchased by San Francisco owners, that she was finally divested of her smoldering cargo. She was completely overhauled, with new sails and new rigging. A new name, *Annie Johnson,* was applied

Wreck of the British ship **STRATHBLANE** between North Head and Leadbetter Point November 3, 1891. Seven crewmen perished in this tragedy. *Courtesy Charles H. Fitzpatrick.*

Like a great stranded whale, the capsized German bark **MIMI** imprisoned many of her crew near the Nehalem River in Oregon in April 1913. The vessel, a few months earlier grounded on Nehalem Beach. Salvage operations were underway when the ship rolled over, causing the death of 18. Only four survived. *Gregg photo.*

148

to her bow and counter and she sailed on for many more years of trading.

*　*　*

Another strange story of fire on a square-rigger involved the steel four-masted bark *Pyrenees,* which departed Tacoma for Leith, October 14, 1900.

At 126° W. when the ship was on the equator it was found that the cargo of grain was on fire, believed caused through spontaneous combustion.

Captain Robert Bryce figured that his only chance of saving his command was to take her to the nearest island which happened to be Pitcairn. By the time the *Pyrenees* was standing off the island her decks were steaming hot. The eager islanders came out to greet the visitors and were asked if there was a beach where the vessel could be put aground. Inasmuch as Pitcairn is bounded by steep rock walls, the governor of the island, McCoy, (related to the Bounty mutineers) offered to pilot the *Pyrenees* to the nearest sandspit in the archipelago (bounded by coral reefs and atolls), some 288 miles away. The offer was readily accepted and the vessel was piloted toward Manga Reva reef utilizing all sail to take advantage of the southeast trades. En route, a dead flat calm plagued the vessel for two costly days and the frantic crew fought the blaze for hours on end, feet burning, prespiring bodies stripped to the waist.

In desperation, Captain Bryce took over command from McCoy with the first breeze and tossing care to the winds guided his ship through a pincushion of coral reefs and tide rips and ran her ashore in Manga Reva Lagoon on December 2. The *Pyrenees* by then was almost glowing red. She was immediately abandoned and all loose gear removed.

All hands, including McCoy and Captain Bryce, were eventually rescued by a French trading schooner.

To all intents and purposes the story should have ended there, the *Pyrenees* burning and rusting away to nothingness. However, when the company of the *Pyrenees* reached San Francisco and told of their plight, two adventurous master mariners named Thayer and Porter, sight unseen, purchased rights to the abandoned ship, gathered a few restless seafarers and went to Papeete by steamer. There they enlisted some eager natives and set out in a small schooner to salvage the *Pyrenees.*

To their dismay they found that the vessel no longer had decks—they had burned through. But this did not discourage the men. After much difficulty and work of the hardest kind, they miraculously managed to refloat the burned out hulk. It took them 12 days more to get her to Papeete where temporary decks were laid. Then, making the best possible use of the standing rigging and some borrowed sails, they set a course for San Francisco passing through the Golden Gate July 27, 1902. At the Bay City, the enterprising Thayer & Porter put out bids to rebuild the vessel. This done, she was renamed *Manga Reva* after the lonely reef. Receiving American registry and home ported in San Francisco, she went on to more successful years of trading until vanishing at sea in 1917.

*　*　*

Though the mutiny on the *Bounty* will forever be a classic of the sea, there have been many

The German bark **MIMI** bound for the Columbia River in ballast went aground near the north entrance of the Nehalem River, Oregon February 13, 1913 and she looked like this the following day. Built as the British bark **GLENCOVA,** the vessel was the target of a major salvage operation which on April 6 ended in horror as the vessel capsized, claiming 18 salvage men and crewmen. *Courtesy Tillamook County Museum.*

Five-masted bark **KOBENHAVN,** one of the largest sailing vessels ever built, left Buenos Aires en route to Australia in 1929 and went missing with all hands. *Photo by Hauersley, from a painting by M. Molsted, 1922.*

attempted mutinies on sailing ships that have received little notice in history books. For example take the case of the attempted mutiny aboard the 2,067 ton British full-rigged ship *Leicester Castle.* She left San Francisco for Queenstown on July 26, 1902 in command of Captain R. D. Peattie, with a polygot mixture of hands in the fo'c'sle. Admittedly, the familiar method of filling empty berths had been used, many of the hands having been shanghaied.

Perhaps the incident here is best told in the captain's own words, on file in the British archives.

September 2, 1902—On the night of September 2, at 10:30 p.m., while we were making 3½ knots under all sail, and while the second mate had charge of the deck, I was lying in my cabin reading before going to sleep, when a man named Ernest Sears, A.B., an American, (shipped at San Francisco), came to my room door and asked me to come out, as a man had fallen from the foreyard and broken his leg.

I immediately did so, and going into the cabin, lighted the lamp so that I could have the table to lay the injured man on. I then went to the port door of the cabin where Sears was standing and asked him where the wounded man was.

He replied: "just outside" and I told him to tell the second mate to bring him into the cabin, when suddenly W. A. Hobbs, A.B., (also an American shipped at San Francisco), stepped into the cabin by the starboard door, and get-

Big German bark **OTTAWA** of Hamburg which also bore the names **MUSCOOTA, BUCKINGHAM** and **FLYING CLOUD,** is seen peacefully at anchor awaiting orders. *Photo courtesy Captain P. A. McDonald, one time master of the vessel when she was the Buckingham.*

ting between me and my own room door, said: —"now then, captain," and fired at me with a revolver, striking me on the left breast immediately over the heart. I attempted to close with him and hit him once, but he fired again hitting me on the arm. He then used a heavy club and began to batter my head. I struggled with him to the deck, where he fired two more shots at me, wounding me again in the arm. The second mate, hearing the noise, came to us, when Hobbs fired at him too and he fell instantly, the bullet evidently piercing his heart.

By that time the steward and a man named Dunning came on the scene. Hobbs had disappeared. I was in a very bad state, as I had five wounds from the revolver, and my scalp was terribly broken and was bleeding profusely. The place looked like a shambles.

The mate now took charge and calling the hands aft, it was decided to endeavor to secure our assailants when daylight broke, but about half an hour after midnight, greatly to our surprise, a raft with three men on it was observed in the dark floating past the starboard side. The men on it were Hobbs and Sears and James Turner, another American shipped at San Francisco. The mate immediately hove the ship to and waited till daylight when, nothing further being seen of the raft, the ship proceeded on her course.

I have not the slightest doubt that the frail raft, which consisted of a few planks and three cork cylinders from the forward lifeboat, went to pieces that night and that the men were lost. My wounds were dressed by R. J. Brennan, A.B., who had some experience, I believe, in a South African ambulance corps, and after one day's rest I was able to resume my duty, though I suffered considerably and do so yet, as the bullets are somewhere in my body, though the wounds have healed well. Mr. Nixon, the officer killed, was buried the day after his death. We were some 300 miles north of Pitcairn Island when it all happened, and the revolver used by Hobbs had been stolen from Nixon.

* * *

Square-rigger mishaps in days of yore were many, so much so that local newspapers sometimes treated them lightly. For instance in the Astoria (Oregon) Daily Budget for December 23, 1913 the following article appeared:

The British bark *Thistlebank* that was in a collision with the British ship *Hinemoa* two days earlier was shifted to the lower harbor

(Columbia River), and the German bark *Mimi* that was stranded recently on Oregon's Nehalem Beach south of Mount Neah-Kah-Nie was broken to pieces during the recent gale. Only two small boatloads of stores and a sail were saved.

* * *

In the early 1890's the downeaster *Gatherer* had a mate named Watts aboard. He was so brutal toward his crew that two seamen jumped overboard to resist torture.

Watts was sentenced to a term in San Quentin for his indescribable brutality, one of the few arrests of an officer in those hard years before the mast.

* * *

Many years back while at Port Angeles, Washington when his ship was loading lumber, Captain P. J. R. Mathieson, master of the *Moshulu,* described her as a "whale of a vessel" with beautiful lines, a clipper bow, and a fine run aft. He further described her as very lofty, with long yards and tall masts; measuring 335 feet in length with a beam of 47 feet and a 26.6 foot depth. Each of her four masts measured 165 feet from deck to trucks and the three lower yards were each 96 feet long. Two thirds of her 1,230 blocks were of steel, and the standing and running rigging, nearly all steel wire line measured no less than 21 miles. The square sails carried on the yards on each of the masts were 1 course, 2 topsails, 2 topgallant sails, and staysails between the masts, 1 fore topmast staysail, and four jibs. She had a total of 35 sails which spread over 42,000 square feet of canvas, and was fitted with a donkey boiler and engine used for working the cargo, shifting the vessel's berth and working the windlass through a wire line messenger. She had six powerful hand winches for hoisting the three upper topsails and three upper topgallant yards; six brace winches for canting the yards, and six capstans for heaving in on the sheets of the courses as well as one capstan for turning the windlass by manpower.

The *Moshulu,* according to Mathieson, was the ultimate in big steel square-riggers.

* * *

In 1909, the *Howard D. Troop,* a British four-mast bark under Captain D. W. Corning, when hurrying across the Pacific in ballast from Hong Kong to Astoria, had only twenty-two days to save her charter after she passed the longitude of Yokohama. She arrived just

One of the largest and finest four-masted barks ever built was the **MOSHULU.** Her last master under the American flag was Captain P. A. McDonald, hale and hearty in his 80's at this writing. This vessel made latter day history under sail taking part in the Australian grain race.

before sunset on the very day that her charter expired.

* * *

When the Boston bark *W. W. Crapo* departed Port Townsend in February 1883, virtually the entire crew was in irons. The vessel, laden with Puget Sound spars, was in command of Captain W. W. Hardy who had his wife and infant child along.

Captain Hardy's son, Captain F. H. Hardy, who in years past was well known as master of Coast & Geodetic Survey ships, has told this story as related to him by his father.

"My father said it was natural for the men to refuse duty. There were many ships in Port Townsend waiting for crews; the men sent up from San Francisco by steamer with the second mate had each received three months' advance wages and in no case in his 50 years at sea had my father seen a more thorough job of robbing the men than the sailor boarding house keepers in San Francisco had done. One man on opening his chest that formerly had contained all he had in the world found everything had been stolen and the chest filled with straw and a few rocks to give it weight.

"At muster when the men were brought on board, my father told them that they had signed articles to go to sea in the ship, that the owners had paid their transportation from San Francisco, and advanced three months pay to each man, that he had plenty of clothes in the slop chest and although the owners were under no obligation to do so, he would see that such articles of clothing as were needed to keep them warm in Cape Horn weather would be

151

The **BALCLUTHA** at Oakland Dock & Warehouse Co. just before being shifted to Pier 43 San Francisco, to serve as a museum ship. She was restored to her original splendor. *Photo by Walter Taylor.*

furnished without expense to them. That as representative of the owners it was his duty to see that the men went to sea in the ship and that they were going to do so. Still refusing duty, they were placed in irons. When they got out of the irons they attempted to take charge of the ship, coming after my father and the mate with drawn knives; they were held at bay with firearms, and in some way the captain of the tugboat found out something was wrong and turned around off Dungeness and returned to Port Townsend. With a baby about a year old, my mother's feelings and fear can be imagined. The men were put back in irons and the ship proceeded toward Boston. The trip took 133 days and there was absolutely no trouble on the entire voyage.

"One of the men mentioned as a ringleader was kept in irons for about a week, the other until the vessel reached the Equator. I often heard my father say that he never saw a man show more spunk, and when he was released he was so weak he had to be helped out of the lazaret where he had been confined. My father said this man was an excellent sailor man (every hair a rope yarn and every finger a marlinspike), one of those men who were more valuable to a ship's company than the best of second mates; one of those sailors who could be de-

pended upon to do the right thing in any emergency, the man who when reefing sail was always on the weather yard arm handling the head gearing. It is apparent that far from any resentment, there developed a deep respect between my father and this man, because he was the only sailor I ever knew my father to keep. on board while in an eastern U. S. port. He remained by the ship while discharging in Boston and loading in Philadelphia and made the trip to Kobe in the ship."

This stubborn sailor who finally relented, gained such respect from the elder Captain Hardy that he was actually recommended to Captain Burnam of the ship *Pactolas* as second mate. The infant son on that voyage that began with the crew in irons was none other than Captain F. H. Hardy, who related this episode.

* * *

Barratry, one of the most vicious words in the maritime vocabulary, is the premeditated destruction of a vessel for the purpose of collecting insurance on the hull and/or the cargo. The *Agenor*, a ship of 1,487 tons came under scrutiny in 1905.

Long employed in Pacific tradelanes, the *Agenor* was aging fast, having been built at East Boston in 1870. In the year 1905 she was sold to the West Coast Commercial Company, of Bellingham, Washington and sent to Alaska to load a cargo of salt dog salmon for Japan. Leaving the northland in October, she turned up at Yokohama 96 days later after having been given up for lost. The cargo in her wooden holds weighed out at little more than half the charter called for and the consignees brought suit, the shippers contending that the long passage over the southern route had caused the cargo to dry and shrink the additional amount.

The ship meanwhile was sold to an American firm in Yokohama and later was loaded with wheat for Kobe. She was wrecked on the passage, and the underwriters were able to prove that only a part cargo had been shipped, insurance being obtained on the full amount, and that the ship had been scuttled, as the holes were found in her bottom when the wreck drifted ashore. The responsible party was sentenced to life imprisonment in 1907 for falsifying bills of lading.

And all I ask is a merry yarn from a laughing fellow-rover,
And quiet sleep and a sweet dream when the long trick's over.
—MASEFIELD

One of the finest New England square-riggers ever built but one which ended her hectic career on the West Coast, was the 2,700 ton ship *Harvey Mills*. Built by Mills & Creighton at Thomaston, Maine, she was "baptised in blood," as the saying goes, when a man was reputedly killed at her launching in the fall of 1876.

Fire broke out aboard as she completed loading cotton at Port Royal for Liverpool three months later. Two of her crew suffocated before the fire was extinguished. She was dismasted in a severe Atlantic gale in February, 1878. Two years later she collided with and sank the bark *Eta* off the English coast. Following many legal problems, crew troubles and setbacks, the *Mills* was tabbed as a "hoodoo ship," and legion were the tales told of ghosts of the dead, for which she was responsible, coming back to haunt her. Such tales made it virtually impossible to crew the *Harvey Mills*.

Then came the curtain closer. On December 12, 1886, she left Seattle, deeply-laden with coal for San Francisco. In a severe Pacific gale, on December 14, the vessel foundered. Captain Crawford, her master, and all but three of his company perished. Two rafts got away but one swamped and the other containing two seamen and first mate Cushing were the only survivors. They were without food or water for four tormenting days until rescued, near death, by the ship *Majestic*, Captain Bergman, and taken to San Pedro.

* * *

"The ship is old, the grub is bad,
Leave her, Johnny, leave her.
I'm getting thin, I'm growing sad;
It's time for us to leave her.
The sails are furled, our work is done,
Leave her Johnny, leave her,
And now ashore we'll have some fun;
It's time for us to leave her."

—Old Sailors' Rhyme

As for this writer, the old rockin' chair near a crackling fire seems like a pretty nice place to be. Sometimes it's just more fun to dream of the past.

Gone are the days—here, still revealing her pleasant lines is the **FALLS OF CLYDE** in drydock at a Seattle shipyard for survey prior to being taken to Honolulu in 1963-64 to become a museum ship. Note her old anchor in foreground at Todd No. 2 drydock. The citizens of Honolulu purchased her and a Navy tug towed her to the islands. She was built in 1878. *Joe Williamson photo.*

Above, breakers lap at the stranded British bark **GALENA** on Clatsop Beach, Oregon in 1906. She was a total loss.

Page from the log of the bark **DAYLIGHT,** New York to Bombay, 1911.

Chapter Eight

Seamen's Missions and Board-ing House Crimps and Runners

The seaman was but a pawn in a seafaring chess game.

Since the beginning of the history of man in the Garden of Eden, the good and the righteous way as set down by the Almighty has always been in dire contrast with Satan and his diobolical temptations that has led humans into debauchery.

So has it been ever since, not only with the world at large but especially with those who have made their living upon the sea.

Perhaps the way of the seaman in the age of the tall ship is best described by Anton Otto Fischer in his book, *Focs'le Days:* He alluded to one of the many Seamen's missions, this one in particular located at Tacoma on Puget Sound, where numerous square-rigged sailing vessels came for a cargo of grain and lumber at the turn of the century. Said Fischer:

"Into the focs'le stepped a very attractive young woman. She was one of two ladies who conducted a Seamen's Mission, and she had come, as she did to every ship arriving in Tacoma, to invite us all up to the Mission. She produced some tracts which she handed around, smiling sweetly at everybody, and ignoring the sarcastic remarks of the crimp, who knew her as a doughty antagonist in their constant struggle for the souls of sailors. Against the promises of the fleshpots of Egypt held out by the crimp, all she could offer was a get-to-gether to sing hymns, have coffee and cake, play games like pool and dominoes, and reading matter. We took the tracts and promised to come to the Mission. Then she departed with a smile for every-body, leaving the field to the crimp, who tried his best to counteract the effect her charm had on us, but who found it useless for the time being to try to add any more of us to the three who were ready to follow him.

"A few of the crew, like myself, were not drinking men and we got in the habit of going to the Sailor's Mission every evening. There was always a surprisingly large number of sailors sitting around, reading, playing pool or checkers. One of the main attractions of the place was a collection of thousands of photographs of ships and crews which had come into Tacoma. The crew pictures especially were examined by the men for former shipmates.

"The Mission was run by two ladies, one in her early twenties and very pretty. Their charm and kindness were the main factors in the Mission's success. The main room contained a parlor organ, and when the ladies discovered I could play the piano, I became somewhat of a privileged character. Sunday afternoons

were always devoted to a hymn-singing session followed by a generous repast of coffee and cake. I would take my seat at the organ, and the two ladies led the aggregation of sailors to the strains of *"Where Is My Wandering Boy Tonight?'* or *'Lead Kindly Light',* and other hymns.

"These two ladies did a wonderful work, and thousands of sailors must hold them in grateful memory. They knew all about the traffic in sailors, and did as much as they could to combat it by warning the sailors how it actually worked."

Fischer was speaking of Mrs. Birgitte Funnemark and her daughter Christine who ran the Seaman's Rest in Tacoma for five years, from 1897 till 1903, and ever afterwards continued to meet the needs of lonely seafarers in various ways. Birgitte died in 1919 and Christine in 1960. Thanks to an historic writing that appeared some years back in the *Oregon Historical Quarterly,* Rowena L. and Gordon D. Alcorn told the history of the ladies and their mission. The setting was the latter part of the 19th century and the early 1900's when scores of the finest merchant square-riggers in the world were calling at Tacoma which was described as the mecca for deep-sea cargo sailing vessels, the port bristling with the masts of graceful ships—full-riggers, barks, barkentines, brigs, brigantines and schooners.

The route of the sailing ships was rather systematic. From European ports they headed west in ballast for New York where they loaded kerosene in five gallon cans, two to a crate, bound for the Orient. Often they made a call at Rio de Janeiro, but usually sailed directly around Africa's Cape of Good Hope and through the Indian Ocean, where they sometimes fell in with flat seas that becalmed them for days under the torid sun of the tropics. On occasion, a devastating typhoon reaped havoc on its victims. Sometimes the vessels would pass south of the East Indies through the Strait and Timor Sea, but more often voyaged around Australia, through the Coral and Tasman seas and north along the Oriental shores to Chinese and Japanese ports. After discharging the oil, they continued across the Pacific, sometimes with cargo, sometimes in ballast, following the great circle route where flows the Japanese Current eastward to the Pacific Northwest. The route from Europe to Puget Sound and Columbia River grain ports often required an entire year to complete. Grain ships often under-went considerable repairs after batterings at sea; also

Despite efforts to refloat her, the British bark **GALENA** was entrapped in the sands of Clatsop's clutches near the south entrance to the Columbia River November 13, 1906. Her skeleton was eventually enveloped in a sandy crypt.

replenishment of stores, chandlery replacement and rest for the sea-weary crews. Several weeks were spent in port where thousands of tons of jute-sacked wheat was loaded.

Departures were sometimes sad affairs as the vessels towed out to open water behind a big steam tug and cast off for the rugged voyage around notorious Cape Horn, which sailors often labeled as "Cape Stiff." Destinations were Queenstown at the southern tip of Ireland or to Falmouth for orders as to what European port they would discharge. The tall ships that went to South Africa sailed directly to Capetown or Delagoa Bay.

Its easy to understand the weariness of sailors on such long voyages and most were easy prey for the crimps. The saloons, gambling houses and brothels were well tenanted by fo'c'sle clientele on shore leave.

Non denominational seamen's missions were located at most of the larger seaports on the Pacific Coast in the age of sail, but the sailors' boarding houses, often used nefarious schemes to win over the sea-weary sailors enticing them with wine, women and song, designed to extract their wages and eventually garner blood money in the art of shangahaiing.

The success of the Seamen's Rest in Tacoma was especially significant for it flourished at a time when the world's most formidable merchant sailing vessels were crowding the port for grain, foreign and domestic

seafarers being in abundance. The *Tacoma Daily Ledger,* noted that in September of 1898, no less than 53 sailing vessels had anchored in Commencement Bay most of which loaded out grain for world-wide ports. The harbor was a forest of tall masts and graceful hulls with unique names. Beneath each bowsprit delicately carved figureheads were intriguing by their very presence.

An earlier chapter of the book discusses two British sailing vessels whose crew members had close ties with the Seaman's Rest, the *Atalanta* and the *Andelana,* both tragically lost, one off the Oregon coast and the other right in Tacoma's Harbor. But for the most part the tall ships frequenting the harbor around the turn of the century made long but successful voyages.

Back in those years the populace gave little thought to a day when such graceful vessels would become scarce as hen's teeth. The progression of sea transportation would soon crowd them off the seas in favor of powered vessels, which though much more costly to operate, were far more reliable, not having to depend on the whims of the winds. They were not hampered by the doldrums nor the ocean currents, and were able to work their way free in tight squeezes. The uncanny navigating abilities of the old seadogs that manned the tall ships is worthy of great praise.

Ironically it took the tragic loss of the *Atalanta* in 1898 to put one of the nefarious boarding house

French ship **BIARRITZ** berthed at San Francisco just after the turn of the century as depicted in a painting by super marine artist Ronald Dean of England. The steel-hulled **BIARRITZ** was built at St. Nazaire in 1901, and measured 282 feet in length. Note the detail artist Dean has recreated in this busy harbor scene.

operators out of business in the ongoing battle between good and evil—Tacoma's Seamen's Rest versus the sailors boarding house, owned and operated by Dave Evans and his hoods. The two installations were continually at loggerheads, and the upper hand was gained by the element for good in the testimony given by the three survivors of the ill-fated *Atalanta*.

George Fraser, one of the survivors claimed at the hearing that a half dozen seamen aboard the *Atalanta* were shanghaied within sight of several policemen in Oldtown Tacoma. Said he:

"One side of my face was wrecked and the other side shanghaied, (pointing to the bruises and scars incurred) This is where Billy Lyon, the ex prize fighter and present boarding house runner billied me. He knocked me senseless when I refused to go aboard the ship after I saw what kind of papers Evans had bound me with. Ryan was the only guy among the 'strikers' who could have forced me into the job. When I resisted I meant business. I pulled my knife and started for my arch enemy, but among the boosters was a big

Swede named Fred. A blow under my eye by him made me helpless and before I knew it, I was aboard the *Atalanta* beyond opportunity for escape. Some of the other lads told me that they had been robbed of their advance and then taken forcibly aboard the ship."

Another survivor, Francis McMahon, claimed to have been abducted after being relieved of his $35 advance by Dave Evans, after which he suffered a clout on the head and was carried aboard the ship unconscious.

Had there not been any survivors from the tragedy off the Oregon coast Dale Evans may not have been exposed. However, fate took a strange twist, and as a result of the testimony, Evans was put out of business by the authorities, ending his reign of brutality and shanghaiing of seamen.

In the early years of the tall ships on San Francisco Bay and Puget Sound ports the anchors were hardly down before the boarding house runners were alongside. The mates endeavored to fend them off from the ships, but the runners watched their opportunity to

157

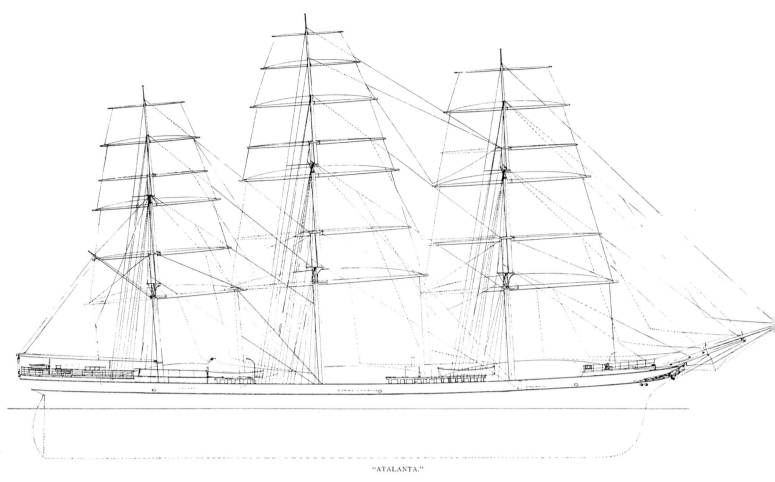

"ATALANTA."

Sail plan of the ill-fated British full-rigged ship **ATALANTA,** owned by the Ninian Hill shipping house of England. The vessel was lost with all but three of her 27 man crew after stranding four miles south of Alsea Bay, Oregon, November 17, 1898 en route to South Africa from Tacoma.

sneak aboard and often hid themselves until the crew was off duty. The fo'c'sle gangs were often like sheep before the slaughter. Crimping and blood money was the name of the game and ship captains often paid so much a head to the crimps in order to complete their complements once sailing time approached...A crimp and his runners employed any and every trick, from drugged rum to sandbagging. The usual method when men were scarce, was to woo crewmen on newly arrived vessels to desert.

In some American Downeast sailing vessels the officers made no attempt whatsoever to stop the culprits from boarding their ships. A well informed seafarer wrote in 1897:

"When the anchor had touched the bottom we stood by for the crimps. Even before we were aware of it the evil creatures began to swarm aboard like a flock of sinister vultures and without ceremony they fell upon their prey. They plied the men from bottles whose black nozzles protruded from their coat pockets. As soon as darkness fell those who were

Seamen's Rest located on North Carr Street, was a popular mission for seafarers on the sailing ships that visited Tacoma at the turn of the century. It was opened in 1897 and was operated by Mrs. Birgitte Funnemark, upper inset, and her daughter Christine Funnemark. The house was still standing at this writing. Courtesy Oregon Historical Society Quarterly.

anxious to desert were removed in a boat which slipped quietly alongside. Though the crewmen were aware they were foolishly giving up a good pay day for a night's spree, once the crimp was in command he would not hesitate to ship them away on a departing vessel within a day or two of their first trick ashore after several previous months at sea. The weakness of the victims were obvious and though they were aware of their fate many such seamen was liable to have his first drink doped if hands were scarce. There were even cases where crimps clubbed innocent citizens on dark streets at night and forcibly carried them aboard outbound vessels."

One such event involved a clergyman, who had never in his life been to sea.

In San Francisco, Columbia River and Puget Sound ports in the early 1890's sailing vessels were so plentiful, and hands so hard to come by, blood money up to $50 a man and more was asked and received. During such periods, a ship's officer had to be very careful he was not paying for corpses rather than drugged, insensible individuals, dumped on the vessel's deck.

If indeed a captain was a good Christian individual who treated his crew with respect and decency, they in turn respected him and remained with the ship voyage after voyage, seldom risking the temptations of the crimps. Even the ignorant fo'c'sle hands knew when they were well off, though sometimes unknown to the shipmaster, the bucko mates were tyrants harshly treating seamen under unwarranted authority. A wise sailing ship captain had his finger on all aspects of his vessel's management and of the personality and activities of his crew, both officers and seamen from the lowest apprentice on up.

———

In Captain A.G. Graham's fine little booklet, *Voyage in a Square-rigger 1913-14,* published by the Columbia River Maritime Museum, he tells of a boarding house master in Portland, Oregon at the turn of the century. He was Larry Mikola Sullivan, (1863-1918) sometimes referred to as "King of the Sailors." Larry Sullivan's Sailors' Boarding House had the local reputation of a shanghai joint where he got his guests drunk, robbed them and shipped them out again for a fee. However, Graham was told by three Yankee seamen that sailed with him on the British bark *Lord Templetown,* that their previous experiences at the establishment were like many other hangouts in various seaports. When one was paid off a ship in a strange port, there was always a runner on hand to welcome and escort him to the local boarding house. But at Sullivan's they reputedly found a safe place for their belongings, a bed, good food and kindred souls from other ships with whom to pass the time. Drinks

King of the sailors, Larry Mikola Sullivan, who ran an infamous boarding house in Portland, Oregon at the turn of the century. Oregon Historical Society photo.

were readily available at barroom prices and credit was good after money ran out up to a month's pay from the next ship. It was paid from the legal advance given on signing for the voyage.

Other inhabitants at Sullivan's had an entirely different story to tell, and whether treated fairly or not all agreed that the "King" was a tough character, as were his lieutenants, Jack and Pete Grant and other members of the staff. Handy with fists and knives they kept the competition to a minimum by holding a near monopoly. Guests were held in subjection whenever they celebrated too much. Sullivan's reputation for shanghaiing was at its peak only when there was an acute shortage of hands before the mast when anxious skippers and mates were willing to pay blood money to man their hungry ships.

Though there were many lawless, deceptive and conniving crimps and runners in the 1880's and 1890's, none could surpass the Barbary Coast butchers in the wake of the California goldrush. Most notorious was Shanghai Kelly, a raw-boned Irishman, with red whiskers, a nasty temper, slovenly and thickset, a man who had no scruples and often reasoned like Satan himself. None was more feared, and local citizens often gave his infamous boarding house a wide berth at 33 Pacific Street. The three story frame structure was a rat trap on the waterfront, where skiffs slipped underneath the barnacle-riddled pilings to take tapped individuals out to waiting windjammers in a stupor from drugged rot-gut or from terrible beatings from Kelly's hoods or from his fists. His two recognized recipes were drugged liquor and opium-loaded cigars.

His most diabolic plot involved the supplying of three vessels at one time with crews when there were no seamen available. One of the ships feared by every man before the mast was the *Reefer,* out of New York, which was listed in maritime annals as a "hell wagon." With the challenge at hand, Kelly sent out his runners to spread the word along the waterfront that he was about to throw a wing-ding cruise to celebrate his birthday, all food and drinks on the house. He invited friends and outsiders as well to join him on a special cruise of the bay on the chartered paddle wheel steam tug *Goliah,* which had wide decks for dancing and drinking. The appeal drew nearly 100 unsavory souls. The merryment began as soon as the vessel cast off. As the paddle wheels churned up the bay water, doped liquor gurgled down the throats of the guests. When they were nearly stoned, the tug pulled alongside the waiting sailing vessels to unload drunks for the traditional blood money. The next thing the victims knew was being awakened by cold seawater being slopped across their faces, wind in the sails above and outbound for a long voyage under demanding task-masters.

With money in his pockets, Kelly continued the cruise on the *Goliah* by picking up the shipwrecked crew of a sailing vessel that had stranded near the entrance to the Golden Gate. When the *Goliah* docked at Market Street Wharf, a cheering crowd greeted the crimp for his rescue effort. Nobody seemed concerned about the riffraff he'd shuffled off for blood money and the city seemed little concerned that they weren't aboard.

Though Kelly could perhaps have put her out of business, he was tolerant of a "crimpess" who had an establishment near his. Perhaps more of a drinking house than a boarding house, the infamous Miss Piggott had teamed up with a Lapland runner named Nikko. The "Piggott Special" was a concoction made of brandy, gin, whiskey and drugs that could put a man out cold in a matter of minutes. Should his resistance be stronger, brother Nikko would bounce a pebble off his crown with his trusty slingshot, or the bar tender would render a knuckle sandwich to his jaw. A springed hatch was then utilized, and the inate victim lowered to an awaiting skiff, much to the joy of the toothless Laplander and the sly Miss Piggott.

Still another female crimp on the San Francisco waterfront made a name for herself in the rip-roaring days of the clippers. She was nothing less than an Amazon, more than six feet tall in her flat, size 12 shoes. Muscular as a man and tough as nails, Mother Bronson ran a boarding house on Stuart Street. She could fight like a tigeress with her fists and if overpowered would sink her teeth into her opponent. Perhaps having been spurned by an early love affair

she enjoyed taking out her revenge on others, though it was said she had paid many men to go after her lover, who weighing the odds had figured escaping to sea would be far better than a life with the wicked witch of the Barbary coast.

San Francisco had many notorious boarding houses run by crimps and runners with colorful sounding names. Some even specialized for the kind of seagoing personnel most preferred on certain ships, such as whaling vessels.

Many names are still recorded in maritime annals for their dastardly deeds. Among them were Horseshoe Brown, Calico Jim, Honest Arnold, Shanghai Brown and numerous others that came and went, including Mike Connor, known as the religious crimp, who allegedly never told a lie. He claimed he never put a man aboard a ship that had not rounded the Horn at least twice. Instead of Cape Horn he referred to a cow's horn in his establishment, which he required all of his guests to go around at least twice.

Nefarious Ship's Officers

The belaying pin, a wooden or iron pin shaped object which fits into a hole in a pin rail, used for making a rope secure on a sailing vessel became a symbol of punishment aboard the Downeaster. Often featured as a weapon rather than a utilitarian tool, bucko mates and tyranical captains frequently used them to beat non-submissive seamen into submission.

Aboard the Downeaster a shipmaster was the all powerful monarch of his small floating islet domain, and woe to the hand before the mast who challenged his position. He had a heart of lead and a mind of steel. Often more cruel than some of the blue water sailing ship skippers were the bucko mates who did most of the dirty work on the crew with his superior's approval. The hand before the mast was often referred to as the lamb before the slaughter, despite the earlier efforts of Richard Henry Dana, whose book, *Two Years Before The Mast,* published in 1840, pointed out the cruel treatment and culinary swill dealt to the men in the fo's'cle.

Take for instance, Captain "Shotgun" Murphy, master of the four-masted bark *Shenandoah.* Outbound from San Francisco for Liverpool, less than a week out to sea, he assembled his mates and complained that they were acting like old women. Said he, "Here, we've been out of 'Frisco, more'n a week and I ain't seen any blood running in the scuppers yet."

He got his wish before the end of the voyage, there being several dented skulls among the crew for performance which in the estimation of the officers was not up to par.

Iron hulled bark **ANNIE JOHNSON** pictured here, was built at Harrington, England in 1872 as the **ADA IREDALE.** She was abandoned afire in the South Pacific October 15, 1876, 2,000 miles east of the Marquesas. Drifting westward in the equatorial current for eight months, she was finally intercepted by a French cruiser and towed to Papeete, her cargo of coal still burning. Not until May 1878, was the fire totally extinguished. Taken to San Francisco she was rebuilt and re-rigged as the **ANNIE JOHNSON.** As a four-masted auxiliary schooner under the name **BRETAGNE,** she foundered en route from Vancouver B.C. to Suva in 1929. She had been sold three years earlier by Matson Navigation Company to Leo Ozanne of Papeete. Photo courtesy Matson Navigation Company.

The Red Record alluded to elsewhere in this book pointed out many of the charges brought against captains and mates before the mast, charges published in the *Coast Seamen's Journal,* the house organ publication of the National Seamen's Union of America. Bringing the charges to court, however, was generally a sham, the guilty parties often disappearing or unavailable for the hearings. The record covered only seven years, from 1888 to 1895, affording details of 64 cases of cruelty and murder on the high seas in the Yankee Cape Horn fleet.

Such charges only seemed to make the officers tougher than ever and above civil decency. In all honesty there were some decent shipmasters, a few who even tried to live by the dictates of the Bible, but even they had to hold the line between the poop deck and the fo'c'sle, for often among the crew were rough, tough uneducated renegades slightly removed from pirates, who only understood the rule of the iron hand. Sailing vessel jobs for seamen were considered beneath the dignity of most other professions, despite the fact that nobody worked harder nor under more difficult conditions for such a paltry stipend.

The cruelty displayed in Jack London's novel, *The Sea Wolf,* though fictionized, was a real live actuality among personnel on Downeasters. Among the worst was Captain William Belchior, better known as "Bucko Belchoir." He committed such atrocities as breaking with his bare fist the jaw of a crewman helplessly ironed in the "tween deck" of a sailing vessel, and then on the same voyage hurtling himself into a circle of men brandishing sheath-knives successfully quelling a mutiny. Never did he make a voyage, especially in the *Wilmington,* without terrifying accounts of his cruel actions, so much so that every seamen steered away from signing aboard his ship. Belchoir enjoyed picking up the malcontents, frequently by the art of Shanghaiing. He was described as a short, broad, beetle-browed grey-eyed bully of unchallenged courage whose makeup lacked any understanding of love or compassion.

An article in *Harpers Magazine* in 1874 written by a United States Consul described a certain Captain Halyard's address from the quarter deck to his newly signed crew.

"Men! My name's Captain Halyard. I'm master of this ship and I want to start square with you. We've got a long voyage before us and there's plenty of work to be done. I want you to understand I'm great on discipline, and you can have hell or heaven on board, just as you please. All you've got to attend to is to do your duty and obey orders: that's what you shipped for, and that's what you're paid for. If you do your duty, it will be all right; and if you don't, it will be all wrong.

"The first man that disobeys my orders I'll put daylight through him—quick, and here's the little joker I'll do it with (exhibiting a revolver). If any of you men try to make trouble aboard of this ship I'll make it hot for you. I'll make mince-meat of some of you quicker'n hell can scorch a feather!

"I hear that some of you are from the *White Swallow,* (the crew of the *White Swallow* mutinied in the China Sea because of harsh treatment) where you gave much trouble. Well, this is not the *White Swallow,* and you've got bloody Jock Halyard to deal with. Now you know who I am, and what you've got to expect. Go forward!"

How would the reader have liked to have shipped before the mast after a speech like that, realizing that he would be facing a rugged voyage around the Horn of several months duration. The temptation would be to jump overboard with the first lifering one could grab.

Captain David Bone, master of the *Brassbounder*, told of an incident with Captain Bully Nathan, master of the *W.B. Flint*, in which the latter stated to waterfront crimps, "Give me grave-diggers or organ grinders, boys, if you kyant get sailormen. Anything with two handan' feet. I guess I'm Jan K. Nathan and they'll be sailormen or stiffs before we reach aout'."

There were many colorful shipmasters in the Downeast fleet, most of which came from the climes of New England, principally Maine, where the bulk of the fleet was constructed of native woods. Thomaston and Searsport probably led the list of contributors, though nearly every New England port on down to Boston made worthy contributions. In some cases all the male members of a family went to sea with long lines of captains following in succession. Each had his own idea of how his ship should be operated, maintained and painted. Take for instance the peculiarities of Thomaston shipmaster Ed Masters. He was so set on preserving his command that he spoiled the appearance of every ship he commanded, his basic material being plain old black tar. When he was master of the pert appearing *Baring Brothers*, he not only ordered her tarred from the waterline to the rail, but also her topsides, so much so that she appeared like the black moria. All the white paint was scraped off the deck houses and replaced with prime Stockholm. Often at sea, superstitious sailors on passing ships feared her as the phantom "Flying Dutchman," that evil omen that haunted seafarers of old.

By sheer contrast with the sometimes tyranical or peculiar ship's officers was a shipmaster named Dave Libby. This unusual man of the sea was endowed with a friendly and understanding personality with all who sailed under his command. His crews would have given their lives for him, and never in his seagoing career was there one who jumped ship, but there was often a line up to sign on with him. He virtually acted as a father to the younger seamen proving that a contented crew can make for a happy well run vessel. It was too bad that his recipe was not followed by others. Just the opposite was generally practised. If a skipper was not known as a strict disciplinarian or taskmaster he wasn't considered much of a man by his peers.

Bucko mate Red Rogers who sailed in the *Columbia*, was claimed to be as foul mouthed as any other in the Cape Horn fleet. He reeled off lines of profanity with alarming profusion and had a bad temper to go along with his speeches. It is said that he once burst a blood vessel cursing out a deaf shipmate who had been shanghaied aboard his ship. Rogers died a few hours

Under the American flag, the **CHILLICOTHE**, registered in Portland, Oregon, was the former German ship **FLOTOW**. She is shown at anchor in the Columbia River. Courtesy Columbia River Maritime Museum.

later and undoubtedly took up his habit with the prince of Hell.

Before the turn of the century, the handsome Bath built ship *St. Paul*, was lying in San Francisco Bay. Captain Bert Williams was in command, and a nefarious second mate by the name of Martin, whose reputation was feared on both coasts wielded the whip over the fo'c'sle gang. Due much to his savagery the vessel was listed as a "Hell Ship" and considerable blood money was paid out to get any kind of a crew to

Climbing the Jacob's ladder, a Puget Sound pilot boards the British bark **GANGES**, owned by J. Nourse of London. Built at Sunderland, England in 1882, the iron-hulled vessel was in later years sold to Norwegian interests. From Joe D. Williamson collection.

people her decks. In the holds was a full load of grain, destination Liverpool, and the Blue Peter was flying. Time was wasting and with no volunteer takers, the mates turned to the masters of the infamous shanghai houses. When word got around the waterfront that the drive was on for hands on the *St. Paul,* business was unusually slow at the grog shops. Out to the streets went the crimps. So desperate did they become that they snatched a prim and proper Baptist minister right off the Market Street board walk, a man who had never been to sea in his life. With a konk on the head the clergyman was hustled to a wharf shed, drugged and rowed out to the *St. Paul* swinging at anchor. Shortly after, sail was made and the preacher man, stripped of his garb and suited out in dungarees gained his senses only to learn to his horror that he was Cape

Horn bound with no chance of escape. With a kick in the ribs and the Satanic prasology, "Minister or Saint—Hell! Up you get and work," second mate Martin leveled a belaying pin at the wretched individual.

One can only imagine the trying experience of that green hand, but somehow he endured, accepting his hardship role with shock and dignity. By the time the ship reached the Horn he was up in the rigging and out on the yardarms handling sail. For 101 days he was part of the fo'c'sle gang, it fortunatly being a splendid passage terminating when the anchor was dropped in the Mersey. Already the consul at Liverpool had received money from the pastor's San Francisco churchmen to bring him back home to an anxious flock.

Copy of the Certificate of Discharge of Able Bodied Seaman C. Hansen from the ship **STAR OF POLAND** at San Francisco, signed by Shipping Commissioner Gibbs in 1919. The vessel was commanded by Captain B.J. Larsen.

Several weeks later, the minister was back in his pulpit, hardened and wind-burned, proving that he was made of true grit. The topic for his first sermon after returning home undoubtedly involved the book of Psalms where in Chapter 107, verses 23-24 it reads: "They that go down to the sea in ships, that do business in great waters, These see the works of the Lord and his wonders in the deep."

Sometimes the hands before that mast became so desperate over harsh treatment on the blood ships that they took their own lives rather than face further torment. On the ship *Gatherer,* Captain John Sparks in command, backed by the infamous mate Charlie Watts, San Francisco newspapers screamed of a despicable voyage shortly after the vessel arrived in the bay. After rounding the Horn, two seamen had committed suicide, one a Scandanavian driven to total distraction by the mate. He climbed to the royal yard shouting curses and insults at the captain and mate. Watts chased after him up the rigging in a rage and as he reached the royal yard the distraught seaman flung himself into the sea and vanished forever.

The other victim, a man named Swanson, later jumped on to the taffrail, drew his sheath knife across his throat and fell backwards into the ship's wake, fist clenched and blood pouring profusely from the wound.

Nor was the drama of horror over, for a third seaman on the same voyage was shot by the enraged mate. Due much in part to the news publicity related to the press by the surviving seamen, Captain Sparks went into hiding, losing his command. The treacherous mate Watts, in one of the few isolated cases of justice being performed, went to prison.

A well known Pacific trader was the ship **TONAWANDA**, built at Greenock, Scotland in 1892. She also sailed under the names **LIDA** and **INDRA**. Pictured here in dock at Astoria, Oregon in bygone years, she became a hulk at New Caledonia in 1926. Courtesy Columbia River Maritime Museum.

Chapter Nine

The Great Star Fleet

Even the tallest, most handsome vessels of sail have numbered days.

Nobody is better qualified to render a brief history of the Alaska Packers Association fleet of sailing vessels than Captain Harold Huycke. Resident of Edmonds, Washington, he is a marine surveyor, master mariner, marine historian and author. Following is his writing on the fleet that gave one last boost to the tall square-riggers on the Pacific Coast. Parts of this article appeared in *Yachting Magazine* several years ago, and reappeared in the *Sparks Journal.*

Even if you lived in the San Francisco Bay area in September, 1930, the chances are you weren't aware of the arrival of the ship *Star of Alaska* from Alaskan waters, rolling easily through the Golden Gate in tow of a hardworking steamer. That was on the 19th of September, and the *Star of Alaska,* a steel full-rigger 44 years old at the time, brought to an end an era in Pacific Coast maritime history.

Star of Alaska was one of 19 ships whose names began with *Star,* that once called the port of San Francisco "home." There was the *Star of Bengal,* gone these 75 years with the bones of a hundred Chinese emtombed in her rusted hulk; *Star of Falkland,* which went out of the Golden Gate in the spring of 1928 and never returned; *Star of England,* which knew the City by the Golden Gate long before the fire of 1906; *Star of Shetland,* which left the Bay several years ago on a voyage to a scrapyard in Japan. There were many more, each as different from her sisters as human beings are from each other.

These ships belonged to the Alaska Packers Association of San Francisco. In 1893 the Association was formed by merging small Alaskan salmon canneries, which had been suffering and expanding alternately with the fluctuating demand for canned salmon. The waters of Alaska and the Pacific Northwest teemed with salmon. The relative inaccessibility of the fishing grounds called for ships that could sail across more than 2,000 miles of open, oft-times stormy seas, and bring a season's pack of salmon home in the fall. Supplies and workmen could be taken to the cannery and fishing sites by sea only. The need for ships of large carrying capacity was thus obvious.

There was at that time a well-established shipbuilding industry on the Pacific Coast to meet the growing shipping demands of the lumbering and logging interests. These yards built sailing vessels suited to the coastwise and limited offshore lumber trades, but except for a few Pacific Coast-built schooners and barkentines, the new Association found the larger square-riggers from the New England shipyards more suitable.

The first few years they chartered an assortment of ships owned mostly in San Francisco. Salmon fishing in Alaska was a seasonal occupation, starting in late spring and running toward the end of August, and by chartering, the Packers avoided the expense of maintaining a fleet during the winter. But they ran into the problem of the limited facilities of the chartered ships. Salmon packers were not exactly considered to be in the deep-sea trade, but rather more like "floating warehouses." Their actual time at sea rarely exceeded three months a year. Within seven years of organization, outright ownership of vessels became established policy and thereafter only extra-large catches forced the Association into the charter market for additional bottoms.

By the turn of the century came the problem of replacements. The large square-riggers the Packers owned were not new, and they were of wooden construction. American shipyards, generally speaking, hadn't turned to steel ships as had the European builders. Then, as now, American law prohibited the use of foreign-built ships in coastwise trade, except for repaired wrecks and ships admitted to United States Registry by Special Act of Congress.

In 1898 the Hawaiian Islands were annexed by a joint resolution of Congress but this did not immediately change the status of ships owned by Hawaiian citizens or ships registered in Hawaii but owned by Americans. However, within two years another Act of Congress provided that all ships that carried Hawaiian registry between June 14 and August 12, 1900, would be entitled to the full rights of American coastwise trade. Several British-built ships were immediately affected, and in the two months' leeway several additional ships were registered in Hawaii.

Thus a good-sized fleet of iron and steel ships became eligible for the Alaska Packers trade. The small ship *Euterpe* was the first of 19 iron and steel square-riggers to fly their swallowtail houseflag. After the turn of the century, the Association bought only iron and steel ships, though there were a half-dozen wooden ships in the fleet for nearly a quarter of a century more. The Downeasters *Indiana, Bohemia, Santa Clara* and *Harry Morse,* veterans of the Cape Horn trade, season after season sailed up to Kvichak,

Anchored in Port Blakely Harbor, Washington during the World War I era are four square-riggers making repairs and being readied for sea voyages. Part of the old lumber mill is seen in the background. The two sailing vessels at the right are the **BENJ. F. PACKARD** and the **J.D. PETERS.** Webster & Stevens photos.

Nushagak, Naknek, Chignik and other canneries in Alaska.

The Association maintained its own dockyard in the Oakland Estuary and here, in winter, the whole fleet would be laid up and repairs and alterations effected. Men who later became masters of American ships, both sail and steam, found employment as riggers and sailors in maintenance crews in their youth in the yard at Paru Street in Alameda. If the jobs on offshore vessels were scarce, a sailor on the beach might be hired by the Alaska Packers to keep the fleet in condition. With the end of winter in sight, a couple of the ships would be sent to the Puget Sound area for cargoes of coal and box shooks, which would be brought to San Francisco and distributed throughout the fleet for transportation to the canneries in southern Alaska or Bristol Bay.

From San Francisco to Alaska was approximately 2,500 miles, not far as sea voyages go. Each ship was loaded with supplies, manned by fishermen who served as sailors, and crowded with cannery workers. The whole summer's operation was sustained by the supplies and manpower carried in the sailing fleet. At the end of the fishing season the salmon, canned and boxed, were loaded in the homeward-bound ships. The operation covered seven months at most. Since each ship carried upwards of 100 men and supplies for the season, alterations were necessary in the ship's living quarters and storage spaces.

On ships like the *Star of Alaska, Star of Holland, Star of France, Star of Iceland* and *Star of Russia,* poop decks were lengthened as much as 75 feet to provide additional living quarters for fishermen and cannery hands. Tween-deck spaces were given over to living quarters, large water tanks and several kitchens or galleys. The Chinese were well represented in the canneries, while Italian and Scandinavian fishermen from San Francisco Bay made up the fishing crews.

Fishing methods in Southern Alaska differed from those in Bristol Bay. The water in southern Alaska was too clear for gillnetting, so traps were used. Trap fishing required smaller crews for the ships that went to the Chignik, Karluk and Alitak. In the early days of the century, fishermen signed on the windjammers as

STAR OF INDIA was built as the **EUTERPE,** flying the British flag. In later years she served as a unit of the Alaska Packers Association, out of San Francisco and is one of the oldest merchant sailing vessels afloat. She is pictured here at America's Bicentennial July 4, 1976 in San Diego Harbor.

sailors, being paid on a quarterly basis; one quarter for the run to Alaska, one quarter for unloading the cannery supplies; one quarter for loading the salmon pack and the last quarter for sailing the ship back to San Francisco. The Bristol Bay ships generally had larger crews than those going to southern canneries, but even so, good sailormen who knew square-riggers were often scarce.

Crews were split into gangs of from 12 to 18. Prior to World War I, gangs numbered 18 men. Two were assigned to keeping quarters on the ship clean, one man to repair and keep nets in order, and the balance of the gang to do the ship's work under way. Upon arrival of the ship at its cannery both anchors were let go and a swivel shackled into the chains so the ship could swing freely. As the stores were unloaded, the upper yards were lowered to improve stability. All hands then turned to in getting the cannery ready for operation, doing everything from carpentry to over-hauling the boats and barges. The chief mate was beach boss, more often than not, and it was he who had to make order out of chaos. With the growing strength of the fisherman's union, delineations were made in the work performed by fishermen, and eventually the carpentry and miscellaneous chores were lessened.

The ships were as varied and colorful a lot as were ever owned by one company. The Alaska Packers were shipowners from 1893 until World War II when the government requisitioned the few steamers they still owned.

During the first few years casualties were rather heavy. The ship *Raphael* was wrecked near Karluk in July 1895, and the following year the ship *James A. Borland* was lost on Gugidak Island. Navigation in fog-shrouded and unmarked channels was hazardous at best, and it is a wonder that more ships weren't lost in those early years. In 1898 the big wooden full-rigger *Sterling* went aground on an un-named and unmarked shoal in the Bering Sea, so far from any assistance that she had to be given up. Today's charts of those waters show "Sterling Shoals."

In 1900 the wooden ship *Merom* was wrecked on the beach at Karluk. The following year, the wooden full-rigger *Santa Clara* was wrecked at Trial Island near Puget Sound, while going after a cargo of coal, but survived to remain in service for 25 years more.

In addition to their own fleet, the Association chartered 57 ships over a period of 18 years, but by 1911 the need for chartering had diminished. At the turn of the century they owned 13 wooden ships. In 1901 the small iron bark *Euterpe* was purchased followed by the iron bark *Coalinga,* and in the following year by the iron bark *Himalaya.* All three, registering a little over 1,000 tons each, were British-

built and had been in the emigrant and colonial trades for over 30 years. Had it not been for their sound construction and relatively heavy iron plates the ships would have been obsolete.

During the next four years the Association bought six more ships and barks from San Francisco owners, and by the end of 1906 had nine iron and steel ships.

Among this group was a quartet of iron Belfast-built ships, which had already acquired some fame as fast windjammers while under the Red Duster of England. A little of their former glory rubbed off on their less glamorous sisters when the names of the other five were changed to conform to the rakish four Irish ships. Thus the *Star of France, Star of Russia, Star of Bengal* and *Star of Italy* formed the nucleus of an American-flag *"Star"* fleet.

With 15 years of seafaring behind her under British ownership, the ship *Balclutha* became the *Star of Alaska. Euterpe,* beginning her 35th year at sea, became the *Star of India; Coalinga* with a colorful past as a competitor of the clipper ships became *Star of Chile; Abby Palmer,* originally the British bark *Blairmore,* became *Star of England;* and the *Himalaya,* of the same vintage and history as *Euterpe,* became *Star of Peru.*

Old deepwater sailors will tell you today that they "lost track" of these ships once they went into the salmon fisheries. But the ships themselves continued to

House flag and insignia of the Alaska Packers Association of San Francisco which from 1893 employed a huge fleet of square-rigged sailing vessels in the Alaska salmon trade.

make their own histories. *Star of Bengal* served only two seasons in the Alaskan trade and came to an agonizing end Sept. 20, 1908, when she was being towed from her cannery station at Fort Wrangell in southeastern Alaska at the start of her voyage home. Heavy weather drove her ashore, despite the efforts of two tugs, and 110 people were lost, most of them Chinese. Those that survived did so under the most trying and tragic conditions. This was by far the worst disaster the Association suffered.

Even in this routine calling, where ships spent nearly nine months a year at anchor or in a berth, navigating skill and weather ken were vital. Ice was not unknown, and fog, unlit channels and strong currents taxed the masters and mates to a high degree.

Captain Nicholas Wagner, who was master of the *Balclutha* in 1906 and the *Star of Bengal* in 1907 and 1908, refused to substantiate the claims of Captain Bill Mortensen, who began his career with the Association before the turn of the century, that the *Star of Alaska* was the fastest ship in the fleet. Even when both men had retired to Sailors' Snug Harbor in their declining years, they most decidedly failed to agree on this point. Captain Wagner died in 1943 at a ripe old age, Captain Mortensen lived for another five years.

End of an Era

In 1908 the bark *Willscott* was bought and renamed *Star of Iceland.* She remained in the company's service until 1925. She was another British-built bark, dating from 1896, a deadweight carrier with no speed records. When only a year old, she had been dismasted off the Japanese coast and sailed under jury rig 4,000 miles in 61 days. She was then sold to San Francisco owners and put in general cargo trades, mostly from Hawaii to the Atlantic Coast via Cape Horn with sugar and back with coal or other cargoes. In 1929 she put to sea for the last time, bound to Japanese scrappers.

In 1909 the bark *Homeward Bound* was bought and renamed *Star of Holland.* She had a few unique twists to her history, too. She had been built as the ship *Zemindar* in 1885 in Belfast, Ireland, by Harland and Wolff for the Indian trade, and had spent nearly 15 years in that service for the Brocklebanks of Liverpool. Then she spent a short time under the German flag as the *Otto Gildemeister* of Bremen, but was dismasted in 1901 on a voyage from Yokohama to Portland, Ore. She came under the American flag when enough money was spent on her refitting to qualify for United States Registry, and for the next eight years the vessel

Alaska Packers Star ships wintering in the Oakland dockyard. **STAR OF FINLAND** in foreground. San Francisco Maritime Museum photo.

sailed in the Cape Horn trade between California, Oregon, and Europe.

Captain Chadwick Thompson had some shares in her, and tried out his own rig which proved rather successful. Captain Thompson rigged her as a sort of bark, but kept a single squaresail on the mizzenmast, followed by an immense ringtail which was typically Pacific Coast stuff. Sold to the Alaska Packers in 1909, she was renamed *Star of Holland* and converted to a conventional bark. After being sold a couple of times as a barge, she was broken up for scrap in 1950.

From 1909 to 1912, the Alaska Packers bought the bark *Kaiulani,* which was renamed *Star of Finland,* and the big four-mast barks *Acme, Astral* and *Atlas,* renamed *Star of Poland, Star of Zealand* and *Star of Lapland.* The Standard Oil Co. of New York, owner of the last-named trio, had commissioned the famous shipbuilding family of Sewall of Bath, Maine, to build three 3,000-tonners for their case-oil trade to the Far East, with an eye to picking up cargoes homeward in the Hawaiian sugar trade, or general and lumber trades from the Pacific Northwest to the Atlantic. They were profitably employed for a little over ten years, but by 1910 the Standard Oil Co. found cargoes hard to obtain in the face of steamship competition. The Alaska Packers bought them as they came on the market, the last being the *Acme* after she completed a westbound passage to Puget Sound in 1913, one of the last such voyages of an American flag ship.

Even the Sewalls of Bath began to dispose of some of their ships. They had built ten steel-hulled sailing ships and for a number of years had operated the British-built four-mast bark *Kenilworth.* They let the latter go in 1908. She became the *Star of Scotland,* a name familiar for many years along the California Coast.

As the competitive deep-water trades in which sailing ships had once been profitably engaged were captured by steamers, the market for sailing vessels was poor. But for the salmon packers, these ships might never have survived the brief period of discard that preceded World War I.

That war found the Association with 16 iron and steel windjammers and about eight wooden vessels. With the shortage of shipping throughout the world, the Association was in a happy position. Shipping people of the coast were anxious to charter sailing ships for general cargo voyages in the Pacific during the off-season when they would otherwise have been laid up in Alameda.

The *Star of Holland* made a couple of voyages with lumber to Australia and Manila, and later returned to Alaska. The *Star of Poland,* formerly *Acme,* was a better offer on charter than her smaller contemporaries, and was chartered in the fall of 1916 for Australia,

Chile and Manila. Homeward bound from the Philippines in the fall of 1918, she was wrecked on the Japanese coast.

Star of Finland returned to old familiar routes when the APA chartered her for a round trip to Hawaii, returning with sugar in 1917. The voyage was not without bad weather and trouble, but she weathered the gales and returned to Alaska in the spring. She continued thus for another decade, being laid up in 1927.

With the entry of the United States into the war, the government seized a number of German ships in United States ports in 1914 and turned them over to the Shipping Board to operate. For three years after the war a boom in world-wide shipping continued, but in 1921 the bottom fell out of freight rates and laid up many sailing vessels and steamers. The former German ship *Steinbek,* which had been seized in 1917 in Eagle Harbor, Wash., and put into operation as *Northern Light,* came into New York in the spring of 1921. In the spring of 1922 the Packers bought her, with money they received from the government over the loss of the *Star of Poland* in 1918, and brought her to San Francisco with a load of coal. She was renamed *Star of Falkland* and put into the Alaska business.

Down in New Orleans one of the most famous sailing ships ever to carry the flag to sea was laid up for lack of cargoes. The *Edward Sewall,* a product of the Sewall yard, now owned by the Texas Co., had lain for over a year in the Mississippi River. Captain Halvorson and a Mr. Iversen of the Alaska Packers looked her over and decided she was a good buy. In February, 1922, she left the Crescent City under tow, the tug *Barranca* taking her as far as Colon. She had a general cargo, likely the last one carried intercoastally by a sailing ship. Early in May she arrived in San Francisco. Renamed *Star of Shetland,* she and the *Star of Falkland,* were the last sailing vessels purchased by the APA.

Throughout the summer and fall of 1922 she lay in the Moore shipyard in Oakland being overhauled. Though the Association doubtless felt it could profitably operate sailing ships indefinitely, 1922 was not a year for brash and optimistic speculating. Shipowners in San Francisco were beginning to cast long looks at their inventories, consisting largely of wooden vessels. Robert Dollar had bought a fleet of large steel square-riggers which had laid idle for six years in Santa Rosalia, Mexico, a small mining port in the Gulf of California, and when they were towed to San Francisco they weren't the best looking of ships. Hind Rolph and Co. owned a few square-riggers, but were bringing them home in 1921 for an indefinite lay-up. None of these ships went to sea again.

It seemed to be a poor time to plan continued

Placid scene at historic Roche Harbor on San Juan Island in Washington State. The little port was a factory town founded by John S. McMillan where lime was produced, beginning in the 1880's. Today the preserved town is a popular resort. The photo here was probably taken in the 1930's. At the far right is the old sailing vessel **ROCHE HARBOR LIME TRANSPORT,** purchased by the firm in 1926. She was the former Scotch-built ship **LA ESCOCESA** (Scottish Lady) ex **COALINGA** ex **STAR OF CHILE.** Built at Dundee in 1868, she had a brief stint under sail during World War II under the name **SCOTTISH LADY.** The Hotel De Haro at Roche Harbor, once hosted President Teddy Roosevelt. From Joe Williamson collection.

operation of large sailing vessels, but the Alaska Packers were not primarily in the shipping business. In the early 1920s the Association began laying up the older wooden ships, followed by the smaller and older iron and steel ships. As buyers were found, most of them disappeared on one-way voyages to obscure corners of the Pacific Ocean, or were sold to the movie moguls of Hollywood who needed authentic-looking props which would burn, sink or explode on command. Steamers replaced the ships whose tall masts had towered above the sheds in Alameda, and the 1930 depression added to the pessimism of the shipping world.

We're back again to the *Star of Alaska,* as she leaves the pier in Alameda, the solitary ship chosen from a dwindling fleet of finely-kept but out-of-date vessels to go north for the annual salmon fishing. But she goes in tow of the company steamer *Arctic* and keeps her sails furled. On Sept. 16 she appeared off the Golden Gate, rolling in the swell, a long towline leading ahead to the steamer *Kvichak.* She had not made her own way at all that year, and when her cargo was unloaded she was tied up with her sisters and offered for sale.

That was more than half a century ago. Where did that great fleet of ships go?

Star of Alaska herself is still in the neighborhood, but she has had her appearance changed considerably. *Star of Chile* was sold in 1926 and became a barge named *Roche Harbor Lime Transport,* making a couple of coastwise voyages under tow, full of limerock, before being laid up in Puget Sound. During the Second World War she was rerigged as a four-masted schooner, but she sat on a rock in British Columbia waters and returned to Lake Washington with a lump of cement in her bottom to keep the water out. After eleven years of idleness she was sold,

Chilean bark **BELFAST,** built for Britain's Brocklebank fleet in 1874 is pictured at a ballast dumping ground at a Puget Sound port in the early years of this century. Sold to England's Shaw, Savill Line in 1901, Chilean owners purchased her five years later. For nearly two decades she operated out of lumber ports in the Pacific Northwest to South America and returned to the Pacific Coast with nitrates. Her master was Captain Parajow. In the lower photo, men are in the ship's hold shoveling out ballast to ready the hold for cargo. From Joe D. Williamson collection.

repaired and used as a barge in Canadian waters.

Star of India, that solid old ship with her heavy Swedish iron plates, was sold in 1926 too, and went to San Diego to become a floating Maritime Museum. She is there today, tied up near downtown San Diego. Her rig has been severely cut down and she needs paint, but there's no mistaking this 1863 vessel.

Star of Peru hoisted the tricolor of France in 1926, took a cargo of lumber from Vancouver, B.C., to the South Pacific Islands and was converted to a hulk there.

Star of Italy was cut down in 1927 to be towed away to Buenaventura, Colombia, for use as a barge. This ship that had such a beautiful rake to her masts and sat so gracefully in the water, was one of the last survivors of the fleet, but she became a hulk in some obscure alien port.

Star of Russia was sold and took a load of lumber from Tacoma to Samoa before being hulked in New Caledonia. She was renamed *La Perouse* for that last voyage. For the next three decades she lay not far from her old sister of Alaska days, *Star of Peru.*

Star of France fell into the hands of some people from Southern California who saw in her only the potentialities of a fishing barge. She was sold in 1934, converted to a barge in Alameda, towed to Redondo Beach and anchored a mile or two off-shore. For the next seven years she suffered the torments of neglect, while rubber-legged landlubbers splattered mackerel slime, soda pop and candy wrappers over her decks. Here was a ship which had raced home from India in the 1870s with jute for the British Isles; a relic of the splendid Victorian era when all the grace of wooden clippers had gone into hulls of iron and lost little in the transition. In 1940 she was shifted to the more lucrative fishing grounds off the San Pedro Breakwater. Then one day in September, 1940, a Japanese steamer cut her down in a thick fog and sent her to the bottom.

Star of Greenland, which had showed her skysail yards to dockside watchers along the Melbourne 'front in her youth, was sold to Swedish owners in 1929. They renamed her *Abraham Rydberg* and kept her busy with cargoes of grain, sailing around the world, training boys for the sea. World War II found her in the North Atlantic, near the Faeroes, where she was ordered to the United States. For a year or two she was a visitor to the Atlantic ports and somehow managed to escape the U-boats, but eventually was sold to Portuguese buyers who converted her to a motorship. She struggled on as the *Foz Do Douro,* finally going the way of all outdated machinery, into a scrap pile.

Star of England was sold in 1932. Her new owners dreamed up a pay-as-you-go, round-the-world cruise, but the money was short and the plans went up in smoke. *Star of England* was again sold, and went to Canada for use as a barge.

Star of Shetland, Star of Lapland and *Star of Zealand* were all laid up in the late 1920s, but weren't sold until 1934. These latter day big carriers were still good, and the Association put considerable money into their upkeep even after the *Star of Alaska* came home for the last time in 1930. But it became hard to find men who would go out in the sailing ships.

One by one, the three big Sewall-built four-masted barks were towed away, loaded with salt and scrap steel cargoes, on one-way passages across the Pacific to Japan where they were scrapped. The *Star of Shetland,* hard old battler of the sea, was the last to go in September 1936.

Then only the *Star of Finland* remained. It was hoped that she would be kept as a relic of the days of sail. The Alaska Packers Association was proud of its past, and much attention and nostalgia were lavished on these ships, so it seemed altogether proper to try to keep the *Star of Finland.* But in 1939 she was sold for a good price and only the steamers were left in the Alameda yard.

The Alaska cannery ports spread out on either side of the Aleutian chain and the lower coast of the Bering Sea afforded considerable employment for the last of the Pacific Coast square-riggers which annually transported workers to the locales and returned with full cargoes of canned salmon. The above map shows the major cannery ports teneted by several famous old windships for many years. In addition to the cannery workers and fishermen, the tall ships also transported the gillnet boats to Alaska annually from which the fishermen caught their bounty of fish for the canneries. Courtesy Sparks Journal.

The darkening horizon of World War II proved to be a form of salvation for this last survivor, and in 1941 she was chartered to load lumber for South Africa. She sailed in September from Grays Harbor, reaching Durban in 126 days, and thence plodded on down to Hobart, Tasmania. Troubles plagued the old bark and she was sold to the United States Army, towed to Sydney and slashed down to a hulk. She survived the war in the Southwest Pacific and was finally taken to the Philippine Islands and shoved upon a beach, where she remains.

Where once the port-painted hulls of Limejuicers could be seen in San Francisco Bay's anchorages, only one remains. The *Balclutha* has completed a cycle of history, in a sense, because she presently lies moored to a San Francisco waterfront wharf, not too far from the spot where she rode at anchor as a new ship back in 1887. She is port-painted today as she was then, but the men who built her, and her old owners, are history. Those who sailed her in her British days can hardly be found in the British Isles, and even around San Francisco one has to look a little harder for the generation of seamen who remember her as the *Star of Alaska.* It is fitting that the *Balclutha* has found her last mooring in San Francisco, which has been her home for several decades.

Chapter Ten

Other Well-Known Vessels

An idle vessel is a sea-oriented pauper

St. Frances

The Alaska cannery fleet under sail suffered many tragedies. Among them was the loss of the *St. Frances.* She was owned by Libby, McNeil and Libby. While bound from San Francisco to Koggiung in Bristol Bay she stranded in the darkness, 3 a.m. May 10, 1917. At the time she was working her way through Unimak Pass and was not far from Cape Sarichef when she struck broadside and was buffeted by heavy seas that commenced breaking across her decks, causing near panic.

With 281 persons aboard, mostly cannery workers and fishermen, their plight in that lonely sector of the globe was a gamble with death. Water was soon up to the 'tween decks and all hands were grabbing for anything that was bolted down as one blockbuster after another struck the impaled vessel.

An SOS was picked up by the Pacific American Fisheries steamer *Norwood,* at the time unloading supplies at the Port Moller cannery on the north side of the Aleutian chain. Lines were cast off, and the steamer ran at full speed to the scene of the wreck. On arrival at 9 a.m. the lookouts could easily spot the stricken vessel writhing with all the pain of an inanimate creation. Those aboard were in fear of their very lives. Heavy seas were still running and breaking clear over the decks, most of the crew and cannery hands hanging in the rigging like bugs caught in spider webs. Rescue efforts would be difficult at best.

E.V. Wampler, the radio operator on the *St. Frances* stuck to his water-filled post, his equipment still working. He maintained an open line with Walt Lachelt and Joe Hammill, the operators on the *Norwood.* It was decided that the survivors would try to make it to the inhospitable shore through the surf on the lee side, while the steamer put over her lifeboats in an attempt to gain the beach and pick them up.

By swimming, clinging to floatable material and drifting in lifejackets, the entire company of the *St. Frances* were able to get to the beach, a near miracle in itself, and almost as much of a miracle that the *Norwood's* boats were able to rescue every last man. Ironically, there was no loss of life and no serious injuries.

The steamer was overloaded, and though most could be accommodated it was decided to proceed to Dutch Harbor to put the survivors ashore to await transport to their destination. Except for the hand of fate the *St. Frances* tragedy could have rivaled that of the *Star of Bengal* where 111 souls perished nine years earlier.

Standard

Howard Cookson tells of the wreck of the three-masted barkentine *Standard* also lost on the barren coast of Alaska. She was built in Maine in 1876 as a full-rigged ship, and shortly before her demise had been cut down to a barkentine. Aboard were 200 persons, Cookson a passenger, going to Nushagak, Alaska to operate the cannery station's KMG. One woman, the cannery superintendent's wife was the only woman aboard.

Sailing from San Francisco in the spring, it took 36 days to sail the 2,000 miles to the entrance of the Nushagak River on Bristol Bay. Near their destination in the darkness of night, the vessel piled up on Cape Constantine, (May 1917) its wooden hull pierced by the sharp outcrops. Flares were useless as there was no population for miles in any direction. The situation looked hopeless, but Cookson cleverly put together a sending set with bits and pieces of equipment and wire he found on the vessel. Even as the ship was pounding on the rocks, he put his contrivance to work and rigged an antenna. Amid the confusion, the rudder post came up through the deck and the pumps were choked with debris. After several tries without success, Cookson contacted the operator at Kvichak calling for immediate assistance. Not many hours afterwards, the skipper of the *Standard* ordered abandonment of the wreck, and all hands took to the boats. For nearly four days, the 200 survivors suffered in the open craft rationed to one sardine, some crackers and a swig of whiskey per day. Whiskey and sardines did little to control the misery of the tossing lifeboats, and those who didn't get seasick suffered from stomach aches. All survived however, picked up finally by rescue tugs sent out from Bristol Bay canneries.

City of Sydney

One of the most unusual square-riggers to play a major role in Pacific waters was the six-masted barkentine *City of Sydney.* She was one of only two vessels of her rig to sail the seas, the other being the *E.R. Sterling,* launched as the four-masted bark *Lord Wolseley* in Belfast, Ireland in 1883 and scrapped in an English shipyard in 1928.

The *City of Sydney* was unique inasmuch as she was built as a steamship, not a sailing vessel. Completed in

Stern quarter view of the barkentine **CITY OF SYDNEY**. After serving Pacific Mail Line for many years, the iron-hulled steamer was converted to sail in 1916 by L.A. Pedersen of the Bristol Bay Packing Company. From 1918 till 1924, she served the Alaska salmon trade and was eventually scrapped in California. University of Washington Library photo.

Outbound from the Columbia River, the veteran ship **ST. NICHOLAS,** of the Columbia River Packers Association heads north for Alaska loaded with cannery workers, fishermen and supplies. Having a rather charmed life, the wooden-hulled Bath-built vessel dating from 1869, was burned for scrap near Portland, Oregon in 1927. Courtesy Columbia River Maritime Museum.

1875, the iron-hulled steamer flew the houseflag of the Pacific Mail Line and was placed in the Australian trade. She was purchased in 1916 by L.A. Pedersen of the Bristol Bay Packing Company and converted into a six-masted barkentine. From 1918 to 1924 she was used in the Alaska salmon trade and finally broken up for scrap in a California shipyard in 1930.

During her latter years under sail, the *City of Sydney,* was commanded by a seasoned sailing ship skipper named B.F. Larsen who had spent 50 of his 70 years at sea. He was proud of the fact that the usual practice of converting a sailing vessel to power had been reversed, his tall ship having had all traces of her former steam plant removed. She proved to be a reasonably good sailer. There was, however, a small diesel engine aboard used for assisting in hoisting the sails and for pulling in the anchor.

During her years as a cannery sailing vessel, a crew of about 40 were necessary, and 160 cannery workers and fishermen were quartered in the ship's hold where bunks were five high. Though many of the other cannery square-riggers carried Orientals to man the Bristol Bay canneries for the season, the *Sydney's* owners had contracted for Mexican workers and carried their own Mexican cook. Many of the fishermen were Italians. In rough weather the hatches were

Six-masted barkentine **CITY OF SYDNEY,** one of only two vessels of such a rig to sail the seas. She was originally a steamer built in 1875.

tightly sealed and the air became extremely stagnant. When the seas were calm the hatches were opened to allow clean sea air to filter through.

The wireless operator who sailed on the vessel in 1924 told of a bizarre incident that happened aboard the *City of Sydney*. A man aboard had succumbed to advanced stages of tuberculosis. The sailmaker sewed up the body in a canvas sack, then weighted it with lumps of coal, while most of the ship's crew assembled on deck to wait for the captain to read a few passages from the Bible. When he failed to appear after a long period of time, the mate ordered a couple of seamen to throw the body overboard. Not being sufficiently weighted, it did not sink immediately. Just at that moment the cook and his assistant appeared with a tub of garbage and dishwater, and not knowing what was going on, heaved it over the side. It hit the water over the partially sunken corpse. About that time the captain arrived with his Bible. Finding his services were no longer needed he returned to his cabin, little concerned about the whole affair.

Star of England

One of the well known square-riggers to join the Alaska Packers fleet had a rough beginning. Built in Scotland in 1893, the *Star of England* was christened *Blairmore*. Her sinking in Mission Bay on San Francisco Bay in 1896 is recorded on page 147, when she rolled over and sank trapping seven men in her hull. Raised, rebuilt and renamed *Abby Palmer*, northbound to Puget Sound at a later date she was struck by a gale that tore out her masts and rigging. Refitted again, a year later she was rammed by the steamer *Queen* which nearly severed her bow. She ended her days as a barge.

Norwegian bark **AUSTRALIA** in Pacific Northwest waters. She was built at Bergan, Norway in 1886 and owned by Rasmus F. Olsen. Joe Williamson collection.

Chapter Eleven

The Lord Templetown, Somali and Glenesslin

A tall ship with wings of canvas is a picture to behold

Lord Templetown

An Irish-built sailing vessel that spent most of her years operating out of Pacific Coast ports was the handsome bark *Lord Templetown*. Constructed by Harland & Wolff at their Belfast yard, she measured 283 feet in length and was of 2,152 registered tons. Her maiden voyage was commenced June 12, 1886 under Captain Robert Hawthorne. Initially she was employed carrying bulk cargoes, principally in the California grain trade.

In 1893, the bark suffered an unfortunate accident. Bound from London to Philadelphia with a crew of 34, six passengers and a cargo of chalk, she was buffeted by gale-force winds off the Newfoundland Banks. Sixteen men were aloft goose-winging (minimizing the risk of sail ripping) the lower main topsail when the yard's truss snapped, letting the yard suddenly drop several feet until stopped by its tie, flipping off the third mate, boatswain and seven hands, catapult fashion. They were all drowned. Others plummeted to the deck, one striking his head and perishing immediately while two others suffered serious injuries.

As a pall of doom fell over the vessel, she ran before the wind for two days following the tragedy, it requiring a week to repair the damage. Captain Hawthorne intended to proceed to Philadelphia, but his disconsolate crew refused to continue the voyage, placing the blame for the accident on the shipmaster and mate. The vessel had to return to Queenstown, Ireland.

Following was an official inquiry. Outcome of the hearing was a decision exonerating the master and officers of blame. The bark was said to have been navigated in a proper manner.

In 1898, Eschen and Minor of San Francisco purchased the *Lord Templetown* for 11,000 pounds sterling, and though they managed the vessel placed her register at Victoria, B.C. under the nominal ownership of R.P. Rithet and Company.

Arriving at Portland, Oregon on April 13, 1900, 167 days out of Newcastle-on-Tyne, she was immediately engaged to carry a full cargo of pine and redwood lumber to South Africa during the frantic days of the Boer War. Despite steam competition, the square-rigger was employed in Pacific trades until 1921, carrying many essential cargoes during the

World War I era. Following her final voyage under-sail, bringing in a cargo of nitrates from Iquique, Chile, she was laid up at Oakland, California.

In 1924, the *Templetown* was acquired by Coastwise Steamship and Barge Company and converted into a barge to carry coal and ore cargoes from British Columbia to Puget Sound. In 1935, Island Tug & Barge purchased the aging hull and used her as a British Columbia log carrier. Finally in 1956, the Zidell Company of Portland bought the hull and scrapped her the following year. Some of her original gear was acquired by the San Francisco Maritime Museum where it is displayed today.

Somali

H.N. Vyvyan, was shipmaster of the British Shire liner *Carmarthenshire* in 1895. His story of a rescue at sea of the huge square-rigger *Somali* was told in his own words in *Sea Breezes,* three decades later.

"I left Yokohama for Singapore in May, 1895. A week later, when just south of the Paracels, we encountered an unusually heavy typhoon, which gave me a good deal of anxiety. The weather improving and the glass showing signs of lifting, I turned in, feeling I deserved a good night's rest. Shortly after 10 p.m. I was awakened by a tap at the door and heard the voice of one of the quartermasters saying, 'A vessel, sir, is showing signals of distress about two points on the starboard bow.' A few minutes later I got on to the bridge just in time to see a rocket sent up by the vessel in distress. The night was very dark, with little wind, but an ugly swell, the souvenir of the typhoon, was tumbling about in all directions. I ported two points, and calling all hands, had two boats made ready for action. An hour later we made out that the vessel firing rockets, was a large four-masted barque (bark) with only the jigger mast standing. Passing close under her stern we were informed that she was the *Somali,* of Liverpool, a vessel over 3,000 tons register (at one time the largest sailing ship under the British flag, 3,410 registered tons) and bound for Singapore to Ylo Ylo to load sugar for New York. Lowering two boats, we managed to get two coir hawsers fast on her, and by 1 a.m. had her in tow for Hong Kong. The next day the swell having subsided, I slowed down and sent a boat for the master. He told me that in the height of the typhoon, the bolsters on the foremast had crushed,

She failed to make it around the tip of South America. The British ship **DUCHESS OF ALBANY**, lies a forlorn relic on the beach today at Tierra del Fuego after grounding in the fog while attempting to round Cape Horn in 1893. National Geographic Magazine photo.

slacking up the lower rigging. Almost immediately afterwards the foremast had gone by the board taking with it the main and mizzen masts, leaving the three skysail yard *Somali* absolutely helpless.

"Two days later we arrived in Hong Kong. Some months afterwards the *Somali* having been refitted, was fixed to load at Hong Kong for San Francisco. When she left the former port it was in the height of the N.E. monsoon, which is almost always a gale of wind in the China Sea. Having been built more for weight carrying than for speed she could not weather the Philippines, and in consequence was obliged to up helm and run down for Anjer and make her easting to the southward of Australia. She was 170 days making a passage which has often been done in 45, and arrived at San Francisco a very hungry ship."

The *Somali,* like many of the great windships of yesteryears had her ups and downs throughout her career. Handsome in appearance, she ended her days as a super barge for the Island Tug and Barge Ltd., of Victoria, B.C., under the name *Pacific Carrier,* not exactly an illustrious finale for a fine old square-rigger.

While operating as a codfish brig for J.A. Matheson, the **HARRIET G** was abandoned by her crew after capsizing off Cape Flattery in 1917. Taken in tow by the halibut schooner **SUMNER,** the battered, dismasted hull was towed to Seattle and re-rigged as the three-masted schooner **ESTHER,** sold to Captain J.E. Shields, and placed in the South Seas copra trade. The vessel was built at Norfolk, Virginia in 1878. She ended her days as an Alaska herring fishery.

178

Graceful bark **LYNTON** registered in London, England is pictured at anchor in Port Blakely Harbor at the turn of the century. Built in 1894, the 2,531 ton vessel was owned by R. Mattson. She was later sold to Finnish owners at Mariehamn. One of the downeast "Saint" ships is seen in the background. Webster and Stevens photo.

Glenesslin wreck

Dramatic and bizarre was the wreck of the handsome, iron-hulled British ship *Glenesslin* on the pockmarked outcrops of unrelenting rocks at the base of Mt. Neah-Kah-Nie on October 1, 1913. After all of these years the unusual circumstances and the perennial photos of the tragedy frequently surface. Down through the years many theories as to the reason for the wreck and of the conduct of the captain and crew have been advanced with a modicum of fact and considerable fancy. The most accepted but never proven were barratry and drunkeness, neither of which were borne out by the hearing held at the British Consulate at Portland, Oregon, on October 9-11, 1913. However, due to the mysterious circumstances there has always appeared to be a missing link amidst the facts.

The vessel in question, under a full suit of canvas and pleasant sea and weather conditions, in broad daylight, sailed directly onto the rocks at the base of Neah-Kah-Nie just as if the wreck had been deliberately planned from the outset.

The salient facts as produced at the hearing differed with some of the accounts given by those who were first at the wreck scene and by those who viewed the strange occurrence from a distance.

Following are the findings of the Naval Court held at the British Consolate in Portland. The British sailing ship *Glenesslin* of Liverpool, official number 91227, was wrecked at Neah-kah-nie Mountain about 30 miles south of the Columbia River while voyaging from Santos, Brazil to Portland, Oregon, on October 1, 1913. The inquiry was held to find the cause of the

English three-masted bark **GLADYS** at dockside on the Seattle waterfront. Built at Bristol, England in 1891, she was owned by the Taltal Shipping Company of the same port and did considerable trading in the Pacific.

stranding and of the conduct of the master, certificated first and second mates and crew of said vessel.

"The *Glenesslin* was a steel (according to Lloyd's Register, iron) sailing full-rigged ship of 1,645 tons registered tonnage, built at Liverpool in 1888. It appears from the evidence before the court that she sailed from Santos, Brazil, on the 28th day of May, 1913, bound for Portland, Oregon, with about 850 tons of rubble ballast and a crew of 23 hands, all told. She was drawing 13 feet. The ballast was properly secured. According to the evidence before the Court, about 8 o'clock in the evening of September 30th the light at Tillamook Bay (Cape Meares) was sighted. At 1:30 a.m. the course was changed to west-south-west to get off shore again, which course was maintained until 8:00 a.m. The course was then set to come in shore again. Sights were taken at 8:30 and land was sighted about 11, but it was very hazy, and latitude at noon was 45° 38′ and 124° 26′ west.

"At about 30 minutes to one the master went to the charthouse to lie down, leaving the second mate in charge of the vessel, with instructions to hold the course set and to call the master at 2 p.m. At five minutes before two, the second mate states that he called the master as the vessel was getting close to the shore, and again called him at five minutes after two, and was told by the master to call him again at 2:30.

The second mate then called the first mate, who came on deck, looked at the shore and went back to his room. In two or three minutes the second mate called

Skeletal remains of the British bark **PETER IREDALE,** wrecked October 25, 1906 on Clatsop Beach near Fort Stevens, Oregon. She was engaged in the grain trade for Peter Iredale & Porter of Liverpool. Dennis Mavity photo.

French ship **ALICE** ran hard ashore January 15, 1909 near Ocean Park, Washington and became a total loss. Built at Bordeaux, France in 1901, she was one of a fleet of French "Bounty" vessels which upgraded France's merchant fleet at the turn of the century.

the first mate again, and the first mate then went to the master, who came on deck and ordered the crew to wear ship, but before this could be done she struck and immediately began to fill with water."

The Court, having regard to the circumstances above stated, determined as follows:

That the master, Owen Williams, was negligent in his duty, and the Court orders that his certificate as master be suspended for three months.

That the first mate, L.W. Howarth, is reprimanded for not acting immediately on his being notified of the threatened danger, but was not notified in time to save the ship.

That the second mate was acting under orders, but showed great negligence in running so close to shore without insisting on the master coming on deck, and, also when the master did not answer his second call, negligence in not taking matters into his own hands and ordering the crew to wear ship in the critical position in which he considered the vessel to be, and the Court therefore orders that his certificate as second mate be suspended for the term of six months

The expenses of the Court, fixed at £26 14s 4d., are approved. Dated at Portland, Oregon, this 11th day of October, 1913

Thomas Erskine,

British Consul
President of the Court.

H.C. Davison,
Master of the British Merchant ship *Lord Templetown,* of Victoria B.C.
Official Number 93156

Ernest Dalton, O.C. 024534
Master of the British merchant ship *Border Knight* of Liverpool,
Official Number 110591

(members of the court)

(Issued in London by the Board of Trade on the 18th day of November 1913)

———

No mention was made in the Court's findings that a lifeline was shot across to the rocks, after the stranding, and all hands safely reached shore. The vessel was impaled on the jagged rocks, and began breaking up almost immediately after the stranding.

With a storm warning out, there was little hope of salvage and with rising surf the *Glenesslin* broke up within a few days.

Rumors that the *Glenesslin* was deliberately wrecked to collect insurance at a time when steamers were becoming predominant in overseas trades, or that the shipmaster was inebriated ran their course. However, such allegations appeared to have little substance despite the fact that some of those at the wreck scene claimed that some of the survivors appeared under the influence of alcohol. The fact that Lloyd's of London paid the insurance on the wrecked ship was evidence they did not consider the ship was deliberately wrecked. Neither did they challenge the shipmaster's previously unblemished 26 years of seafaring. It was evident the vessel did carry relatively inexperienced mates; that the vessel was caught in a windless pocket and that Captain Williams had spent many hours trying to get proper sextant readings in dense offshore haze the two previous nights before the wreck occurred.

The fact that second mate Colefield did not insist much earlier that the captain get up on deck to take charge, undoubtedly was largely responsible for the wreck.

Hardly a position for a lady of the sea—the Britisher **KILBRANNAN** hard aground near Point Wilson, Port Townsend, Washington in the early months of 1896. A major salvage job eventually refloated the vessel after which she was sold and renamed **MARION CHILCOTT**.

APPENDIX A

COMMERCIAL SAILING VESSELS, BUILT ELSEWHERE, BUT OWNED ON THE PACIFIC COAST—1900-1969

(OVER 100 TONS)

(For list of West Coast-built windjammers see book: *Windjammers of the Pacific Rim,* Schiffer Publishing Ltd. 1986)
Based on the research of the late Dr. John Lyman
(Key to Abbreviations)

(W)	. . .	wood construction	(5m)	. . .	five-masted	(Schr.)	. . .	schooner-rigged
(S)	. . .	steel construction	(6m)	. . .	six-masted	(Bktn.)	. . .	barkentine-rigged
(I)	. . .	iron-construction	(Ship)	. . .	full-rigged	(Brig)	. . .	brig-rigged
(4m)	. . .	four-masted	(Bark)	. . .	bark-rigged	(Bgtn.)	. . .	brigantine-rigged

(Ship-Bark), or similar designation implies vessel has had various rigs.

NOTE: Only the final fate of each vessel is listed. Many had various serious mishaps other than their final disposition, but lack of space precludes mention of same. A large share of these vessels were lastly used as barges having been crowded off the high seas in their latter years by steamers.

Name	Rig	Tonnage	Built	Place	Final Fate
A. J. Fuller	Ship (W)	1,848	1881	Bath, Me.	Sunk collision, Seattle Harbor 1918
Abbie M. Deering	Schr. (W)	101	1883	Kennebunk, Me.	Wrecked Akutan Pass, Alaska 1903
Abbey Palmer (see Star of England)					
Abner Coburn	Ship (W)	1,972	1882	Bath, Me.	Scrapped, Puget Sound 1929
Academy (ex Earnest)	Schr. (W)	114	1875	Baltimore, Md.	Laid up, Martinez, Calif., broken up about 1920
Agate	Bark (W)	626	1868	Newburyport, Mass.	Scrapped about 1910
Agenor	Ship (W)	1,487	1870	E. Boston, Mass.	Scuttled in Pacific 1905 (baratry proven)
Alaska	Bark (W)	340	1867	Mattapoisett, Mass.	Wrecked in Bering Sea 1900
Alden Besse	Bark (W)	842	1871	Bath, Me.	Registry dropped 1920, Los Angeles
Alexander (ex Astoria) (whaler)	Aux. steam bark	294	1855	New York	Wrecked 1906 Cape Parry, Alaska
Alex. Gibson	Ship (W)	2,194	1877	Thomaston, Me.	Wrecked New Jersey Coast 1915
Alexander McNeil	Ship (W)	1,122	1869	Waldoboro, Me.	Wrecked Pratas Shoal, Manila for P.S. 1902
Alice McDonald	Schr. (W)	656	1888	Bath, Me.	Went to pieces at Oakland boneyard 1918
Alta	Bktn. (S) (4m)	1,385	1900	Pt. Glasgow, Scotland	Vanished, San Pedro for Bellingham 1923
America	Ship (W)	2,054	1874	Quincy, Mass.	Wrecked False Bay, San Juan Is., W. 1914
Americana	Schr. (S)	900	1892	Grangemouth, Scotland	Vanished, Astoria for Sydney 1913
Amy Turner	Bark-Bktn. (W)	991	1877	E. Boston, Mass.	Foundered, Newcastle to Manila 1923
Andrew Hicks (whaler)	Bark (W)	303	1867	Fairhaven, Mass.	Foundered, Cape Henry, Va. 1917
Andrew Welch	Bark (I)	903	1888	Pt. Glasgow, Scotland	Afloat Norway 1940's, as MS Canis
Andromeda (ex Kenyon)	Bktn. (I)	1,243	1862	Liverpool, England	Afloat at S.F. 1939, as barge King No. 1
Annie Johnson (ex Ada Iredale)	Ship (I)	1,049	1872	Harrington, England	Foundered, Vancouver, B.C. to Suva 1929, as Bretagne
Annie M. Reid (ex Howard D. Troop)	Bark (S) (4m)	2,165	1892	Glasgow, Scotland	Broken up, Alameda, Calif. 1935
Antiope	Ship (I)	1,496	1866	Pt. Glasgow, Scotland	Storeship at Beira, Africa 1940's
Archer	Bk.-Bktn. (I)	900	1876	Sunderland, England	Wrecked in Philippines 1936 as MS Marie
Aryan	Ship (W)	2,123	1893	Phippsburg, Me.	Burned, N.Z. to San Francisco 1918
B. P. Cheney	Ship-Bark (W)	1,322	1874	Bath, Me.	Registry abandoned 1929 at Antioch, Calif.
Balclutha (See Star of Alaska)					
Baroda	Bark (S)	1,417	1891	Dumbarton, Scotland	Barge in B.C., 1940's
Battle Abbey (ex Royden)	Ship (I)	1,559	1875	Liverpool, England	Burned, Newcastle, NSW to Vancouver, 1913
Bear (sealer) (USCG Cutter)	Steam Bark (W)	703	1874	Greenock, Scotland	Foundered in North Atlantic 1967
Belfast	Ship-Bark	1,957	1874	Belfast, Ireland	Broken up 1924, San Francisco
Beluga (ex Mary & Helen) (whaler)	Aux. steam bark	508	1882	Bath, Me.	Sunk by German raider off Fanning Is. 1917
Belvedere	Steam whaling bark (W)	440	1880	Bath, Me.	Crushed in ice Cape Serdze, Siberia 1919
Benj. F. Packard	Ship (W)	2,156	1883	Bath, Me.	Purposely scuttled off New York 1939
Berlin	Ship (W)	1,634	1882	Phippsburg, Me.	Wrecked at Chignik, Alaska 1922
Big Bonanza	Ship-Bark (W)	1,472	1875	Newburyport, Mass.	Laid up San Francisco 1920, rotted away
Bohemia	Ship (W)	1,633	1875	Bath, Me.	Purposely blown up for movie 1931 at San Diego
Bowhead (ex Haardraade) (whaler)	Steam whaling bark (W)	381	1871	Christiania, Norway	Purposely beached and burned by movie firm after 1912
Boxer (government vessel)	Aux. Brigantine	346	1905	Portsmouth, N. H.	Sold out of service 1940's (Dept. of Interior) (as motorship)

Barge **FRESNO,** in tow of the tug **GOLIAH** on Puget Sound in the 1920's. She was built as a bark at Bath, Maine, in 1874 and was burned on the shores of Seattle's Lake Washington April 4, 1923.

Built for Flint & Co. by John McDonald at Bath in 1888 was the schooner **ALICE McDONALD.** She is seen aground here near Point Loma, California, in 1910, but was later salvaged and returned to service.

WILLIAM H. SMITH, serving as a fish barge, is seen here after being driven aground off Monterey, Calif., April 14, 1933. The vessel was built as a full-rigged ship at Bath in 1883, and later cut down to a five-masted schooner.

184

Name	Rig	Tonnage	Built	Place	Final Fate
British Yoeman	Bark (I)	1,953	1880	Southampton, England	Sunk in South Atlantic 1917 by von Luckner's Seeadler
Brodick Castle	Ship (I)	1,820	1875	Glasgow, Scotland	Vanished, Portland, Oregon for England, 1908
C. D. Bryant	Bark (W)	929	1878	Searsport, Me.	Last reported laid up, Port of Spain 1922
C. F. Sargent	Ship (W)	1,704	1874	Yarmouth, Me.	Became Navy barge, 1918
Callao	Bark (SI)	1,014	1885	Belfast, Ireland	Burned off Chilean coast 1925
Carondelet	Ship (W)	1,438	1872	Newcastle, Me.	Foundered off Prince Rupert, B.C. 1911
Carollton	Ship (W)	1,450	1872	Bath, Me.	Wrecked Midway Is., Honolulu to Newcastle, NSW, 1906
Centennial	Ship (W)	1,286	1875	E. Boston, Mass.	Burned for movie, at Long Beach, 1930
Ceylon	Bark (W)	1,438	1856	Boston, Mass.	Wrecked on Laysan Island 1902
Charger	Ship (W)	1,376	1874	E. Boston, Mass.	Foundered off Prince of Wales Island, Alaska 1909
Charles Levi Woodbury	Schr. (W)	105	1889	Essex, Mass.	Foundered off Pt. Arena, Calif. as Mexican schooner Alliance 2 in 1915
Charles B. Kenney	Bark (W)	1,128	1878	Bath, Me.	Laid up Antioch, Calif. 1919, rotted away
Charles E. Moody	Ship (W)	2 003	1882	Bath. Me.	Burned at Naknek, Alaska 1920
Charmer	Ship-Bark (W)	1,885	1881	Bath, Me.	Wrecked, Chesapeake Bay 1912
Chillicothe (ex Flotow)	Ship (S)	1,862	1892	Glasgow, Scotland	Hulked at New Caledonia 1928
Chin Pu (ex Amstel)	Bark (IW)	1,594	1874	Amsterdam, Holland	Wrecked in typhoon 1919, broken up at Shanghai
City of Sydney (ex steamer)	Bktn. (I) (6m)	2,903	1875	Chester, Pa.	Burned out for scrap at S.F. 1930
Clarence S. Bement	Ship (I)	1,998	1884	Philadelphia, Pa.	Burned, Newport News for S.F. 1904
Coloma	Bark (W)	852	1869	Warren, R. I.	Wrecked off Cape Beale, B.C. 1906
Colorado	Bark (W)	1,075	1864	Medford, Mass.	Wrecked Wrangell Narrows, Alaska 1900
Columbia	Ship (W)	1,475	1871	Bath, Me.	Wrecked at Unimak Pass, Alaska 1909
Coronado (ex Waikato) (J. C. Pfluger)	Ship-Bktn. (I)	1,189	1874	Sunderland, England	Foundered, Gulf of Georgia, B.C. 1913
Coryphene	Bark (W)	811	1878	Millbridge, Me.	Wrecked Prince Wales Is., Alaska 1905
Crowley (ex SS City of Panama)	Bktn. (I)	1,364	1873	Chester, Pa.	Sold to Brazil 1920
Dashing Wave	Ship (W)	1,054	1853	Portsmouth, N.H.	Wrecked Shelter Pt., Vancouver Island, B.C. 1920
David Dollar (ex Prince Robert)	Bark (S) (4m)	2,832	1893	Liverpool, England	Scuttled as breakwater, Alameda, Calif. 1930
Daylight	Bark (S) (4m)	3,756	1902	Pt. Glasgow, Scotland	Converted to "leg of mutton" auxiliary in Vancouver, B.C. 1941, sold in So. America
Diamond Head (ex Gainsborough)	Ship-Bark	1,012	1866	London, England	Burned for scrap, Everett-Seattle 1950
Dirigo	Bark (S) (4m)	3,004	1894	Bath, Me.	Torpedoed S.W. of Eddystone Light 1917
Drumburton	Ship (I) (4m)	1,891	1881	Glasgow, Scotland	Wrecked below Cliff House, S.F., 1904
Drumcraig	Bark (I) (4m)	1,979	1885	Barrow, England	Vanished, Astoria for Manila 1906
Drummuir	Bark (I) (4m)	1,844	1882	Liverpool, England	Sunk by German Navy off Cape Horn 1914
Drumrock	Bark (S) (4m)	3,100	1891	Leith, Scotland	Wrecked Tukush Bay 1927
Dunsyre	Ship (S)	2,149	1891	Pt. Glasgow, Scotland	Wrecked near Vancouver Island 1936
Everett G. Griggs (see E. R. Sterling)					
E. R. Sterling (ex Lord Wolseley ex Columbia, ex Everett Griggs)	Ship (I) (4m) Bktn. (6m)	2,577	1883	Belfast, Ireland	Dismasted, So. Atlantic 1927, scrapped England 1928
Eclipse	Schr. (W)	233	1852	Greenpoint, N.Y.	Wrecked Cape Romanzoff, Alaska, 1900
Eclipse	Ship (W)	1,594	1878	Bath, Me.	Abandoned, Newcastle to S.F. 1906
Edward May	Bark (W)	928	1874	Boston, Mass.	Register abandoned, Antioch, Calif. 1934
Edward Sewall (see Star of Shetland)					
Electra	Bark (W)	985	1868	Boston, Mass.	Sold as barge 1909, S.F.
Elwell	Ship (W)	1,461	1875	Damariscotta, Me.	Burned for scrap, Puget Sound 1932
Emily Reed	Ship (W)	1,564	1880	Waldoboro, Me.	Wrecked near Nehalem River entrance, Ore. 1908
Emily F. Whitney	Ship (W)	1,317	1880	E. Boston, Mass.	Burned on purpose, S.F. 1940
Emma F. Harriman	Bark (W)	385	1862	Searsport, Me.	Registry dropped, S.F. 1901
Empire	Ship (W)	1,131	1870	Kennebunkport, Me.	Destroyed by fire, S.F. 1901
Enoch Talbot	Ship-Bark (W)	1,242	1857	Freeport, Me.	Abandoned 1924 as Navy Coal Barge II
Evie J. Ray	Bark (W)	956	1878	Harrington, Me.	Registry dropped at Portland, Ore. 1906
Erskine M. Phelps	Bark (S) (4m)	2,998	1896	Bath, Me.	Oil barge L.A. Harbor 1940's
Falls of Clyde	Ship-Bark (I) (4m)	1,809	1878	Port Glasgow, Scotland	Afloat at Honolulu (1969), now a museum attraction at Honolulu
Fearless (ex Elida)	Steam whaling bark (W)	220	1883	Sandefjord, Norway	Lost in Arctic ice 1901
Ferris S. Thompson	Bark (W)	531	1874	Setauket, N.Y.	Dropped from registry S.F. 1917
Florence	Ship (W)	1,684	1877	Bath, Me.	Vanished, Tacoma for Honolulu 1902
Fort George	Bark (I) (4m)	1,769	1884	Belfast, Ireland	Vanished, N.Y. for Honolulu 1908
Frank W. Howe	Schr. (W)	573	1891	Boston, Mass.	Wrecked near Seaview, Wash. 1904
Fremont (ex steamer)	Bktn. (W)	345	1850	Philadelphia, Pa.	Registry abandoned N.Y. 1921
Fresno	Bark (W)	1,244	1874	Bath, Me.	Burned on Lake Washington 1923
Gatherer	Ship-Bark (W)	1,874	1874	Bath, Me.	Foundered off Virginia Coast 1909
Gay Head	Steam whaling bark (W)	265	1877	Mattapoisett, Mass.	Wrecked Chignik, Alaska 1914

JABEZ HOWES, driven ashore in a gale at Chignik, Alaska, in April, 1911. Fortunately the 114 crew and cannery workers aboard were rescued. The venerable old wooden ship, built at Newbury-port, in 1877, was a total loss.

Standing out to sea, the huge 3,756 ton British bark **DAYLIGHT.** She and her sistership, the **BRILLIANT,** were the largest four-masted sailing vessels ever built. They were built at Port Glasgow by Russell & Co. for the Anglo-American Oil Co., a branch of Standard Oil, to carry case oil.

Freak ship—the only one of her kind—four-masted vessel **OLYMPIC** was square-rigged on the two forward masts and schooner rigged on the other two. The vessel ended her days as a fishing barge off Los Angeles in the 1940's. She was built by the New England Shipbuilding Co. at Bath in 1892. *H. H. Morrison photo.*

One of the few foreign-built sailing ships to come to the West Coast with a fore 'n aft rig was the schooner **HONOLULU,** constructed of steel at Port Glasgow, Scotland, in 1896 by R. Duncan. Coming under U.S. registry in 1900, the schooner departed Shanghai for Port Townsend March 26, 1905, and went missing with all hands. She was purposely built for operation in the Pacific and was under Hawaiian registry until 1900. The vessel is seen here flying the Hawaiian flag.

Name	Rig	Tonnage	Built	Place	Final Fate
General Fairchild	Bark (W)	1,427	1874	Freeport, Me.	Last owned at Seattle 1920
George Curtis	Ship-Bark (W)	1,837	1884	Waldoboro, Me.	Registered abandoned Seattle 1928. Burned
George Skolfield	Ship (W)	1,313	1870	Brunswick, Me.	A hulk at Nagasaki after stranding 1900-01
Gerard C. Tobey	Bark (W)	1,459	1878	Bath, Me.	Wrecked Seymour Narrows, B.C. 1914
Germania	Ship-Bark (W)	995	1850	Portsmouth, N.H.	Broken up in 1900
Glory of the Seas	Ship (W)	2,102	1869	E. Boston, Mass.	Burned for metal Endolyne (Seattle) 1923 (fish barge)
Golden Gate (ex Lord Shaftesbury)	Ship-Bark (S) (4m)	2,332	1888	Whitehaven, England	Broken up at Alameda 1935
Governor Robie	Ship (W)	1,712	1883	Bath, Me.	Foundered off Highland Light, N.J. 1921
Gratia	Bark (S)	1,582	1891	Pt. Glasgow, Scotland	Grounded near Redondo Beach, Calif. 1932
Great Admiral	Ship (W)	1,596	1869	E. Boston, Mass.	Foundered off Washington Coast, Pt. Townsend to San Pedro 1907
Guy C. Goss	Bark (W)	1,572	1879	Bath, Me.	Broken up in Australia about 1927
Harriet G.	Brig-Schr. (W)	252	1878	Norfolk, Va.	Abandoned, Uyak, Alaska 1932 (floating cannery)
Harry Morse	Ship (W)	1,356	1871	Bath, Me.	Sunk in collision near Texas Coast 1916
Harvard (ex Sam Skolfield II)	Ship-Bark (W)	1,603	1883	Brunswick, Me.	Foundered, So. Pacific 1919
Harvester	Bark (W)	754	1871	Newburyport, Mass.	Vanished on leaving Tonga Islands 1920
Hawaii (later Ethel Sterling)	Bktn. (S) (4m)	1,095	1900	Dumbarton, Scotland	Mexican flag MS Hidalgo in 1940's
Haydn Brown	Bark (W)	864	1876	Newburyport, Mass.	Wrecked, Montague Is., Alaska 1911
Hecla	Ship-Bark (W)	1,529	1877	Bath, Me.	Broken up at Antioch, Calif. 1928
Henriette	Bark-Schr. (I) (4m)	735	1874	La Seyne, France	Wrecked Nukulaila, Ellice Islands, 1922
Henry Failing	Ship (W)	1,976	1882	Bath, Me.	Foundered, Block Is., N.Y. 1918
Henry Villard	Ship (W)	1,552	1882	Bath, Me.	Burned for metal, near Seattle 1929
Henry B. Hyde	Ship (W)	2,583	1884	Bath, Me.	Wrecked south of Cape Henry, Va. 1904
Herman	Steam whaling bktn. (W)	471	1884	Bath, Me.	Sold Mexican 1923 as MS Chapultepec
Highland Light	Ship-Bark (W)	1,314	1874	Bath, Me.	Foundered off Vancouver Is., Tacoma for Honolulu 1901
Honolulu	Schr. (S) (4m)	982	1896	Pt. Glasgow, Scotland	Vanished, Shanghai for Port Townsend in 1905
Hunter (whaler)	Bark (W)	355	1851	Bath, Me.	Wrecked in Bering Sea 1900
Indiana	Ship (W)	1,478	1876	Bath, Me.	Grounded at Long Beach, Calif. 1936, purposely burned on Harbor Day
Invincible	Ship-Schr. (W) (4m)	1,460	1873	Bath, Me.	Burned for metal, S.F. Bay 1927
Isaac Reed	Ship (W)	1,541	1875	Waldoboro, Me.	Foundered off Bodega Bay, Calif. 1924
J. B. Brown	Ship (W)	1,550	1874	Kennebunkport, Me.	Broken up at S.F. in 1904
J. D. Peters	Bark (W)	1,085	1875	Bath, Me.	Destroyed by fire at Crescent Beach, Wash. as oil barge 1930
Jabez Howes	Ship (W)	1,648	1877	Newburyport, Mass.	Wrecked Chignik, Alaska 1914
James Dollar (ex Comet)	Bark (S) (4m)	3,017	1901	Pt. Glasgow, Scotland	Canadian hog fuel barge, Forester 1950
James Drummond	Ship (W)	1,556	1880	Phippsburg, Me.	Wrecked Seaforth Channel, B.C. 1914
James Nesmith	Ship-Bark (W)	1,735	1877	Bath, Me.	Registry dropped S.F. 1915
James Rolph (ex Celtic Monarch)	Ship (S)	2,108	1884	Liverpool, England	Broken up at Bay Point, Calif. 1935
Janet Dollar (ex Eclipse)	Bark (S) (4m)	3,091	1902	Pt. Glasgow, Scotland	Hulk on Yangtze River 1927, in Japanese hands 1938
Jeanie	Aux. Steam Schr. (W)	1,071	1883	Bath, Me.	Registry dropped at Tacoma 1913
John Currier	Ship (W)	1,945	1882	Newburyport, Mass.	Wrecked Nelson Lagoon, Alaska 1907
John Ena	Bark (S) (4m)	2,842	1892	Pt. Glasgow, Scotland	Broken up at Los Angeles 1934
John McDonald	Ship (W)	2,281	1883	Bath, Me.	Caught fire, foundered in North Pacific 1901
John A. Briggs	Ship (W)	2,110	1878	Freeport, Me.	Foundered off Barnagat, N.J. 1909
John C. Potter	Ship (W)	1,244	1869	Searsport, Me.	Beached and broken up on Cunningham Is., B.C. as barge, 1929
John & Winthrop (ex whaler)	Bark-Schr. (W)	338	1876	Bath, Me.	Hulk at Launceston, Tasmania about 1925
Joseph Dollar (ex Schurbek)	Bark (S) (4m)	2,409	1902	Pt. Glasgow, Scotland	Hulked in China 1929
Joseph B. Thomas	Ship (W)	1,938	1881	Thomaston, Me.	Foundered off Cape Cod 1913
Julia E. Whalem	Schr. (W)	101	1884	Essex, Mass.	Out of registry at S.F. 1900
Kailulani (see Star of Finland)					
Kate Davenport	Ship-Bark	1,248	1866	Bath, Me.	Hulk, out of registry 1916
Katherine (ex County of Linlithgow)	Ship (I) (4m)	2,205	1887	Glasgow, Scotland	Greek MS Frieda (5m) (aux. tanker) afloat 1940's, later scrapped
Kennebec	Ship (W)	2,126	1883	Bath, Me.	Foundered off Sandy Hook 1917
Lasbek (ex Ben Dearg)	Ship (S)	2,335	1894	Glasgow, Scotland	Broken up S.F. Bay 1930
Letitia	Schr. (W)	245	1867	Salem, Mass.	Sank in So. San Francisco in gale about 1915
Levi G. Burgess	Ship-Bark (W)	1,616	1877	Thomaston, Me.	Burned for scrap near Portland, Oregon 1928
Lizzie Colby	Schr. (W)	150	1882	Essex, Mass.	Wrecked Anadir Bay, Siberia 1907
Llewellyn J. Morse	Ship (W)	1,392	1877	Brewer, Me.	After movie role, burned in Catalina Harbor 1926
Lord Templetown	Bark (S)	2,152	1886	Belfast, Ireland	Canadian hog fuel barge 1950's

Bark **STAR OF FINLAND** serving the Alaska Packers was the largest vessel of her rig (1,699 tons) ever built in the United States. She was launched as the **KAIULANI** by A. Sewall & Co. at Bath in 1899 for H. Hackfield & Co. of Honolulu and managed by Williams, Dimond. She became the Star of Finland in 1910. At this writing, the vessel last having served as a barge in the Philippines was given back to the U.S. to be restored as a museum ship at Washington, D.C. She is still idle at Subic Bay (1987) but has her original name Kaiulani. The vessel appeared in the movie Souls At Sea in 1936-37.

Grace personified—all sails set—British bark **LYNTON,** in 1913. *Photo by G.E. Plummer.*

Name	Rig	Tonnage	Built	Place	Final Fate
Louis Walsh	Ship (W)	1,556	1861	Belfast, Me.	Wrecked Dutch Harbor, Alaska 1902
Louise J. Kenney	Schr. (W)	163	1889	Essex, Mass.	Sold to Australian owners about 1905
Louisiana	Ship-Bark (W)	1,436	1873	Bath, Me.	Sold to B.C. owner as barge 1920
Lucille	Ship (W)	1,402	1874	Freeport, Me.	Wrecked Ugashik, Alaska 1908
Lydia (ex whaler)	Bark (W)	329	1840	Rochester, Mass.	Registry dropped S.F. 1901
M. P. Grace	Ship (W)	1,928	1875	Bath, Me.	Stranded Shinnecock, N.Y. 1906
Mae Dollar (ex Somali, ex Alsterdamm, ex Adolf Vinnen)	Bark (S) (4m)	3,410	1892	Pt. Glasgow, Scotland	Canadian barge Pacific Carrier, still afloat 1950
Manga Reva (ex Pyrenees)	Bark (S) (4m)	2,214	1891	Glasgow, Scotland	Vanished, London to Hampton Roads 1917
Marion Chilcott (ex Kilbrannan)	Ship (I)	1,738	1882	Pt. Glasgow, Scotland	Broken up, Trinidad in 1930's
Martha Davis	Bark (W)	870	1873	E. Boston, Mass.	Destroyed by fire at Hilo, T.H. 1905
Mary Ann (ex steamer)	Schr. (W)	102	1852	Philadelphia, Pa.	Wrecked Unga, Alaska 1905
Mary Dollar (ex Hans)	Bark (S) (4m)	3,102	1904	Pt. Glasgow, Scotland	Became 6 mast schooner Tango in 1942; afloat 1950 as Portuguese MS Ciudad de Oporto
Mary L. Cushing	Ship-Bark (W)	1,658	1883	Newburyport, Mass.	Wrecked at Mazatlan, Mexico 1906
Mauna Ala (ex Pak Wan)	Composite Bark	820	1863	Sunderland, England	Wrecked on bar, Topolobampo, Mexico 1903
May Flint (ex SS Persian Monarch)	Bark (S) (4m)	3,576	1880	Dumbarton, Scotland	Sank after collision in S.F. Harbor 1900; remains blown up
McLaurin	Ship (W)	1,374	1878	Newburyport, Mass.	Burned for metal S.F. Bay 1927
Melanope	Ship (I)	1,686	1876	Liverpool, England	Became breakwater at Royston, B.C. about 1947
Mercury	Ship (W)	1,156	1851	New York, N.Y.	Wrecked near Skagway, Alaska 1898
Merom	Ship (W)	1,204	1870	Phippsburg, Me.	Wrecked at Kodiak, Alaska 1900
Mildred E	Schr. (W)	118	1884	Meteghan, N.S.	Out of registry, Seattle 1901
Mohican	Bark (W)	852	1875	Chelsea, Mass.	Burned at San Diego, Calif. 1926
Monongahela (ex Balasore, ex Dalbek, ex Red Jacket)	Bark (S) (4m)	2,782	1892	Glasgow, Scotland	Became Canadian log barge 1936; afloat several years thereafter
Monterey (ex Cypromene)	Ship-Bktn. (I) (4m)	1,854	1878	Southampton, England	Broken up at Los Angeles 1935
Moshula (ex Kurt, ex Dreadnaught)	Bark (S) (4m)	3,116	1904	Pt. Glasgow, Scotland	Hull still afloat at Stockholm, Sweden 1969
Muscoota (ex Buckingham, ex Bertha, ex Ottawa, ex Flying Cloud)	Bark (S) (4m)	2,660	1888	Liverpool, England	Became hulk at Sydney, N.S.W. 1921
Nellie Coleman	Schr. (W)	160	1883	Lamoine, Me.	Vanished, Squaw Harbor, Alaska for Seattle 1905
Nicolas Thayer	Bark (W)	584	1868	Thomaston, Me.	Vanished, Seattle for Seward 1906
Northern Light	Bark (W)	384	1851	Rochester, Mass.	Lost on voyage, Puget Sound to Hawaii 1900
Nuuanu (ex Highland Glen)	Bark (I)	1,028	1882	Leith, Scotland	Last owned in Philippines as auxiliary schooner San Bernardino in 1930's
Oakland	Bark (W)	534	1865	Bath, Me.	Wrecked near Port Clarence, Alaska 1901
Occidental	Ship (W)	1,533	1874	Bath, Me.	Laid up New York 1930; rotted away
Olympic	*Vessel (W) (4m)	1,469	1892	Bath, Me.	Afloat as fish barge at Los Angeles 1940's
Oregon	Ship-Bark (W)	1,430	1875	Bath, Me.	Wrecked at Nome, Alaska about 1905
Orient	Brig-Schr. (W)	312	1865	Brunswick, Me.	Registry dropped, San Francisco 1912
Oriental	Ship (W)	1,688	1874	Bath, Me.	Abandoned at Seattle 1930; later burned
P. N. Blanchard	Ship (W)	1,582	1876	Yarmouth, Me.	Destroyed by fire near Cape Horn, Baltimore for S.F. 1900
Pactolus	Bark (W)	1,673	1891	Bath, Me.	Broken up, S.F. Bay 1937
Palmyra	Ship (W)	1,359	1876	Bath, Me.	Burned by movie interests at Catalina Is. 1929
Paramita	Ship (W)	1,582	1879	Freeport, Me.	Wrecked Unimak Pass, Alaska 1914
Phyllis (ex Australia, ex Elisa Lihn)	Bark (S) (4m)	2,258	1886	Pt. Glasgow, Scotland	Broken up for scrap 1925
Poltalloch	Bark (S) (4m)	2,253	1893	Belfast, Ireland	Wrecked on British Coast 1916
Prins Valdemar	Bark-Bktn. (S) (4m)	1,361	1892	Elsinore, Denmark	Sank at Miami in 1926; raised, afloat in 1930's
Prussia	Ship-Bark (W)	1,212	1868	Bath, Me.	Wrecked off Staten Is., Tierra del Fuego 1907
Quatsino (ex British Merchant, ex Arther Fitger)	Ship (I)	1,700	1880	Belfast, Ireland	Wrecked in Dixon Entrance, Nanaimo, B.C. for Cordova 1909
R. D. Rice	Ship (W)	2,263	1883	Thomaston, Me.	Destroyed by fire at Hiogo, Japan 1901
R. P. Rithet	Bark (I)	1,097	1892	Glasgow, Scotland	Destroyed by fire in Pacific, Honolulu for S.F. 1917
Reaper	Ship-Bark (W)	1,468	1876	Bath, Me.	Destroyed by fire at Port Ludlow, Wash. 1906
Reinbek (ex Windermere, ex Lord Rosebery)	Bark (S) (4m)	2,765	1889	Whitehaven, England	Broken up about 1930
Reuce	Ship (W)	1,924	1881	Kennebunk, Me.	Wrecked 114 days out of Omaesaki, Japan 1924
Richard III	Ship (W)	985	1859	Portsmouth, N.H.	Wrecked Clarence Straits, B.C. 1907

* Carried two square-rigged masts and two fore n' aft masts.

The **SNOW & BURGESS,** built as a full-rigged ship at Thomaston, Maine, in 1878 by Thomas Watts, this vessel was converted to a five-masted schooner on the West Coast in 1904. She also served as a bark after being sold to A. P. Lorentzen at San Francisco in 1890. This vessel was burned for junk in 1922, after arriving at Port Townsend from Manila with a broken back, a year earlier. *O. Beaton photo, 1912.*

Ship **STAR OF ALASKA** sailing for the Alaska Packers Association out of San Francisco. *Courtesy San Francisco Maritime Museum.*

Name	Rig	Tonnage	Built	Place	Final Fate
Riversdale (ex Harvesthude)	Ship (S)	2,181	1894	Pt. Glasgow, Scotland	Became B.C. barge; afloat till 1950's; scrapped
Robert Kerr	Bark (W)	1,123	1866	Quebec City, Canada	Wrecked Danger Reef, Thetis Is., B.C. 1911
Roderick Dhu	Bark (I)	1,534	1873	Sunderland, England	Wrecked Pt. Pinos, Monterey Bay, Calif. 1909
Rufus E. Wood	Ship-Bark (W)	1,477	1875	Deering, Me.	Dropped from registry 1927
Ruth (ex Sharpshooter, ex Madeleine)	Bark-Bktn. (I)	488	1860	Sunderland, England	Beached after collision, Oakland mudflats 1923
S. C. Allen	Bark (W)	690	1888	Bath, Me.	Wrecked off Diamond Head, Hawaii 1913
S. D. Carleton	Ship (W)	1,882	1890	Rockport, Me.	Out of registry, New York 1914
St. David	Ship (W)	1,595	1877	Bath, Me.	Wrecked Yakutat, Alaska 1917
St. Frances	Ship (W)	1,898	1882	Bath, Me.	Wrecked Unimak Pass, Alaska 1917
St. James	Bark-Bktn. (W)	1,578	1883	Bath, Me.	Hit reef at Oeno, Tuamotos 1918
St. Katherine	Bark (W)	1,201	1890	Bath, Me.	Broken up, S.F. Bay 1927
St. Nicholas	Ship (W)	1,798	1869	Bath, Me.	Burned for scrap near Portland, Oregon 1927
St. Paul	Ship (W)	1,893	1874	Bath, Me.	Became part of breakwater Oyster Bay, B.C. 1942
Santa Clara	Ship (W)	1,535	1876	Bath, Me.	Let sink in L.A. Harbor 1939
Santiago	Bark (S)	979	1885	Belfast, Ireland	Scrapped as oil barge 1940's
Sea King	Ship (W)	1,491	1877	Bowdoinham, Me.	Burned for her metal, Scotland, Va. 1924
Sea Witch	Ship (W)	1,289	1872	E. Boston, Mass.	Foundered off Cape Flattery, Wash. 1906
Seminole	Ship (W)	1,442	1865	Mystic, Conn.	Hulk at Adelaide, Australia about 1901
Servia	Ship (W)	1,866	1883	Bath, Me.	Wrecked Julia Pt. Karluk, Alaska 1907
Shirley	Ship-Bark (W)	1,049	1850	Medford, Mass.	Register abandoned Alaska 1919 (floating hotel)
Simla	Bark (S) (4m)	2,237	1890	Pt. Glasgow, Scotland	Scuttled in S.F. Bay 1933 after capsizing in 1930
Sintram	Ship (W)	1,656	1877	So. Freeport, Me.	Wrecked Egegak, Alaska 1915
Sir Thomas J. Lipton	Schr. (W) (4m)	1,558	1918	Brunswick, Ga.	Became Canadian barge in 1940, later broken up
Snow & Burgess	Ship-Bark Schr. (W) (5m)	1,655	1878	Thomaston, Me.	Burned for junk, Puget Sound 1922
Sonoma	Bark (W)	1,061	1868	Chelsea, Mass.	Foundered off Pt. Reyes, Calif. 1911
Spartan	Ship (W)	1,448	1874	E. Boston, Mass.	Wrecked off Spreckelsville, Hawaii 1905
Speedway	Aux. Schr. (W)	613	1917	Littlebrook, N.S.	Used as rumrunner; burned, sank off Vancouver Island late 1920's
Standard	Ship (W)	1,534	1878	Phippsburg, Me.	Lost Cape Constantine, Alaska 1917
Star of Alaska (ex Balclutha)	Ship (S)	1,682	1886	Glasgow, Scotland	Afloat 1969, as S.F. Maritime Museum ship
Star of Bengal	Ship (I)	1,877	1874	Belfast, Ireland	Wrecked Coronation Is. Alaska 1908
Star of Chile (ex La Escocesa, ex Coalinga)	Ship-Bark (I)	1,001	1868	Dundee, Scotland	As barge, sank off north end Vancouver Island about 1960
Star of England (ex Blairmore)	Ship-Bark (S)	2,123	1893	Dumbarton, Scotland	Became B.C. barge Island Star 1935
Star of Falkland (ex Durbridge)	Ship (S)	2,163	1892	Pt. Glasgow, Scotland	Wrecked Akun Head, Unimak Pass, Alaska 1928
Star of Finland (ex Kaiulani)	Bark (S)	1,699	1899	Bath, Me.	Hull afloat 1969, Subic Bay, P.I.; planned as maritime museum at Washington, D.C.
Star of France	Ship (I)	1,766	1877	Belfast, Ireland	As fish barge Olympic II, sank off L.A. Harbor 1940 after collision
Star of Greenland (ex Hawaiian Isles)	Ship-Bark (S) (4m)	2,179	1892	Glasgow, Scotland	Became Portuguese MS Fos do Duro 1943; traded for many years thereafter
Star of Holland (ex Zemindar, ex Otto Gildemeister, ex Homeward Bound)	Ship-Bark (S)	2,121	1885	Belfast, Ireland	Became B.C. sawdust barge 1937, afloat many years thereafter. Scrapped
Star of Iceland (ex Willscott)	Bark (S)	2,165	1896	Pt. Glasgow, Scotland	Towed to Japan after abandonment at sea 1929; scrapped
Star of India (ex Euterpe)	Ship-Bark (I)	1,318	1863	Ramsey, Isle of Man, England	Marine Museum at San Diego, Calif., still afloat 1987
Star of Italy	Ship-Bark (I)	1,614	1877	Belfast, Ireland	Last owned as hulk in Colombia 1940's
Star of Lapland	Bark (S) (4m)	3,381	1902	Bath, Me.	Broken up in Japan in 1936
Star of Peru (ex Himalaya)	Ship-Bark (I)	1,027	1863	Sunderland, England	Became hulk at New Caledonia 1926 under name Bougainville
Star of Poland (ex Acme)	Bark (S) (4m)	3,288	1901	Bath, Me.	Wrecked at Katsumura, Japan 1918
Star of Russia	Ship (I)	1,981	1874	Belfast, Ireland	Became hulk in New Hebrides 1926 under name La Perouse
Star of Scotland	Bark (S) (4m)	2,598	1887	Pt. Glasgow, Scotland	Sunk by Nazi submarine in So. Atlantic as a 6 masted schooner 1943
Star of Shetland (ex Edward Sewall)	Bark (S) (4m)	3,206	1899	Bath, Me.	Broken up in Japan 1935-36
Star of Zealand (ex Astral)	Bark (S) (4m)	3,292	1900	Bath, Me.	Broken up in Japan 1936-36
Susie M. Plummer	Schr. (W) (4m)	920	1890	Thomaston, Me.	Capsized off Cape Flattery, Wash., 1909
Tacoma	Ship (W)	1,738	1881	Bath, Me.	Crushed in ice Cape Craig, Alaska 1918

Journal from New York towards San Francisco

H	K	F	COURSES	WINDS Direction Force	LEEWAY	THERMOMETER Air Water	BAROMETER	REMARKS
1				Southerly				
2				Backing				
3								
4								
5								
6								
7								
8								
9								
10								
11								
12								
1								
2								
3								
4								
5								
6								
7								
8								
9								
10								
11								
12								

35 Days Out

Course	Distance	Diff. of Lat.	Departure	Lat. by D. R.	Lat. by Ob	Variation	Diff. of Lon	Lon. by D. R.	Lon. by Ob
				9..00	9..72			30..58	

H	K	F	COURSES	WINDS Direction Force	LEEWAY	THERMOMETER Air Water	BAROMETER	REMARKS
1				Southerly				
2				Backing				
3								
4								
5								
6								
7								
8								
9								
10								
11								
12								
1								
2								
3								
4								
5								
6								
7								
8								
9								
10								
11								
12								

36 Days Out

Course	Distance	Diff. of Lat.	Departure	Lat. by D. R.	Lat. by Ob	Variation	Diff. of Lon	Lon. by D. R.	Lon. by Ob
				9..48	9..60			30..43	

Page from the logbook of the ship **ST. PAUL** in 1894, on a voyage New York to San Francisco.

Name	Rig	Tonnage	Built	Place	Final Fate
Tanner	Brig-Bgtn. (W)	291	1855	Smithtown, N.Y.	Stranded in Juan de Fuca Strait 1903; refloated, register abandoned 1907, Port Townsend
Theobold	Bark (W)	981	1861	Richmond, Me.	Registry dropped 1903, Seattle
Thetis (sealer, whaler, cutter)	Steam aux. Bark (W)	711	1881	Dundee, Scotland	As power vessel broken up 1934 in Newfoundland
Thrasher (whaler)	Steam aux. Bark (W)	671	1883	Bath, Me.	As diesel schooner Kamchatka, burned off the Aleutians in 1921
Tillie E. Starbuck	Ship (I)	2,032	1883	Chester, Pa.	Abandoned off Cape Horn, N.Y. to Honolulu 1907
Tonawanda (ex Lita, ex Indra)	Ship (S)	1,745	1892	Greenock, Scotland	Became hulk in New Caledonia 1926
Top Gallant	Ship-Bark (W)	1,280	1863	E. Boston, Mass.	Registry dropped 1900, at Port Townsend
Two Brothers	Ship (W)	1,382	1867	Farmingdale, Me.	Herring fishery S.E. Alaska 1912
Undaunted	Ship-Bark (W)	1,764	1869	Bath, Me.	Foundered off Forked River N.J. 1913
Vidette	Bark (W)	616	1865	Bath, Me.	Coal barge at Oakland till 1940's
W. B. Flint	Bark (W)	835	1885	Bath, Me.	Burned for metal on Puget Sound 1937
W. F. Babcock	Ship (W)	2,130	1882	Bath, Me.	Navy coal barge 1917
W. J. Pirrie	Ship (I) (4m)	2,516	1883	Belfast, Ireland	Broke up at sea off Cape Johnson, Wash. 1920
Wachusett	Ship (W)	1,599	1878	Kennebunk, Me.	Registry dropped at S.F. 1901
Wanderer (whaler)	Bark (W)	303	1878	Mattapoisett, Mass.	Wrecked on Cuttyhunk Reef, Mass. 1924
Will W. Case	Bark (W)	582	1877	Rockland, Me.	Coal barge 1920 in British Columbia
William Baylies (whaler)	Bark (W)	380	1886	Bath, Me.	Crushed in Arctic ice 1908
William Dollar (ex Alsterberg, ex Walkure)	Bark (S) (4m)	3,238	1902	Dumbarton, Scotland	Wrecked 1936 as B.C. barge Island Gatherer in Queen Charlotte Sound, B.C.
William Taylor	Schr. (W) (4m)	1,358	1917	Brunswick, Ga.	Sold as fish packing plant Helen Conrad, Seattle 1946
William E. Burnham	Schr. (W) (4m)	772	1909	Rockland, Me.	Registry dropped at Mobile, Alabama 1930
Wm. H. Harriman	Schr. (W) (4m)	1,450	1919	Thomaston, Me.	Scuttled at sea, after collision 1941
William H. Macy	Ship (W)	2,202	1883	Rockport, Me.	Wrecked on Virginia Coast, 1915
William H. Smith	Ship (W)	1,978	1883	Bath, Me.	Stranded near Monterey, Calif., as fish barge 1933
William T. Lewis (ex Robert Duncan)	Bark (S) (4m)	2,517	1891	Pt. Glasgow, Scotland	Became Canadian barge Fibreboard, afloat in 1940's at Victoria, B.C.

High-masted beauty of surpassing grace symbolizes bark **STAR OF INDIA** towing up the Oakland Estuary, near the Alaska Packers yard. Still afloat as a marine museum in San Diego Harbor, this iron-hulled square-rigger dates back to 1863, with a chronicle that reads like fiction. *Courtesy San Francisco Maritime Museum.*

Shipshape and Bristol fashion—the **COUNTY OF LINLITHGOW** puts to sea.

The big steel four-masted bark **BARMBEK** off the Columbia River. Built as the **GILCRUIX** in 1886, she flew the German flag when this photo was taken. Her owners were Knohr & Burchard and she hailed from Hamburg.

Picking up a little breeze off the Golden Gate—ship **DUNSYRE,** steel 2,149 ton Scottish-built vessel launched in 1891. She ended her days as a Canadian sawdust barge and was wrecked near Vancouver, B.C., in 1936.

In the foreground—the 1,085 ton bark **J. D. PETERS** and four-mast schooner **ERIC** await a tow into Puget Sound shortly after the turn of the century.

Homeward-bound after a wearisome voyage at sea—British square-rigger enters the Strait of Juan de Fuca.

APPENDIX B

RECORD PASSAGES IN THE PACIFIC
BY COMMERCIAL SAILING VESSELS

Compiled by the late Captain P. A. McDonald, veteran in sail
Courtesy Marine Digest

Material in the following list has been well checked and substantiated by logbooks and other reliable sources of proof. Here are the best passages on the most travelled trade routes of the commercial sailing ships of yesteryear. Unless otherwise specified the vessels listed were American flag.

NO. 1—SAILERS IN THE WEST COAST-HAWAII ROUTE

DECADE OF THE 1850s

Phoenix, clipper ship, in July, 1853; bound from San Francisco to Hongkong; passed Diamond Head, 8 days and 17 hours at sea.

Swordfish, clipper ship; sailed from San Francisco 2 p.m., June 17, 1853; made Maui in 8 days and 22 hours; days' runs as per log were 236, 340, 280, 250, 225, 202, 201, 142 and 208 nautical miles.

Kingfisher, clipper ship, in June, 1855; from San Francisco to Honolulu, 9 days and 20 hours.

Ocean Express, medium clipper; sailed from San Francisco June 9, 1858, arrived Honolulu June 17; time, 8 days and 17 hours out.

DECADE OF THE 1860s

Fairwind, clipper ship; sailed from San Francisco January 12, 1861, anchored at Honolulu January 21, or in 8 days and 18 hours from anchorage to anchorage.

Comet, bark, in December, 1861, Honolulu to San Francisco, 10 days and 19 hours.

DECADE OF THE 1870s

William L. Beebe, schooner; arrived in Port Townsend February 5, 1878, from Honolulu, 11 days and 18 hours.

Malolo, schooner; arrived at Cape Flattery, in July, 1879, from Honolulu, 10 days and 12 hours.

Catherine Sudden, barkentine; from Honolulu to Cape Flattery in November, 1879, in 9 days and 13 hours.

DECADE OF THE 1880s

W. C. Irwin, brig; in November, 1881, from San Francisco to Kahului, in 8 days and 11 hours; best day's work, 282 miles; poorest, 250 miles.

Lizzie Marshall, bark; arrived in Port Townsend December 24, 1883, in 14 days from Honolulu.

Emma Claudina, schooner, Capt. Matson; in December, 1884, from Hilo to San Francisco, in 9 days and 20 hours.

W. C. Irwin, brigantine; in February, 1884, from Honolulu to San Francisco, 10 days and 12 hours.

Consuelo, brigantine; in December, 1884, from Honolulu to San Francisco, 10 days.

Rosario, schooner; in December, 1884, from Kahului to San Francisco, 10 days.

Hesper, bark; in 1886 from Honolulu to Cape Flattery, in 9 days and 12 hours.

C. O. Whitmore, bark; in 1886 from Honolulu to Port Townsend in 13 days (10 days and 12 hours to Cape Flattery.)

Amelia, barkentine; in 1888, from Honolulu to Port Townsend in 11 days.

DECADE OF THE 1890s

Irmgard, barkentine; from Honolulu to San Francisco in 1892 in 10 days and 12 hours.

Irmgard, barkentine; in 1897 from Honolulu to San Francisco in 10 days and 12 hours.

Spokane, schooner; in 1899 sailed from Honolulu to Cape Flattery in 8 days and 16 hours; she covered 2,288 miles on the voyage.

DECADE OF THE 1900s

Oakland, bark; in February, 1901, arrived off Cape Flattery, 11 days from Hilo.

Annie Johnson, bark; as per her logbook, she passed Fort Point, the Golden Gate, at 3 p.m. on May 13, 1903; was abreast of Diamond Head at 9 a.m. on May 22 and at 10 a.m. anchored in Honolulu Harbor, having made the voyage in 8 days and 18 hours. Best speed, 13 knots; least speed, 9 knots; days' runs as per log 285, 313, 304, 275, 227, 240, 234, 251 and 236 miles.

Irmgard, barkentine; in April, 1903, from San Francisco to Honolulu in 8 days and 20 hours.

Thomas P. Emigh, barkentine; sailed from Honolulu March 10, 1909, made Cape Flattery March 17, or in 7 days and 22 hours.

UNDATED and UNCONFIRMED

Lurline, brigantine, commanded by Capt. Matson; it is claimed she made the voyage from San Francisco to Honolulu in 8 days and 8 hours; no date or details available.

Early San Francisco Bay scene showing a host of square-riggers at anchor. The unidentified vessel in the foreground appears to be a survey steamer. *Photo courtesy San Francisco Maritime Museum from Bortfeld collection.*

Excellent example of a typical steel bark of yesteryear jamming a little breeze off Cape Flattery.

NO. 2—IN SOUTH AMERICA - SOUTH AFRICA TRADES

DECADE OF THE 1850s

Sea Witch, clipper ship; on July 24, 1850, arrived in San Francisco from Valparaiso, Chile, 38 days.

Queen of Sheba, British; on April 12, 1851, arrived in San Francisco from Valparaiso, 38 days.

Telegraph, clipper ship; on April 16, 1854, arrived in San Francisco from Valparaiso, 38 days.

Veloz, British ship; on January 11, 1857, arrived in San Francisco from Valparaiso, 38 days.

DECADE OF THE 1870s

Agenor, ship; on April 11, 1874, arrived in San Francisco from Callao, Peru, 30 days.

Martha, clipper ship; on January 24, 1878, arrived in San Francisco from Callao, 29 days.

DECADE OF THE 1880s

Guardian, ship; on February 3, 1885, arrived in Port Townsend from Valparaiso, 40 days.

Cambria, British bark; in 1886 arrived in Astoria, Oregon, from Valparaiso, 38 days and 12 hours.

DECADE OF THE 1890s

A. J. Fuller, ship; in 1891 from Puget Sound to Cape Town, South Africa, 88 days.

Cambrian Princess, British ship; on November 16, 1891, arrived in Astoria, Oregon, from Valparaiso, 38 days.

Collessie, British iron bark, Capt. McMurtry; on December 8, 1891, arrived in San Francisco from Cape Town, South Africa, 78 days.

Endeavor, schooner; in 1897 arrived in Port Townsend from Callao, 31 days.

Glenclova, British ship; in December, 1897, arrived in Puget Sound from Cape Town, South Africa, 81 days.

DECADE OF THE 1900s

John Currier, ship; in 1901 arrived in Port Townsend from Cape Town, 78 days.

Hawaii, barkentine; on March 23, 1902, arrived in Cape Town from Bellingham, 85 days.

Koko Head, barkentine; in 1903 arrived in Delagoa Bay, South Africa, from Port Townsend, 86 days.

Muskoka, British ship; in 1903 arrived in Cape Town from Tacoma, 83 days.

Georgina, barkentine; in 1903 arrived in Port Townsend from Callao, 30 days and 12 hours.

DECADE OF THE 1910s

Samar, schooner; on August 22, 1911, arrived in Port Townsend from Mollendo, Peru, 30 days.

Wilbert L. Smith, schooner, Capt. Ross; in 1913-14 arrived in Puget Sound from Callao, 35 days.

Tug **STORM KING** tows bark **GOLDEN GATE** through the Golden Gate. This tall ship was built at Whitehaven, England, in 1888 as the **LORD SHAFTESBURY**. James Rolph, her owner in 1911 renamed her **GOLDEN GATE** at San Francisco. She was broken up at Alameda in 1935.

Sea of sand—British bark **POLTALLOCH** imprisoned on the sands on the outer fringes of Willapa Bay entrance yearns for her freedom. She grounded in the fall of 1900 and spent nearly a year and a half on the shoals before being refloated. Her master, Captain Young, stood by her to conduct salvage operations.

British bark **PINMORE** over on her beam ends off the Washington Coast in 1901. The vessel was abandoned but later towed to port and repaired.

NOTE: The best sailing passages from the Pacific Northwest ports to the Orient, given below, were compiled by Capt. McDonald from his own research work with logbooks and customs reports and from data furnished him by the late Frederick C. Matthews, author of "American Clipper Ships," with whom Capt. McDonald carried on a correspondence until Mr. Matthews' death. They exchanged data. Mr. Matthews found the files of the Commercial News of San Francisco a valuable source of information on the lumber carriers. Beginning July 1, 1887, it published the data on the lumber cargoes and ships from California, Puget Sound and the Columbia River and some of those from British Columbia.

The following list covers the sailing passages of definite record that were made from the Pacific Northwest ports to the Orient in less than 60 days; the average passage in that transpacific route ran between 70 and 80 days and some took as long as 90 days. The vessels are American unless otherwise specified.

DECADE OF THE 1880s

Earl Granville, British iron ship, Capt. Copp; sailed from Gig Harbor, Puget Sound, October 12, 1889, arrived in Shanghai December 11; time, 59 days.

Coloma, bark, Capt. Noyes; sailed from Astoria, Oregon, October 19, 1889, arrived in Hongkong December 11; time, 52 days.

DECADE OF THE 1890s

Hesper, bark, Capt. Sodergren; sailed from Port Gamble, Puget Sound, July 1, 1891, arrived in Shanghai August 27; time, 56 days.

Tam O'Shanter, barkentine, Capt. Patterson; sailed from Port Gamble May 9, 1893, arrived in Yokohama June 15; time, 36 days.

Thermopylae, British clipper, Capt. Winchester; sailed from Astoria September 15, 1893, arrived in Hongkong October 29; time, 43 days. (On her next voyage this famous ship took 67 days from New Westminster, B.C., to Shanghai.)

Aida, schooner, Capt. Anderson; sailed from Moodyville, B.C., May 28, 1895, arrived in Shanghai July 25; time, 57 days.

Quickstep, barkentine, Capt. Hansen; sailed from Port Blakely, Puget Sound, June 4, 1895, arrived in Shanghai July 30; time, 55 days.

John Smith, barkentine, Capt. Goth; sailed from Port Hadlock, Washington, June 6, 1895, arrived in Shanghai July 29; time, 52 days.

Golden Shore, schooner, Capt. Henderson; sailed from Tacoma July 20, 1895, arrived in Shanghai September 17; time, 58 days.

Robert Sudden, barkentine, Capt. Berkholm; sailed from Port Blakely July 22, 1895, arrived in Shanghai September 16; time, 55 days.

William H. Talbot, schooner, Capt. Bluhm; sailed from Port Blakely August 25, 1895, arrived in Shanghai October 7; time, 42 days.

Eclipse, ship, Capt. Peterson; sailed from Moodyville, B.C., March 13, 1896, arrived in Shanghai May 12; time, 59 days.

William H. Talbot, schooner, Capt. Bluhm; sailed from Burrard Inlet, B.C., April 10, 1896, arrived in Shanghai May 31; time 52 days.

Prosper, schooner, Capt. Johansen; sailed from Port Blakely April 14, 1896, arrived in Shanghai June 6; time, 52 days.

Charles F. Crocker, barkentine, Capt. Piltz; sailed from Vancouver, B.C., April 28, 1896, arrived in Shanghai June 23; time, 55 days.

Aida, schooner, Capt. Anderson; sailed from Tacoma September 12, 1896, arrived in Shanghai November 10; time, 58 days.

Fred E. Sander, schooner, Capt. Roos; sailed from Port Blakely November 14, 1896, arrived in Yokohama December 13; time, 28 days.

Willie R. Hume, barkentine, Capt. Brown; sailed from Tacoma November 17, 1896, arrived in Shanghai January 2, 1897; time, 45 days.

Robert Sudden, barkentine, Capt. Berkholm; sailed from Port Blakely November 23, 1896, arrived in Haiphong December 31; time, 37 days.

Nomad, schooner, Capt. McAllep; sailed from Tacoma September 18, 1897, arrived in Shanghai November 17; time, 59 days.

Newsboy, barkentine, Capt. Mollsted; sailed from Chemainus, B.C., March 1, 1898, arrived in Taku Bar April 28; time, 57 days.

DECADE OF THE 1900s

Jane L. Stanford, barkentine, Capt. Mollsted; sailed from Port Blakely May 19, 1904, arrived in Tsingtau July 15; time, 56 days.

William H. Talbot, schooner, Capt. Banneche; sailed from Portland, Oregon, May 20, 1904, arrived in Shanghai July 18; time, 58 days.

David Evans, schooner, Capt. Whits; sailed from Portland June 30, 1904, arrived in Shanghai August 26; time, 56 days.

NO. 4—ORIENT TO PACIFIC NORTHWEST

It will be noted that in this list of record passages under sail from the Orient to Puget Sound and the Columbia River, a number of the vessels came from the Far East loaded, while others came in ballast.

DECADE OF THE 1870s

Excelsior, American schooner, arrived in ballast at Port Townsend February 28, 1878, from Shanghai, 27 days.

Jeremiah Thompson, American ship, arrived in Victoria, B.C., May 18, 1879, with cargo from Yokohama, 24 days.

DECADE OF THE 1880s

Taunton, British iron ship, arrived in Astoria, Oregon, July 6, 1881, with 390 coolies and a cargo from Hongkong, 34 days.

Ericsson, American ship, former steamer, arrived in Victoria, B. C., January 20, 1882, in ballast from Shanghai, 28 days.

Jonathan Bourne, American bark, arrived in Victoria, June 17, 1882, with cargo from Hongkong, 34 days.

State of Maine, American ship, arrived in Victoria in April, 1885, in ballast from Shanghai, 28 days.

Winnipeg, British ship of Quebec, arrived in Astoria November 21, 1885, in ballast from Shanghai, 31 days.

Aida, American schooner, arrived at Port Townsend in February, 1886, in ballast from Shanghai, 23 days.

Bylgia, German iron bark, passed Cape Flattery in August, 1886, with cargo from Yokohama, 22½ days.

Lucy A. Nickels American ship, arrived in Royal Roads, B.C., September 29, 1886, with cargo from Hongkong, 38 days.

DECADE OF THE 1890s

Ranee Rickmers, German bark, arrived at Astoria September 29, 1890, in ballast from Yokohama, 28 days, fastest to that time in run from Yokohama to Astoria.

Oberon, British clipper ship, former auxiliary steamer, arrived at Astoria, April 20, 1891, in ballast from Yokohama, 24 days.

Peterborough, British iron ship, arrived at Astoria December 11, 1892, in ballast from Yokohama, 24 days.

Katie Flickinger, American barkentine, arrived in Port Townsend January 12, 1897, with cargo from Kobe, 25 days.

Lyman D. Foster, American schooner, arrived at Port Townsend in February, 1899, in ballast from Shanghai, 24 days.

Manchester, British iron ship, arrived at Port Townsend, September 14, 1899, in ballast from Shanghai, 22 days.

Taken just after the turn of the century this scene in Tacoma's Commencement Bay shows several square-riggers loading lumber over the stern. Another is seen at anchor in the background while the **USS CHICAGO** takes on supplies in foreground. *From the collection of Pete Hurd.*

RETURN FROM THE ORIENT

In return passages to the Northwest from the Orient, the barkentine *Jane L. Stanford,* Capt. McDonald, made the run in 1920 from Chin-wang-tao to Cape Flattery in 40 days and to Victoria in 42 days. In 1922, the American four-masted bark *William Dollar,* Capt. McDonald, sailed from Woosung Forts March 22, arrived off Cape Flattery April 22 and towed to Port Townsend the following day. On that voyage, from one Saturday noon to the next Saturday noon, she sailed 1,865 miles, an average of 266. The same ship in 1902 made a passage from the River Plate via Cape Horn to Port Townsend in 69 days. The *William Dollar* was one of the largest steel square-riggers to have sailed under the American flag.

NOTE: Of the 25 passages from the Pacific Northwest to the Orient, it is interesting to know that 12 were made by vessels built by the Hall Brothers of Puget Sound.

DECADE OF THE 1900s

Peru, German iron ship, arrived in Port Townsend April 16, 1900, with cargo from Yokohama, 21 days.

Herzogin Sophie Charlotte, German bark, arrived in Astoria, December 12, 1900, in ballast from Hiogo, 21 days.

Solano, American schooner, arrived in Port Townsend March 27, 1902, in ballast from Shanghai, 24 days.

Endeavor, American schooner, arrived in Port Townsend March 31, 1902, in ballast from Manila, 38 days.

Wilbert L. Smith, American schooner, passed Cape Flattery June 1, 1905, in ballast from Kobe, 23 days.

NOTE: It was claimed that the American barkentine *Amaranth,* Capt. Bowes, made the run from "open water" off Shanghai to Astoria in 1908 in 23 days, but according to the data of the late F. C. Matthews, the dates of sailing and arrival make the passage 28 days, port to port.

The American half-clipper *Dashing Wave* made an unconfirmed passage from Yokohama to Port Townsend in 18 days in the 1870's, and the bark *Vidette* made a run in ballast from Shanghai to Port Townsend in 24 days, but the date is unconfirmed.

Columbia River bar tug **ONEONTA** prepares to take the **LAWHILL** in tow for Portland. She was one of the largest commercial sailing vessels calling at West Coast ports, boasting a length of 317 feet and a registered tonnage of 2,942. She was built at Dundee in 1892.

This is believed to be the steel four-masted bark **CARRABIN,** built as the skysail yarder **NORTH STAR** for A. Bilbrough & Co. of London, in 1892, at Alloa, Scotland. As the **SUZANNE VINNEN,** she was sunk by a submarine off the Irish coast in 1917.

Nature's porthole—through a great open knot in a gnarled driftwood log is seen the forward section and bowsprit of the wreck of the **PETER IREDALE,** visible on Oregon's Clatsop Beach since 1906. *Tee Jay Views.*

One of the last American flag full-rigged ships to visit Pacific Coast ports was the New York-owned ship **TUSITALA.** Several views of her appear here taken by Walter P. Miller in 1926 while the vessel was off Cape Flattery. Owned by James A. Farrell, the vessel was built in Scotland in 1883 and was 261 feet in length. She was famed in the late 1920's as the only sailing vessel in the world operated the year-round in an ocean route. She loaded lumber or magnesite ore for Baltimore from Seattle and carried sulphate of ammonia from New York to Honolulu and then loaded ballast sand from Waikiki Beach for the run to Seattle. Captain James P. Barker was her master, and Farrell, her owner and a lover of sailing ships, was president of the U. S. Steel Corp.

NO. 5—FROM SAN FRANCISCO TO MANILA

Under this heading there are four authenticated passages, three made in the 1850s and one in the 1860s as follows:

DECADE OF THE 1850s

Westward Ho, clipper ship; sailed from San Francisco in ballast February 16, 1853, arrived in Manila 40 days out.

Flying Fish, clipper ship; sailed from San Francisco in ballast February 18, 1853, arrived in Manila 41 days out.

Greenfield, full-modeled bark; sailed from San Francisco in ballast February 9, 1854, arrived in Manila 38 days 4 hours out.

DECADE OF THE 1860s

Galatea, clipper ship, sailed from San Francisco in ballast December 17, 1862, arrived in Manila 43 days out.

Riding high—British four-mast bark, believed to be the **CEDAR-BANK,** gathers a Pacific breeze in her sails.

NO. 6—FROM MANILA TO SAN FRANCISCO

Under this heading there are 11 authenticated passages in the decades of the 1850s and 1870s, all the vessels being cargo-laden.

DECADE OF THE 1850s

Dominga, bark; arrived in San Francisco October 19, 1850, from Manila, 48 days out.

Brenda, clipper schooner, Capt. Stone; arrived in San Francisco October 24, 1854, from Manila, 43 days. out.

Jane A. Falkenburg, barkentine; arrived in San Francisco May 16, 1855, from Manila, 39 days out.

John R. Mora, bark, Capt. Bartlett, arrived in San Francisco July 2, 1856, from Manila, 39 days out.

DECADE OF THE 1870s

Wildwood, ship, Capt. Frost; arrived in San Francisco August 28, 1874, from Cebu, 48 days.

McNear, ship, Capt. Carter; arrived in San Francisco March 12, 1874, from Manila, 48 days.

Comet, ship, Capt. Bray; arrived in San Francisco March 5, 1875, from Manila, 46 days.

Joseph Hayden, German bark, Capt. Kruse; arrived in San Francisco March 14, 1875, from Manila, 48 days out.

Oregon, ship, Capt. Cushing; arrived in San Francisco October 20, 1876, from Manila, 47 days.

Antelope, ship, Capt. Chaney; arrived in San Francisco June 18, 1878, from Manila, 48 days out.

Cormorant, British bark, Capt. Williams; arrived in San Francisco March 14, 1878, from Manila, 44 days.

To be sure, the sailors of the four-mast ship **COUNTY OF LIN-LITHGOW** were anxious to set foot on land after a long voyage around the Horn for a cargo of Northwest grain.

Pert British bark **LORD ELGIN,** a veteran English merchantman, was well known at Columbia River, Puget Sound and California ports at the turn of the century.

This photo is believed to be the Chilean bark **LAKE LEMAN** putting to sea for Latin America. She was built in 1867.

The British four-masted bark **CROMPTON,** a 310 footer operated by MacVicar Marshall & Co., Liverpool.

British square-rigger **ELGINSHIRE** sails proudly along. Out of Glasglow, she was owned by T. Law & Co.

The view from the stern quarter. Vessel is believed to be the German iron ship **EMILIE,** ex **BRITISH AMBASSADOR.**

NO. 7—FROM SAN FRANCISCO TO HONGKONG

Here are the best passages under sail from San Francisco to Hongkong. They number eight, all authenticated. It will be noted that seven of the eight were made in the decade of the 1850s, the eighth being made in the 1860s. All the vessels in this list were in ballast:

DECADE OF THE 1850s

Memnon, ship; sailed from San Francisco November 8, 1850, arrived in Hongkong 35 days out.

Celestial, clipper ship; sailed from San Francisco November 20, 1850, arrived in Hongkong 33 days out.

White Squall, clipper ship; sailed from San Francisco February 23, 1851, arrived in Hongkong 35 days out.

Gamecock, clipper ship; sailed from San Francisco October 29, 1851, arrived in Hongkong 34 days out.

Pampero, clipper ship; sailed from San Francisco February 15, 1854, arrived in Hongkong 33 days out.

Golden Eagle, clipper ship; sailed from San Francisco September 16, 1855, arrived in Hongkong 34 days out.

Indiaman, clipper ship; sailed from San Francisco December 16, 1858, arrived in Hongkong 35 days out.

DECADE OF THE 1860s

Oracle, British ship; sailed from San Francisco October 28, 1864, arrived in Hongkong 35 days out.

NO. 8—FROM HONGKONG TO SAN FRANCISCO

Under this heading we have four passages that have been duly authenticated, one in the decade of the 1850s, one in the decade of the 1860s, one in the decade of the 1870s and one in the decade of the 1890s, as follows:

Challenge, clipper ship; arrived in San Francisco April 22, 1853, in ballast from Hongkong, 34 days out.

Phantom, clipper ship, Capt. Sargent; arrived in San Francisco May 7, 1863, with cargo from Hongkong, 34 days out.

Wandering Jew, full-modeled ship, Capt. Talpey; arrived in San Francisco August 1, 1878, with cargo from Hongkong, 33 days out.

William H. Macy, full-modeled ship, Capt. Amesbury; arrived in San Francisco July 12, 1890, with cargo from Hongkong, 33 days out.

Old sailing vessel's kedge anchor was recovered accidently off Seattle's Pier 67 by commercial diver Leiter Hockett in 1968 while weighing the anchor of his diving vessel. Weight 800 pounds.

This big steel bark is believed to be the **STAR OF LAPLAND,** ex **ATLAS.**

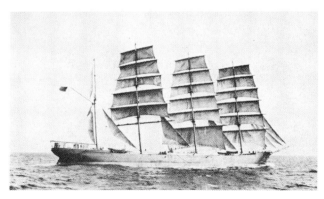

NO. 9—FROM JAPAN TO SAN FRANCISCO

DECADE OF THE 1860s

Viscata, British ship, Capt. Drummond; arrived in San Francisco January 9, 1867, in ballast from Yokohama, 23 days out.

DECADE OF THE 1870s

Gerard C. Tobey, bark, Capt. Crowell; arrived in San Francisco April 23, 1879, with cargo from Yokohama, 24 days out.

DECADE OF THE 1880s

Gerard C. Tobey, bark, Capt. Crowell; arrived in San Francisco December 7, 1880, with cargo from Hakodate, 25 days out.

Carondelet, bark, Capt. Stetson; arrived in San Francisco October 30, 1881, in ballast from Yokohama, 22 days out.

James Stafford, British bark, Capt. Reynolds; arrived in San Francisco January 2, 1885, in ballast from Yokohama, 21½ days out.

Aleous, British ship, Capt. Brown; arrived in San Francisco January 16, 1887, in ballast from Yokohama, 24 days out.

Great Admiral, ship, Capt. Rowell; arrived in San Francisco September 4, 1887, with cargo from Hakodate, 25 days out.

DECADE OF THE 1890s

Swanhilda, British iron ship; arrived in San Francisco in 1891 with cargo from Hakodate, 23 days out.

Clan Buchanan, British iron ship, Capt. Harris; arrived in San Francisco April 29, 1891, with cargo from Hakodate, 25 days out.

Wrestler, barkentine; arrived in San Francisco December 25, 1895, in ballast from Kobe, 24 days out.

DECADE OF THE 1900s

Nile, British iron ship; arrived in San Francisco April 25, 1900, with cargo from Kobe, 23 days out.

Garnet Hill, British ship; arrived in San Francisco May 17, 1902, in ballast from Kobe, 24 days out.

NO. 10—FROM SHANGHAI TO SAN FRANCISCO

Under this heading we have five record passages, so scattered that it is hardly worthwhile classifying them by decades, They follow:

Ringleader, British ship; arrived in San Francisco August 1, 1878, in ballast from Shanghai, 30 days out.

Dallam Tower, British ship; arrived in San Francisco January 20, 1881, in ballast from Shanghai, 28 days out.

Oakworth, British ship; arrived in San Francisco April 22, 1881, in ballast from Shanghai, 28 days out. (NOTE: The *Oakworth* in a period of 18 consecutive days in April sailed 4,525 miles, or 251.4 miles per day.)

Andelana, British ship; arrived in San Francisco August 10, 1891, in ballast from Shanghai, 31 days out.

Queen Victoria, British ship; arrived in San Francisco May 18, 1902, in ballast from Shanghai, 30 days out.

NO. 11—FROM SAN FRANCISCO TO SHANGHAI

There are three records under this heading, all made in the decade of the 1850s. They follow:

Sword Fish, clipper ship; sailed from San Francisco June 17, 1853, in ballast and arrived in Shanghai in 32 days and 9 hours.

Golden City, clipper ship; sailed from San Francisco February 28, 1854, in ballast, and arrived in Shanghai in 36 days.

Romance of the Seas, clipper ship; sailed from San Francisco November 17, 1856, and arrived in Shanghai in 34 days.

German bark **KURT** in tow. This vessel was later known as the **MOSHULU,** under the American flag.

German ship **FLOTTBEK** in trouble near White Rock, south of Cape Flattery in January, 1901. The crew was removed and the water-filled vessel towed in and repaired.

Alaska Packers' cannery ship **STAR OF SCOTLAND** at Loring, Alaska on July 4, 1909.

Though generally conceded to be the first steamer to sail the waters of the North Pacific, the **BEAVER** sailed to the Columbia River as a brig and had her paddle wheels connected after she reached Fort Vancouver. Thus she qualifies as one of the early commercial square-rigged ships to come to the West Coast. She arrived in 1836 for service with Hudson's Bay Co. and was wrecked in service as a tug in 1888 near Vancouver, B. C.

Pencil sketch of the bark **PAMIR** off Cape Flattery, Australia-bound, in a gale, January 6, 1946. The sketch is by Edward Goodall of Vancouver, B.C. made from Hugh Frith's photo. The Pamir was the last commercial square-rigger to sail out of the Strait of Juan de Fuca. *Courtesy Island Tug & Barge Ltd., Vancouver and Victoria, B.C.*

Decks squeaky clean and paint whiter than snow mark the huge four-masted bark **EDWARD SEWALL,** one of the most beautiful sailing vessels ever built in an American shipyard. She is pictured here at the old Seattle coal dock. Built and owned by A. Sewall & Company of Bath, Maine, the vessel was built in 1899 and measured 332 feet in length with tonnage of 3,206, one of the largest square-riggers then afloat. In later years, the bark was purchased by the Alaska Packers Association and renamed **STAR OF SHETLAND.** She was broken up in Japan in the mid 1930's. From Joe Williamson collection.

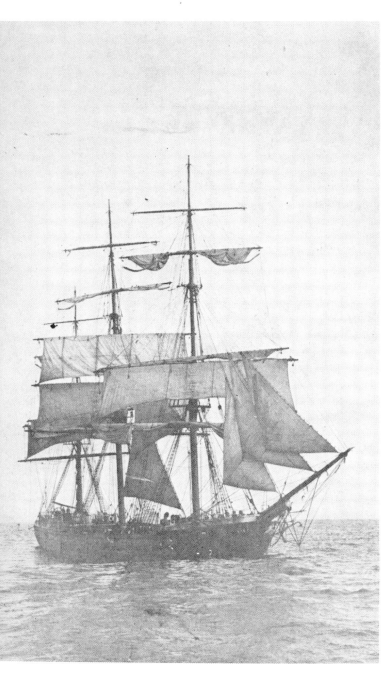

"Far as the breeze can bear, the billows foam,
  Survey our empire and behold our home."
"Our Ships all in motion once whitened the ocean,
  They sailed and returned with a cargo."

Entering the Strait of Juan de Fuca in search of cargo, the German ship **NIXE,** a 228 foot iron-hulled vessel was built at Vegesack in 1887 for a Bremen shipowner.

"Unless the tide abate,
 you cannot make it through the strait."
Promptly the tug's signal was returned:
"As long as you have steam and coal,
 you steam ahead, God bless your soul."

The four-mast American bark **DIRIGO,** was the first steel sailing vessel built in North America. She was built for and by A. Sewall of Bath in 1894, and owned for a brief spell on the Pacific Coast in later years. Torpedoed off the English coast in 1917, she went down with the loss of one of her crew. *Photo by G.E. Plummer in 1912.*

"A wet sheet and a flowing sea,
   A wind that follows fast,
And fills the white and rustling sail,
   And bends the gallant mast."—A. Cunningham

This photo taken by Captain Plummer in 1914, is believed to be the **DIRIGO** plunging into a North Pacific swell, wild spray flying. "The way of the ship is like nothing else."

"Even in a practical workaday world stripped of its myths and legends, a ship at set is still somehow touched with romance."
   —Richard Hanser

Another view of the handsome **DIRIGO** in 1912. "A good master keeps his kites up till the last moment." G. E. Plummer photo.

British ship **CLAVERDON,** a vessel which spent many years hauling grain to the United Kingdom from Portland, Oregon and Tacoma, Washington. In 1902, on a 218 day passage from Cuxhaven to San Francisco, she was struck by mammoth seas near Cape Horn which drowned five of her crew and injured nine.

Captain G. E. Plummer took this fine photo of the British steel bark **LYNTON** in 1913 in North Pacific waters. "Watchfulness is the law of the ship, watch on watch, for advantage and for life."

The **DRUMCRAIG,** pictured here, went missing on a passage from Portland and Astoria, Oregon with lumber for Manila in 1906. This beautiful vessel, measuring 280 feet in length, was a unit of Gillison and Chadwick's Drum fleet of England.

Bone in her teeth, the gallant steam tug **TATOOSH** heads out for the Strait of Juan de Fuca from Seattle to bargain for a sail ship tow. *O. Beaton photo 1912.*

The powerful steam tug **PIONEER** probably towed more sailing vessels to and from Cape Flattery than any other tug on Puget Sound in the early days. Here she is seen as a unit of the Puget Sound Tug Boat Co.

With a good head of steam the tug **PROSPER** heads out for Cape Flattery to tow in a sailing vessel.

One of the most powerful steam towing craft on the West Coast in her day, was the Canadian tug **LORNE,** which catered to the needs of scores of sailing vessels, mostly out of B.C. waters.

A Puget Sound seagull challenges the steam tug **TYEE** to a race.

"Now would I give a thousand furlongs of sea for an acre of land."

Towing up the Strait of Juan de Fuca in tandem—a British bark and an American barkentine. The year was 1914.

This salty British steel bark is believed to be the **CLAN BUCHANAN** off the Columbia River, outbound with grain.

They that go down to the sea in ships, that do business in great waters;
these see the works of the Lord, and His wonders in the deep."
—*The 107th Psalm of David*

"But it's the landsman mostly, who talks about the 'romance' of the sea. Those who live on it, and get their living from it, usually have scant sentiment for it."

Bow on view of the **SOLWAY.** Note lengthy yards supporting canvas on the foremast like the wings of a great bird.

Employed here by the Northwestern Fisheries Co., is seen the spritely bark **GUY C. GOSS.** She was first owned on the Pacific by the Western Commercial Co. in 1900. That firm later became Pacific Steam Whaling Co. The Goss was built in 1879.

C. Arthur Foss made an effort to preserve the fine old ship **ST. PAUL** as a museum ship in the 1930's at the Ballard Locks in Seattle. Funds gave out after she had served in that capacity for a few years. The St. Paul, a fine Downeaster, built in 1874, is pictured here in better days shortly after the turn of the century. She was owned on the Pacific Coast from 1901 and brought to San Francisco under ownership of Pacific Packing and Navigation Co.

A view of the venerable ship **ST. PAUL** taken by O. Beaton in 1912. This affords a fine study of sail.

"A Yankee ship sailed down the river, Blow, boys, blow! Her masts
and spars they shine like silver, Blow, my bully boys, blow!"
—*Old Sea Chantey*

Big German steel ship **LASBEK** in a calm sea off Tatoosh Island, about 1913. An ex British vessel, she
was scrapped in 1931. C. Connel & Co. built her in 1894, as the **BEN DEARG.**

"O, blow the man down, bullies, blow him right down! Give me
some time to blow the man down."—*Old Sea Chantey*

Built at Rockland, Maine in 1882, the ship **S. D. CARLETON,** came to San Francisco for ownership under the California Shipping Company in 1899, and ended her days as a barge a decade later.

Life aboard a big square-rigger was a hard life.
"Six days shalt thou labor and do all thou art able,
And on the seventh, holystone the decks and scrape the cable."

Seen here is the steel bark **MUSKOKA** in the choppy Pacific.
She was a 300 foot limejuicer.

Bark **ARROW**

LAST OF THE WINDJAMMERS

By 1860 the peak of the clipper construction was over and only the British continued to build square riggers for the Australian grain and wool trade. They were iron or steel, four-masted barques and ships of around 1900 tons and 270′ in length.

Wire rigging enabled them to carry huge spreads of canvas, sometimes as much as 30,000 square yards, and with favorable winds they made good speed. Steam finally replaced them all, although they fought a valiant battle until the last grain race in 1938.

"Even when all hands escape, it is a dreadful thing for sailors to watch a ship drown, to see her die." —*Richard Hanser*

Index

In addition to the general index check appendix A and
B for factual information on individual ships.